JOLt

Challenge

THE SELF INTELLIGENCE EXPERIENCE

Dea Michael,

Hope you enjoy
Book # 1   ☺

W[signature]

Praise for JOLT Challenge

"JOLT Challenge is an incredible tool for stimulating change and growth in self. When you start with that cornerstone of self-trust, the life you build reflects your core values, affecting every aspect of your world. Your health, wealth, and relationships will benefit, helping you maximise results and create positive change."
Stephen M. R. Covey
Author of *The Speed of Trust*

"After more than 30 years of experience as a consultant and trainer, I can say without hesitation that JOLT Challenge is the most comprehensive and effective life-skills program I have seen. If you're interested in personal and career success, I strongly recommend JOLT Challenge to you."
Dr Ken Hultman
Author of Making Change Irresistible and Balancing Individual and Organizational Values

"JOLT Challenge takes complex, theoretical ideas and makes them truly accessible to the lay person. It presents material in engaging, concise prose and provides excellent and relevant examples. This book will appeal not only to those aiming for business success and personal growth, but also to the thinking practitioner and business academic. I congratulate the authors on this eminently thoughtful, useful and practical volume."
Dr Rachel Morrison
Senior Lecturer, Faculty of Business, AUT University
Co-host of TV's *Brain Power*

"An outstanding book, which together with the JOLT Challenge sessions gives the reader a wonderful launch pad for personal and business success."
Tony Falkenstein
CEO Just Water International
NZ Business Hall of Fame

"I am a passionate believer in the basic fact that we shape our own destiny and that we can all make wondrous things happen. However like all things, there are techniques to be learned to unleash our potential and we have to know ourselves well to do it. I would not have started my own business or become Mayor of Auckland without learning these techniques. JOLT Challenge is a well put together summation of these techniques and its step-by-step approach should effectively stop any temptation to read and not learn and practise. I might have gone for Prime Minister if I had access to this book!"
Dick Hubbard
Founder of Hubbard's Foods
Former Mayor of Auckland

"Continual improvement involves an appreciation that there is always a better way to do things irrespective of how much you have achieved or how comfortable you might be with where you currently are in life. As a young international rugby player I learnt a valuable lesson about sacrifice. The bottom line was the phrase 'long after the price is forgotten the quality remains'. Undertaking JOLT Challenge involves sacrifice but it is well worth it as you explore creative and innovative ways of challenging yourself for constant improvement in many areas of life."

Nick Farr-Jones
Australian Rugby Union Player 1984 –1993
1991 Rugby Union World Cup Winning Captain

"JOLT Challenge is a valuable book. I loved the quotes, and its terrific layout means the information is in the right-sized chunks to keep the reader interested. I was especially impressed by the breadth of information that is delivered without the reader feeling overwhelmed. It is very clear why all sections are important to digest if you are serious about making a change. The reference to movies makes the learning fun, helps reinforce the content and is also an ideal way to explain and share what you are doing with someone else."

Marie-Ann Billens
General Manager, Estée Lauder Companies

"A fascinating program. Definitely the most comprehensive compilation of personal change techniques that I have ever come across."

Phillip Mills
Creative Director, Les Mills International
2004 NZ Entrepreneur of the Year

"JOLT Challenge, the great new big little book. It captivated me from the very beginning with so many fabulous quotes and quirky stories. I have identified some of my own personal weaknesses but equally it reinforced my strengths. Some may say they can't afford the time but I say you can't afford not to. I believe this is an inspiring book to improve your mental clarity and emotional and spiritual well-being."

Dame Susan Devoy
Four-time World Squash Champion
Number One Ranked Player 1983–1992

A catalogue record for this book is available from the National Library of New Zealand.

JOLT Challenge™ is a trademark name and is a product of Mind Warriors Limited.

Published by Star Books, Private Bag 102950, North Shore Mail Centre for Mind Warriors Limited
www.mindwarriors.com
First published 2009
Copyright © Mind Warriors Limited 2009

Illustrations by Wayne Logue (www.cartoon.co.nz)

Hedonism (Just because you feel good) Written by Dyer D/ Arran L (Mushroom Music Publishing)
TS Eliot, from 'Little Gidding' in Four Quartets, Faber and Faber Ltd

Disclaimer: It is not the intention for JOLT Challenge to replace any professional medical treatment.

ISBN 978 1 86979 266 4
Printed in China by Everbest Printing Co Ltd

Dedications

Steve says...

JOLT Challenge is dedicated to my loving wife and soulmate Helen, who died of breast cancer in June of 2007 during the final stages of development of JOLT Challenge. She was an exceptional mother to our two boys Kane (8 years) and Niko (6 years). Her generosity, passion and love for life inspired many, leaving fond memories with those she knew. Her journey through cancer taught us many things about ourselves and life, in that the more you look inside yourself the more you realise you don't know. It is sad in a way that it is only when such adversity hits us that we make an effort to look inside. Yet looking in and understanding our inner selves more, can help us to overcome such adversities when they arise. I love you, Helen, for all that we shared and you will always be in our hearts.

Big thanks to Wade for being so compassionate through the challenges the boys and I faced. His amazing ability to accumulate mounds of knowledge and translate it into sensical prose is nothing short of brilliant. Thanks for your passion, dedication and commitment keeping us on our sometimes wobbly track.

Wade says...

Thank you to my partner in crime Steve for his genius, vision, creativity, ability to deconstruct and analyse, kindness and generosity.

Thank you to my family of origin for all their love and support over the years.

Thank you to my beautiful wife Evie who has been the number one supporter of JOLT Challenge and who originated the challenge concept. In the period of researching and writing this book, my wife Evie gave birth to our daughter Sabina. In her first year Sabina has taught me to have an appreciation of life that I marvel at every time I see her.

It is with all my love that I dedicate this book to Evie and Sabina, the two most important people in my life.

Contents

Hats off to...

JOLT Challenge was created by Steve Hill and Wade Jackson, co-founders of Mind Warriors. It was written by Wade, with creative direction by Steve.

However, it went from being an idea to a reality only with the time, energy, support, and genius of many people. So we take our hats off to...

The Mind Warriors team, both past and present, our trainers and researchers, especially Edward Prince and Jessica George who have spent many, many hours dedicated to the cause.

- Wayne Logue, who has the special ability to turn our ideas into brilliant illustrations and capture exactly what we're trying to say.
- Biunca Hooper, who cracked the whip and made sure we stayed on track.
- Our advisory team: Dr Rich Allen, Dr Jim Bartley, Dr Peter Blyde, Dr Helena Cooper-Thomas, Dr David Hopcroft, and Dr Ken Hultman, for all their expertise, advice and guidance that they so generously gave. A special mention goes to Dr Jane Davidson for designing the measurement component within her self-imposed deadline of giving birth to twins in a hot summer.
- Karl von Randow and Matt Buchanan at Cactus Lab for their assistance with design.
- Richard Griffiths for his generosity and leaving no bones on the manuscript unpicked and Gary Carter for his business assistance.
- Atesh Bhej and his team at Biz Solutions for all their support over the years.
- Scott Goodwin at Davenport Harbour Lawyers for his legal acumen.
- Mike Hutcheson for being a wonderful sounding board and a great lunch companion.
- Chris Richardson at Les Mills for green-lighting the initial pilot and providing all the guinea pigs.
- Bob Ross, who has helped guide us through the world of publishing.

We acknowledge the time Phillip Mills generously spent sharing his knowledge and expertise and Hugh Markham at the University of Auckland Recreation Centre for his input.

A huge thank you to all those who provided invaluable feedback on the program over the years.

To all the wonderful authors and teachers, who have shared their insights and been a major source of inspiration for us. There are too many of you to name here but we salute you and are eternally grateful for your contribution to the world.

All the corporate clients past, present and future who have allowed and will allow us to be let loose on their staff and put all the theory and exercises to the test.

Finally, we thank you for holding this book in your hands. Because if you weren't, it would just be taking up space on our bookshelf. We hope JOLT Challenge helps you make a positive change in some way, big or small.

Welcome to JOLT Challenge, the Self Intelligence experience

"Knowing others is wisdom;
knowing the self is enlightenment."

—TAO TE CHING

It's not necessary for you to read this chapter if you are holding this book in your hot little hands and don't have the JOLT Challenge journal and/or aren't enrolled in the JOLT Challenge workouts. You can go straight to the Introduction on Self Intelligence on page xxi. If interested, please contact us via our website (*www.joltchallenge.com*) to find out how to get the journal and/or workouts brought to you.

Our intention is to guide you towards positive change. The next nine weeks is designed to be a fun and stimulating experience, giving you the opportunity to develop your Self Intelligence. Self Intelligence is being aware of and managing your thoughts, emotions, behaviour and capabilities. You'll come to understand yourself more and learn to get the best out of life. By the end of the Challenge you will have looked at the different parts that make up your life and know how you can maximise results so you achieve fulfilment.

Not another one!

Right about now you might be thinking, not another bleeding self-help program! Yes, we know the shelves are full of self-help books on a huge variety of topics ranging from mending relationships to fixing your tap and possibly including mending your relationship while fixing your tap. We're not interested in fixing or mending you. JOLT Challenge is a journey of Self Intelligence. Being smarter about your current *self* allows you to create positive change in your life.

"It's a funny thing about life; if you refuse to accept
anything but the best, you very often get it."

—W. SOMERSET MAUGHAM, PLAYWRIGHT

While this book is a powerful tool in itself, maximum value comes from the overall experience.

The JOLT Challenge program is divided up into four parts: the book, the journal, the workouts and the measurement. Just like fish 'n' chips are incomplete without salt and tomato sauce, so too is JOLT Challenge not fully complete with one component missing; as the saying goes – *"The whole is greater than the sum of its parts."*

JOLT Challenge

There are four components that make up the JOLT Challenge program.

1. The JOLT Challenge Book

There is information based on nine weekly themes, each divided into five parts. We have kept the reading down to an absolute minimum so you can concentrate on the exercises and tools to create positive change. We recommend you read the week you will be exploring in the workout first so you know what we're taking you through.

You only need to read each day as you do it. Read the concise information and then go to the journal to do the exercises. Look to incorporate the tool into your daily routine. There is no need to read the book from cover to cover. That's just crazy and a waste of your time, as you won't take it all in.

Book guides

We use these icons to help cement your understanding of the information.

> **Story**
> Stories are how you make sense of information. They help shape your reality. We've used traditional stories along with case studies from past workout experiences.

> **Movie**
> These are movies that in some shape or form touch on the points we're covering. Sometimes we just reference them, other times we suggest you actively watch them (again, if need be) and use them as a learning experience. Watch them on DVD rather than on TV so you don't get interrupted by commercials. It's even better if you watch them with someone else so you can talk about the movie afterwards. You may want to discuss particular characters, decisions they made, actions they took, different choices you might make in that situation, or any emotions that arose for you.

> **Cliff Says...**
> Cliff Says is a piece of trivia for you. Cliff is your stereotypical know-it-all, the kind of person that hangs around bars waiting to drop pieces of trivia into conversations at random to look like a genius.

2. The JOLT Challenge Journal

This is YOUR journal. Its purpose is to inform and provide you with the necessary tools and exercises for growth in all areas of your life. Colour it in, record your thoughts and feelings throughout the Challenge, doodle all over it – it's yours to enjoy! Make sure you keep it in a safe place. You may or may not want to show other people.

There are exercises and easy-to-use tools to help you maximise the benefits.

Some of the exercises build on previous ones and some are self-contained. We recommend you do them all. Remember, this is an investment in yourself!

3. The JOLT Challenge workouts

One 90-minute session a week for nine weeks.

At every session you'll be coached by an accredited JOLT Challenge trainer who will take you through a variety of exercises that will invigorate your mind and the way you see yourself.

There is a maximum of sixteen people per class, and the workouts are conducted in a non-judgemental environment. This means you're safe to let any barriers drop and unleash your full creative self.

> *"Be not afraid of changing slowly; be afraid only of standing still."*
>
> —CHINESE PROVERB

4. Self Assessment Module (SAM)

The JOLT Challenge program is complete with an online measurement tool that helps you measure positive change.

As each person is at a different stage and is looking for different things from JOLT Challenge, the benefits will be different. The following are just some of the benefits people have told us they experienced after completing the JOLT Challenge:

- More confidence – lost inhibitions
- Increased creativity – not being stuck for ideas
- Overcame procrastination
- Increased happiness
- More energy
- Achieved peak performance
- Better time management
- Deeper awareness and appreciation of their self
- Improved quality of life
- Less stress
- Improved concentration – eliminated distractions
- Enhanced communication skills
- Adapted to change more readily
- Goal setting became easy
- Discovered more opportunities for growth

To get the most out of SAM, you must complete the experience. If you don't do the minimum then it's highly improbable you'll get the results others have enjoyed.

The JOLT Challenge impact

Because JOLT Challenge works on your Self Intelligence it has an impact on all areas of your life.

These areas we call **The Big 3**: Health, Wealth and Relationships

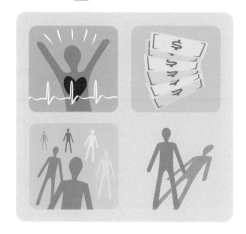

1. Your Health   – mental, physical, emotional, spiritual
2. Your Wealth   – career, business, savings, investments
3. Your Relationships – intimate, family, family of origin, friends, work related

All major issues in life can be brought under these three headings. These big three areas of your life are interconnected. It's hard to be all smiles and giggles at work if things aren't good at home. Likewise, if you're under stress at work then your health and relationships will suffer. So the JOLT Challenge is a holistic way of looking at your life and the life you desire by understanding more about your *self*.

What you need to bring to JOLT Challenge

> *"Minds are like parachutes; they only function when they're open."*
> —THOMAS DEWAR, BUSINESSMAN AND WHISKY MAKER

JOLT Challenge is an opportunity for you to experience, experiment and enjoy learnings that will bring more fulfilment into your life. There are always areas in life that can be improved. We've spent years researching and testing a myriad of the latest, the greatest and even the most obscure works on human development, so now it's over to you to rise to the challenge. Remember what Morpheus said to Neo in the unexpected smash hit movie, *The Matrix*, about freeing his mind and only being able to *show* him the door. Neo is the one who has to walk through it.

So, dear chosen one, the following are what you need to bring to JOLT Challenge:

1. **Desire/need for change**

   This is fundamental for you to succeed. Think of any area in your life you'd like to improve and there's your desire. Some will be stronger than others. Be sure that you don't confuse fulfilment with comfort. Many people are comfortable but they're not always happy or fulfilled. Everyone has desire at some level, so it's a sure bet that there's an area of your life that can be improved as a result of this experience.

   The key to create positive change in your life is to get leverage over yourself. Someone who has just been diagnosed with lung cancer doesn't usually need much in the way of motivation to stop smoking. Don't fall for the comfort trap or wait for things to go bad before you look to make changes. You must actively look for ways to get leverage on yourself so create a life you're thrilled to live.

2. **An open mind**

   In Malcolm Gladwell's book *Blink*, he tells two stories about police officers making snap decisions. One group of officers makes a snap decision and shoots an innocent man forty-one times. Another officer has a youth draw a gun on him but this officer doesn't shoot. He delays judgement long enough for the youth to drop his gun. The difference? One group made assumptions, didn't delay judgement and someone wound up dead. Extreme example, yes, but if you close up your mind to the content within JOLT Challenge you do yourself a great disservice. Keep an open mind, you may not necessarily save a life but you will definitely improve yours.

3. **Commitment**

   We've made JOLT Challenge simple, fun and stimulating. If you commit to the challenge and follow the guidelines, you will enjoy positive change. Simple.

And that's pretty much it. You bring these three things with you and you'll experience an uplift in your daily life. It's what any top performance athlete knows. If you want to be in peak physical and mental condition at game time then you have to put the work in on the off-season. You know, the old "you only get out what you put in" message.

> ### 📖 The Two Wheeler
>
> Imagine you've entered a bike race and when you get to the start line you notice that everyone else has the latest aerodynamic bikes with thirty-six gears and the streamlined clothes. You realise that your ten-speed is not even in the same league. However, you are determined to do well so you put in extra effort. You do okay but you were never going to win the race, as you just didn't have the latest technology.
>
> So you go out and buy the latest thirty-six speed bike and get all the accessories that the top people use. In the next race, you are feeling so confident that you just cruise and to your surprise you finish in about the same place you did with the old bike.
>
> What went wrong? Just having the latest technology by itself isn't enough. You still need to put in the effort in order to win the race.

Wherever you are in life, there's something in JOLT Challenge for you. You'll gain crucial life skills in a fun, unique way without all the usual effort it takes to work on self-development. All change starts with you and these positive changes will set you up for life!

> *"You must be the change you wish to see in the world."*
>
> —MAHATMA GANDHI, SPIRITUAL LEADER

Why change is difficult

Have you ever had a desire to change a habit but found it difficult? Even though you really wanted to change and were totally committed, you still found yourself slipping back to your old ways.

The reason for this is because the conditioning you've gone through has created a certain chemical balance in your brain. When you try and do something different, it throws the mind and body into chaos and you lose the identity you are so familiar with. Your mind and body will seek to return to the familiar, often ending your hopes of making that change.

> ### 📖 The Voice Within
>
> One of our JOLT trainers has a family member who decided to give up smoking. One night, after a few days this person woke up with a voice in his head telling him quite clearly to have a cigarette. He told us:
>
> *"I distinctly heard a voice saying, 'Go on, have a cigarette. Just one.' It was as if there was someone in the room beside me. It really was an overpowering sensation."*

The good news is that you can overcome this conditioning to create positive change in your life. Just as the person in the previous story resisted the voice and the urge to have a cigarette, you too can rise above the seductive feeling of the familiar, and use the tools and exercises in this Challenge to achieve what you truly desire.

Be aware that your inner voice can be cunning. It will create all sorts of reasons for you not to pursue positive change and remain where you are.

Let's look at people who invest in self-development for example. Statistics bandied around show that only 1 in 20 people who ever purchase a how-to book or CD, or go to a seminar, ever read, listen or implement the information imparted. That's 5%. So, statistically speaking, the odds appear stacked against you for completing JOLT Challenge. You may even know of someone holding this book right now that has a self-help book sitting unread and unloved on a bookshelf somewhere.

However, statistics don't tell us why the 95% of people who invest in themselves financially never implement the program or stop using it. Our research revealed very common reasons that people come up with to stop them from achieving their desires. The trick is, you need to find reasons to take action – not reasons not to. We've provided a little remedy as well to help you complete this Challenge and defy the statistics.

The five most common reasons people don't follow on their investment, in order:

1. **Lack of time**
2. **Lack of money**
3. **Lack of constant motivation**
4. **Lack of fun**
5. **Lack of support**

> *"Life is what happens to you while you're busy making other plans."*
>
> —JOHN LENNON, MUSICIAN

1. Lack of time

REASON: You are so busy that you just don't have the time to design your life the way you want. You've got to go to work/school, pay the mortgage/rent, be a loving partner/sibling/parent, and maybe raise a family and/or pet. Who has time to work on developing the extraordinary mindset that will impact the way you think and everything you do in order to take you where you want?

REMEDY: Now – YOU have the time! JOLT Challenge is constant with regular classes on a weekly basis with a simple program to follow. All you have to do is make one change in your busy schedule and that is: make time for yourself. Give yourself a maximum of one hour a day, five days a week for nine weeks, on top of your classes. It's a total of approximately 60 hours. We're suggesting that you give yourself a total of two and a half days to design your life. We even make it easier by giving you tools to help you prioritise your time.

> *"You may delay, but time will not."*
>
> —BENJAMIN FRANKLIN, SCIENTIST & POLITICIAN

The one thing you need to accept right now is that you are worth taking the time for yourself. You probably make time for everyone else in your life, you've got to start making time for you or there won't be any more left of you that's worth giving. From this one change you'll experience all you need to start achieving major results in your life. We even show you how to do this.

2. Lack of money

REASON: You find that the seminar is out of town or out of the country, the last lot of books weren't worth the money or the CDs are an ongoing cost requiring monthly payments and you're just not prepared to make that commitment.

REMEDY: JOLT Challenge is designed to empower you so that you don't need to keep buying other books and materials. We don't want you dependent on this program or on anything else. That's why we've assembled so many tools and exercises to keep you going.

> *"Money is better than poverty, if only for financial reasons."*
>
> —WOODY ALLEN, COMEDIAN

3. Lack of constant motivation

REASON: Your motivation to become who you want to be soon wears off when you put the book down, turn the CD off or leave the conference. The desire to improve yourself is still there but life just seems to get in the way of taking any action that gets long-term results. Like the joke, *'I bought a motivation book but just can't be bothered reading it'*, you need someone to read it for you. You need to be close to the source of inspiration.

REMEDY: JOLT Challenge provides you with a framework that allows you to get results. These results will inspire you to stay engaged. We can't motivate you, as the only person who has the ability to do that is YOU! We help you make this happen by providing you with the best tools, exercises and experiences possible.

4. Lack of fun

REASON: The course is boring. It's tiresome and feels too much like hard work to be constantly motivating and monitoring yourself.

REMEDY: JOLT Challenge is fun. That doesn't mean because it's fun the program can't have life-changing results for you. It just means you enjoy the journey as you go. There's plenty of laughter and learning happening in the workouts. And yes, you may well end up laughing at yourself. This is a huge strength as not only does it help put personally challenging issues into a different perspective – it makes life a whole lot easier!

> **Cliff Says...**
> *It's a little known fact that...* 7 out of 10 people who lose their jobs do so, not because of a lack of technical skill, but due to personality conflicts. If you can laugh at yourself, you'll go places you want to go. If you can't laugh at yourself, you'll also go places, just probably not to places you want to go!

> *"If you're looking for self-help, why would you read a book written by somebody else? That's not self-help, that's help."*
>
> —GEORGE CARLIN, COMEDIAN

However, while we laugh with George Carlin, we disagree with his methodology of only needing 30 or 40 shots to the head with a golf club to motivate you. You'll find JOLT Challenge a lot less painful in comparison.

A helpful maxim to remember is:

Take what you do seriously; just don't take yourself too seriously!

5. Lack of support

REASON: This is a real killer. You want to make the change, you schedule the time to focus on you, you feel motivated but you're all alone. Or worse, your partner or associates at work don't support you. Change can be scary for most people so you end up with good intentions but no action.

REMEDY: With JOLT Challenge you are surrounded by like-minded people in a supportive and positive environment with a trained instructor. You're not alone. You have the opportunity to develop your very own support network with real people and not just those over the internet. If a lack of support does arise *after* the challenge you will have the knowledge and tools to manage the situation.

But wait there's more

There were three other reasons that people gave as to why they never followed through on self-development. We include them here because some of them may or may not apply to you and hinder you completing JOLT Challenge.

i) 'Same wine, different bottle'

It was said in different ways, but we call it the 'same wine, different bottle' syndrome.

This is when people say that all the self-development stuff is all the same. Another variation on this theme is when people say, "*I know this already*" or "*it's just common sense".*

We agree. On some level, you probably do know some of this stuff. If you want to lose weight, you know you've got to eat the appropriate amount of healthy food, cut out the junk and exercise regularly. You know what to do – you just don't do what you know. The difference is taking action and JOLT Challenge makes it easy to do.

> *"The only true wisdom is in knowing you know nothing."*
>
> —SOCRATES, PHILOSOPHER

As soon as you say, *"yeah, I know this"* be aware that you'll switch off and are stopping yourself from having a learning experience. We suggest you keep your mind open.

CALVIN AND HOBBES © 1995 Watterson. Dist. By UNIVERSAL PRESS SYNDICATE. Reprinted with permission. All rights reserved.

ii) Instant gratification

This Calvin & Hobbes cartoon pretty much sums it up. People want instant changes the easy way. They want abs in three minutes a day, food in sixty seconds or less and an instant online degree that's only a credit card away. True success doesn't come that way. Think of how long you have been practising and embedding your old habits. In order to get the results from JOLT Challenge you're going to have to do it. This is one of the reasons why it's called a Challenge.

iii) Fear

Fear may take on many different masks – fear of the unknown, fear of being judged, fear of failure, fear of success or fear of pain. It's the number one killer of creativity and growth and we tackle this issue in JOLT Challenge.

> *"Courage is resistance to fear, mastery of fear, not absence of fear."*
>
> —MARK TWAIN, WRITER

Providing you follow the guidelines, there is no right or wrong way of doing JOLT Challenge. You will be 100% correct. It's about accepting yourself and delaying judgement about yourself while being open to learn.

It's a set-up!

This Challenge is set up for you to succeed. Surround yourself with positive supporters and detach from detractors whether the judgements come from within you or people around you. You are responsible for your actions. And that's exactly what we are inviting you to do. Take action and create the life you desire. Our intention is quite clear. It's to give you simple and effective tools, exercises and experiences for you to increase your Self Intelligence.

> *"The important thing is not to stop questioning."*
> —ALBERT EINSTEIN, PHYSICIST

And now we begin...

The scene is set, the trumpets have sounded, it's time now to draw back the curtain and... let the games begin!

If you have any queries, thoughts, suggestions, comments before, during or after JOLT Challenge then please contact us at info@joltchallenge.com

We're here to support you on this journey and have fun together while we do it. Make the most out of your JOLT Challenge!

The Mind Warriors Team

Introduction: Self Intelligence

"Know thyself"
—INSCRIPTION AT THE TEMPLE OF DELPHI

All great philosophers, spiritual teachers and the smartest people to walk the face of the earth have basically said the same thing – the most important thing you can do is to know yourself better than you know yourself now. Through self-examination you will come to understand yourself better and enjoy the associated fruits of success. This process is called increasing your Self Intelligence. People have different levels of Self Intelligence, which is why people may react differently to the same experience.

"There are three things extremely hard: steel, a diamond, and to know one's self."
—BENJAMIN FRANKLIN, SCIENTIST & POLITICIAN

Self Intelligence is cyclic in nature and made up of two parts: awareness and management.

Self-awareness is the cornerstone of understanding your *self*. Namely, your:
- Thoughts
- Emotions
- Behaviour
- Capabilities

From awareness comes choice. Every experience provides you with feedback. The greater your self-awareness, the better choices you're able to make. This is the second part of Self Intelligence: self-management. These choices then influence your awareness and so the cycle continues.

"A mind stretched to a new idea never goes back to its original dimensions."
—OLIVER WENDELL HOLMES SENIOR, PHYSICIAN & POET

EXAMPLE: You're having a conversation with friends when one angrily tells you that you don't listen and cut people off while others are talking.

REACTION: You take offence and defend yourself.

SELF INTELLIGENCE: The next time you're in a conversation you catch yourself cutting someone off. You realise that you do cut people off and you say to yourself that you won't do it again. That's self-awareness. Later in the conversation you're about to cut the person off again but you catch yourself and remain listening till they've stopped speaking. Now, you're managing yourself by consciously choosing to listen. You practise this choice in following conversations and it becomes a habit. That's Self Intelligence in action.

> *"It is where we place our attention and on what we place our attention that maps the very course of our state of being."*
>
> —JOE DISPENZA, CHIROPRACTOR & AUTHOR

It doesn't have to be someone else who makes you aware of an element of your behaviour. You yourself can become aware of your own strengths and opportunities regarding your thoughts, emotions, behaviour and capabilities simply by making the effort to do so. JOLT Challenge doesn't require any Herculean effort, just a little bit of attention to your reactions to daily stimuli, and a commitment to experiment with your current set thought, emotional and behavioural patterns.

Conscious mind vs Unconscious mind

The conscious mind, despite its extraordinary ability, can only effectively have one thought at a time. We call this paying attention. It is a limited resource and if you doubt this then try holding an in-depth conversation with someone while watching TV, or ponder over a problem at work while doing a crossword. Like a radio, it can only be tuned in to one station at a time.

Multi-tasking isn't so much doing multiple tasks at the same time, but rather rapidly switching attention from one task to another to give the impression that it's all happening at once. Stirring a casserole on the stove while talking on the phone or switching your attention from a book to the TV are examples of this. The beauty is that you can choose where to focus your attention. This is the real power of creating positive change in your life.

The unconscious mind is the sum total of all neurological and biochemical functions that take place below the level of conscious awareness. It's what beats your heart, filters your blood, regenerates your cells, and performs many other functions in the body that you don't even consciously think about. Although there is still debate about the role of the unconscious mind, it is widely accepted that it is on 24/7 taking in information that you are not consciously aware of. Your beliefs, actions and behaviour are often the result of what lies in your unconscious mind. It can determine what you do, how you do it and how you feel about it. Your unconscious mind is there to serve you. When you tap into your unconscious mind, you are tapping into a wealth of knowledge and experience.

Although commonly used, the term *subconscious mind* is avoided in most academic settings as it's deemed unscientific, with the term *unconscious mind* preferred. For consistency purposes, we've chosen to use 'unconscious mind', but we're talking about the same thing.

JOLT Challenge is about taking things that you may know at an unconscious level, and bringing them into your conscious awareness. So some things may already be familiar to you. That's good. Through repetition and practice of the exercises and activities, the principles for fulfilment will become a part of you as you reach a 'higher conscious competence' level, which is explained fully in the Growth Cycle (Week 1 Day 1).

The super computer

While the brain is often compared to a super computer, it's fair to say that it's much more impressive than any computer. Using this analogy however, let's grossly over-simplify things. If your actions are the computer screen where we see the results of your behaviour, then your five senses are the keyboard that programs your brain, and the hard drive is your unconscious mind that records everything.

George Thurman Fleet, a chiropractor, developed this Stick Person Model in 1934 to show the connection between the conscious mind and unconscious mind. All senses feed our conscious mind. Our emotions influence our thoughts and behaviours.

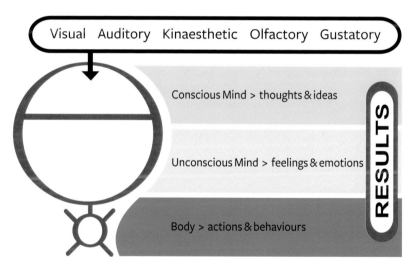

Brain function studies show that the conscious mind is like the tip of the iceberg and only makes up 5% of the mind while the unconscious mind makes up 95% of the mind.

The 4 components of behaviour

As a human being, morning to night, birth to death, you behave.
Your behaviour is made up of four inseparable components:

1. Perceiving – you use your five senses to gather information
2. Feeling – you feel emotions like love, anger, sadness
3. Thinking – you reason, imagine, analyse, ponder
4. Acting – you move, walk, eat, play, exercise, have physiological responses

You experience these components at the same time. Right now you're reading this book. You are seeing the written words on the page and may be feeling the texture and weight of the book. You have some feelings about what you're reading and are thinking about what you're reading. You're physically reading the pages and your body is holding a posture while you do so.

These four components are often, for convenience's sake, lumped into one verb – doing. However, all four parts are at work no matter what you are doing. The famous psychiatrist Carl Jung believed that your preferences for gathering information are innate. However, it's important to know that although you have direct control over the thinking and acting components, you only have indirect control over your feelings. This means that:

**You change the way you feel
by changing your thoughts or acting differently**

This gives you great freedom knowing that with enough determination, ultimately you can control your behaviour.

At times you'll feel negative emotions or have negative thoughts, but you'll discover in Emotions (Week 5 Day 1) these can often serve you. There are those that don't, so your job is to recognise which ones do and choose accordingly. This is Self Intelligence.

All behaviour has a positive intention

People do what they do for a reason. Every action is an attempt to meet a need, regardless of how others may evaluate it. Even the most destructive behaviour has a positive intention underneath it for that person. When you're unable to understand someone else's behaviour, it's because you don't see the world as they see it, and therefore have a different reality.

EXAMPLE: Someone may attempt to mug someone and end up murdering them. Where's the positive intention? The mugger may have wanted the money to buy food, drugs or alcohol. They may have wanted to feel powerful and mugging someone gave them that. Whatever their reason for doing so, they thought it was their best option. Obviously looking from outside in there are better options, but to that person it was their best choice at the time.

That's an extreme example and we're not judging the morals of the mugger, simply the intention. You can probably think of a time in the past when you've behaved in a way that you've since become ashamed of, embarrassed about, or you've looked back and laughed at. At the time, that behaviour seemed the best way forward to you. In hindsight, you now know there were different choices available to you. There is a word for this process: learning.

JOLT Challenge is all about giving you more options and new choices in life. The most powerful thing you can do is to be aware and manage your own behaviour as it leads you to personal fulfilment.

WEEK ONE:

Strengthen Your Foundations

Purpose

To gain a holistic view of how you grow, and to understand any barriers that may hinder you from learning and taking action to achieve fulfilment.

Overview

DAY 1: The Growth Cycle
DAY 2: S.U.C.C.E.E.D.
DAY 3: Overcoming Internal Barriers
DAY 4: Overcoming External Barriers
DAY 5: Procrastination

Benefits

This week's experience in the Challenge guides you to:

- understand the learning process
- learn how to set small, first steps towards achieving your desires
- learn to identify and overcome any thought, emotional or behavioural barriers that hinder you from moving forward
- beat procrastination
- have the conscious ability to induce physical and mental relaxation
- reduce stress and rejuvenate your energy levels
- increase your calmness under pressure and ability to cope with stressful situations
- heighten your creative mindset and ability to enter the play state
- increase self-confidence
- improve concentration and heighten focus and awareness
- connect better with people through eye contact, listening and accepting ideas.

Week 1 Day 1:
The Growth Cycle

"One can choose to go back toward safety or forward toward growth. Growth must be chosen again and again; fear must be overcome again and again."

—ABRAHAM MASLOW, PSYCHOLOGIST & AUTHOR

The Growth Cycle is how we grow as human beings. This cycle reflects the different stages of learning, incorporating the 'conscious competence' learning model. As you progress through JOLT Challenge you will encounter information, exercises and tools that may challenge what you know and believe. As a result you will experience some chaos as your comfort zone extends. You will adapt to these challenges and find yourself becoming quite competent at them. Then you'll start to have fun, and desire another challenge to take you to the next level.

As is the microcosm, so is the macrocosm

Your journey through JOLT Challenge is a microcosm of your journey through life.
Use the Growth Cycle as a way of navigating your way through both the challenge and your life.

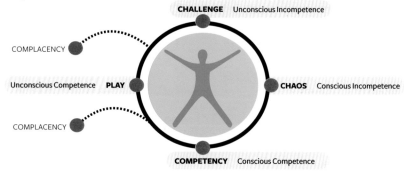

Challenge (unconscious incompetence)

"Small opportunities are often the beginning of great enterprises."

—DEMOSTHENES, STATESMAN AND ORATOR

When you begin something new it challenges you on different levels. New endeavours may challenge your emotions, behaviours, values, beliefs and thinking. New challenges provide opportunities for growth. They're either self-selected or ones you have no control over. Challenges may include a setback, a crisis, a promotion, a new project, a decision to get into shape, a death in the family, a birth in the family, learning a new skill, stopping smoking or a change in job description.

The famous psychologist Richard Lazarus, a pioneer in the study of emotions and stress, believed that anything you experience in life can be appraised as a loss, threat or challenge and those people who choose to reappraise losses and threats as challenges are happier and more effective.

The first three words of psychiatrist M. Scott Peck's book *The Road Less Traveled* are "*Life is difficult*". You need to accept that life isn't always fair or predictable. Hanging onto the illusion that it is, can mean that you'll end up disappointed and angry.

Think back to a challenging time, like learning to ride a bike as a kid or learning to drive for the first time. In the traditional competency model, unconscious incompetence is when you don't know you're not good at something until you try it.

Chaos (conscious incompetence)

> "*Life belongs to the living, and he who lives must be prepared for changes.*"
> —JOHANN WOLFGANG VON GOETHE, POLYMATH

As you work to make sense of the challenge, there may be areas where you fall into chaos and quickly become conscious of your incompetence. Taking the riding the bike or driving the car example, as soon as you fell off your bike or stalled the car, you became conscious of the fact that you sucked at it.

At work or home, this chaos may represent fear, distress, uncertainty, a lack of confidence, knowledge, skills or a desire to change. It is a perfectly natural state and part of the process of growing. If you are open to the challenge, willing to persevere and adapt accordingly, then these areas often provide you with the greatest opportunities for self-development. Gaining knowledge will help take you through the chaos stage.

There are only two types of knowledge: first-hand and second-hand knowledge.

i. First-hand knowledge is gained by personal experience. This takes time, repetition and trial and error.
ii. Second-hand knowledge is gained from other people. This includes educating yourself, seeking guidance from others and gaining different perspectives.

Competency (conscious competence)

> "*Great ability develops and reveals itself increasingly with every new assignment.*"
> —BALTASAR GRACIAN, WRITER

Once you break through the chaos you will feel a sense of achievement and pride as you reach your first level of competency. Things become easier as you focus on the task at hand whether it's pedalling, balancing, steering, changing gears, being aware of other vehicles, indicating and overtaking.

You feel you not only have a handle on things but you're getting quite good at it. As you increase your competency you will reach a point where you almost become automated in your behaviour in dealing with the challenge based on the existing rules and structure.

Play (unconscious competence)

> *"Play is the only way the highest intelligence of humankind can unfold."*
> —JOSEPH CHILTON PEARCE, AUTHOR

Unconscious competence is when you can do the task without even having to think about it. However, this is not enough, as you could be at the complacency stage of the cycle, doing things without thinking about it. The way to avoid complacency is that once you feel competent, start looking for ways to play. Look to have fun in what you do, whatever the challenge is. You've still got to ensure that objectives are being met but you can bring more of yourself to the task. As the saying goes, *'you've got to know the rules before you can break them'*. What can you do that allows you to bring your true self to whatever it is you're doing and keep yourself stimulated and engaged?

> *"Life isn't about striving for certainty but rather enjoying yourself in the midst of uncertainty."*
> —KEN HULTMAN, PSYCHOLOGIST & AUTHOR

Of course, there are those people who have a natural competence. They are good at a task but don't know how they actually do it. You may know of someone who has this natural ability in sports, music, leadership, investing or any activity. They are usually those annoying people who just know how to do something but can't explain it. They may have skipped the conscious competence stage, which means they will never reach the higher conscious competence level. You must know how you achieve success and do things well. If you don't, you will never be able to re-create that experience. The remedy for this is to reflect on the process involved and become aware of it. It may require you re-learn, un-learn or just become aware of the skills accordingly.

> *"Every child is an artist. The problem is how to remain an artist once he grows up."*
> —PABLO PICASSO, ARTIST

Play is your natural state when you are at your best. It is an exercise in self-definition; it reveals what we choose to do, not what we have to do. You've probably achieved this state a lot more as a child than as an adult. Not only children, but young animals too engage in play to aid their development. In fact, humans are among the very few animals that don't play as adults. Yet in the animal kingdom, play increases, rather than decreases, with increasing complexity of the brain.

> *"The day we stop playing is the day we stop learning."*
>
> —WILLIAM GLASSER, PSYCHOLOGIST & AUTHOR

Some psychologists say that William Glasser hasn't gone far enough in his quote above. They argue that when you stop playing, you start dying. When you are in a play state you reduce stress levels, heal emotions, stimulate creativity, attract people to you, improve your biochemical flow of information, gain new perspectives on issues that confront you, and are open to learning. You'll be exploring this play state further in Peak Performance (Week 7 Day 2).

Life is an adventure and no matter what it is you choose to do, you may as well enjoy it. If you're not enjoying your work, then take responsibility and rectify this. You must find ways to incorporate play. You are being most human when you are at play.

New challenge

> *"We shall not cease from exploration*
> *And the end of all our exploring*
> *Will be to arrive where we started*
> *And know the place for the first time."*
>
> —T.S. ELIOT, POET

You may reach the point where you're all played out and once again you run the risk of falling into the downward complacency spiral. This is when you need a new challenge. You're at the start of the cycle again but this time with more skills, knowledge and experience that has added to your personal growth and helped shape who you are.

Challenges are never going to go away. Nor should you want them to, as it's these very challenges that help you grow as a person. Welcome the many challenges you will face in life, and on this JOLT Challenge, knowing that they are simply opportunities for you to grow.

> *"There is nothing in a caterpillar that tells you it's going to be a butterfly."*
>
> —BUCKMINSTER FULLER, INVENTOR & AUTHOR

The Butterfly

A child was keeping caterpillars as part of a science project for school. She was fascinated when she looked into the glass container one day to see they had spun their cocoons. Each day she watched and one day she saw a tiny opening and could tell that a butterfly was trying to emerge. It seemed to be going well but after a while, things stopped happening. The little girl could tell that the butterfly had stopped struggling to get out. So she decided to help. She got a pair of scissors and cut part of the cocoon so the butterfly could escape.

The butterfly did indeed slide easily out of the cocoon but the little girl could tell something was wrong. The butterfly did not fly. It just lay there crawling around and the little girl noticed that its shape was all wrong. The body was large and the wings were too small. The butterfly unable to fly, soon died.

The girl upset, ran to her mum to tell her what happened. The mother comforting her daughter explained why this had happened. She pointed out that although she thought she was being kind and helpful to the butterfly by cutting the cocoon, the butterfly actually needed to struggle. The act of struggling actually sent fluid from the butterfly's body to strengthen its wings. The challenge of getting out of its shell makes the butterfly stronger, and by enduring this process in its own time it is ready for flight.

Complacency

If you become too automated in your thoughts and behaviour it highlights that the stimulation and meaning of the challenge is lost and this can result in you becoming complacent. It may come about because you are either over-skilled for the challenge or you do not suit that particular role.

This stage is not accounted for in the traditional competency model. However, feelings of complacency are a warning sign. It tells you, you have detoured from the Growth Cycle. From here, things can even shift towards disruption, an even bigger telltale sign that you need to get back on track. Disruption has many faces. It may be obstruction to getting things done, gossiping, procrastination or sabotaging ideas and actions. Disruption can be resourceful if you acknowledge it and do something positive towards changing your situation. Alternatively, if not addressed, disruption results in atrophy, or worse, it may lead to destruction, such as a manager of a business unit being responsible for creating a dysfunctional team.

Higher conscious competence

There is also a level of Self Intelligence that encompasses the Growth Cycle. We call it having a higher conscious competence. This is the ability to be aware of the task you did while being aware of your thinking and performance at the same time. You are in the moment but also aware of where you are at that moment. The expert can step outside of themselves while doing a task and be conscious of their unconscious competence.

Imagine that you are dealing successfully with the new computer system that has just been rolled out company wide. You are in the Play stage, getting work done, when someone interrupts your flow to ask you how you do it. This takes you out of Play and immediately into the Challenge stage. You find this interruption an annoyance but a part of you recognises this shift and you take the time to explain it to the person. Being able to explain your mastery and know where you are on the Growth Cycle is putting your higher conscious competence into action.

> **You can leave your hat on**
> Watch the movie *The Full Monty* from the viewpoint of the Growth Cycle and see how the characters go through the different stages both as individuals and as a group.

REMEMBER:

1. Chaos is a part of learning. Welcome it and know that it too shall pass.

2. Be aware of complacency. You need to get back into the cycle.

3. Play is your natural state and an indication you are fulfilling your potential.

Week 1 Day 2:   S.U.C.C.E.E.D.

Stepping Up Constantly and Consistently Each and Every Day

"We are what we repeatedly do. Excellence then is not an act but a habit."

—ARISTOTLE, PHILOSOPHER

In life it's the little things that matter – the little things that you do each and every day.

If you focus on improving your *self* and your situation just by a little bit every day in **The Big** 3 : Health, Wealth and Relationships, then you will reap the benefits.

Stepping Up

Life requires ACTION. That's why initially you must step up. It's difficult to do the things you know you should be doing when you've gotten yourself stuck in a pattern or are following an unresourceful strategy. Often the hardest step is the first one. It feels more like striving than stepping, so make the first step a small one. The payoff that comes from Stepping Up Constantly and Consistently Each and Every Day is that it gets easier each day.

Soon you'll realise that you're no longer striving on your path but actually stepping. And as your momentum builds you'll find yourself stepping faster, easier and taking bigger steps till you're literally spiralling upwards – success begets success as you cultivate a winning mindset and effective strategies. This is the Growth Cycle (Week 1 Day 1) in action.

"A journey of 1000 miles begins with a single step."

—LAO TZU, PHILOSOPHER

> **Cliff Says...**
> *It's a little known fact that...* more power and energy is used at the initial blast-off than any other stage of a space shuttle's voyage. It's at the first stage that resistance is at its greatest and once that's cleared almost no power is used to do the other things.

S.U.C.C.E.E.D. based on the Japanese concept of Kaizen (continuous improvement), is the best way to build up your confidence levels and create empowering habits. Success becomes self-perpetuating as you strengthen both your belief and ability to achieve your desired goals. Making these small steps regularly helps create positive change by bypassing the fear of trying something new.

> **My precious!**
>
> In *The Lord of the Rings: The Return of the King,* Frodo and Samwise have trekked through nine hours of film to get to Mordor where their final path is blocked by the enemy. When Frodo complains that they'll never make it, Samwise suggests, *"Let's just make it down the hill for starters."* That's S.U.C.C.E.E.D.!

Imagine you want to get fit but you're 10 kilos overweight. Rather than cutting all junk food out of your diet and running eight miles a day – take a small step. Cut down on junk food and go for a daily walk around the block. This way you avoid being hit with the physical and emotional pain of the extreme change in behaviour. However, if you start walking then you might like the difference, associate positively with exercise and build up an appetite for more change.

–ISH

And if you find that in certain areas of your life that 'constantly' is too big an ask then we're going to introduce you to a special word that stops all guilt and self-sabotaging thoughts and actions.

That word is –ish!

Just as there will be times in your life when you can't do what you'd like to do, there will be times throughout this Challenge where you can't do the exercises or required reading. That's where-ish comes into play. Be consistent-ish. Do it constantly-ish. Absolute thinking leads to pain, discouragement and disappointment if you constantly judge yourself by what you do or don't do.

While self-discipline is a prerequisite for success, there's no point being so absolute in your standards that you throw all your good work away because you fall behind a day or two. Just as it would be foolhardy to stop exercising altogether because you missed some workouts, it would be the same to give up during this JOLT Challenge or any other worthwhile goal.

This concept of -ish isn't an excuse for low standards but rather a way of keeping perspective on your journey towards your fulfilment.

Many ways to fulfilment

Gregory Bateson, anthropologist and social scientist, in his book *Steps to an Ecology of Mind,* has a conversation with his daughter. She asks why things always get into a muddle for her. He discovers it is only when she has her paint box on her desk in the right place and has it straight, is it considered tidy. He tells her the reason why things get muddled is *"just because there are more ways which you call 'untidy' than there are ways which you call 'tidy'"*.

So you may find when striving for your desired level of fulfilment, you have only one way of being fulfilled but have many ways to fail. So set yourself up for fulfilment by having more than one way of achieving it.

Imagine you have set the target of spending more quality time with your family. You measure this by your ability to stop taking work home on weekends. However, as soon as you get an urgent demand from work and take some work home you have failed this goal. You could have set other tasks such as: taking the kids to the park on Saturday morning, scheduling time with your significant other, picking the kids up after school, even doing chores with your partner.

Time

> *"Life is a checkerboard and the player opposite you is time. You are playing against a partner who will not tolerate indecision!"*
>
> —NAPOLEON HILL, AUTHOR

One of the most important decisions you make every day is how you spend your time. Are you spending it on pursuits that delay you living the life you desire or are you investing your time wisely on a daily basis? Are you living purposefully or are you unwittingly stuck on automatic pilot doing pretty much the same thing each day?

Research by the renowned psychologist Mihaly Csikszentmihalyi shows that your time can be broken down into the following activities:

i.	Production – working, studying,	24–60% of our time
ii.	Maintenance – housework, eating, grooming, driving	20–42% of our time
iii.	Leisure – watching TV, reading, hobbies, sports, resting	20–43% of our time

No wonder that one of people's biggest complaints these days, is that they can't find the time. And here's the reframe of the age-old problem of trying to find enough time to better yourself.

Don't find the time – MAKE the time!

Parkinson's Law: Work expands to fill the time available for its completion.

If you try and find the time, you never will. As Parkinson's Law states, you will always find more things to do, or work according to your available time, resulting in there never being enough time left over at the end of the day to do your really important things.

> *"Time is a created thing. To say 'I don't have time,' is like saying, 'I don't want to.'"*
>
> —LAO TZU, PHILOSOPHER

> **Got The Time?**
> One JOLT Challenge participant came to the trainer with their diary open showing them how full it was, complaining that they just didn't have time to do the journal's exercises. The trainer noticed that 7 am was booked out every morning and asked what happened then. The participant said that was when they went for a morning bike ride for 45 minutes.
> They said, *"You can't ask me to give up that time, it's my exercise time."*
> The trainer replied, *"I'm not asking you to give up that time. All I'm asking is for the next nine weeks, make JOLT Challenge exercises as important as your exercise time."*

ME-Time

Therefore you need to make the time to do the important things in your life. Make the time to do this Challenge, use the tools and do the exercises. It will help you in all areas of your life. Allocate a certain time of the day eg: first thing in the morning, last thing before going to bed. Make it your 'ME-Time'. You give everyone else so much of your time whether it's at your work or family, that giving yourself one hour a day isn't too much to ask of yourself.

Investing that time in yourself is probably on your list of things you should do. You probably have a long list of 'shoulds'.

You know you should exercise more, you should spend more time with the family, you should finish off the work project that's been on your to-do list for two months now, you should get up earlier, you should drink less alcohol, you should drink more water, you should drive slower, you should cut down the junk food, you should read more, you should be more considerate of your colleagues, you should, you should, you should!!

As Albert Ellis, psychologist and founder of Rational Emotive Behavioural Therapy, the predecessor to Cognitive Behaviour Therapy (CBT), puts it, to achieve fulfilment you've got to *"stop 'should-ing' on yourself!"* and turn some of those shoulds into action. Throughout JOLT Challenge, you have the opportunity to discover, create, consider, reflect and decide what is important to you. Some of your shoulds may just evaporate under this process as you realise they're not as important as you once thought them to be. You will then be spending your time on things that really matter to you. Other things on your list of shoulds will rise to the top. These are the things that you no longer should do. They are your must do's!

Remember: People often know what to do – they just don't do what they know!

Think of some of the things you'd like to have achieved but haven't. You probably know very well the reason why you haven't achieved these things. How about the things you're proud of achieving? What characteristics did you show to achieve these things? Your knowledge and actions can be divided in the following way:

Know / Don't Do	Know / Do
Don't Know / Don't Do	Don't Know / Do

"All know the Way; few actually walk it."
—BODDHIDARMA, SPIRITUAL LEADER

When confronted with a project or goal people tend to want to get it done right away rather than doing a bit at a time. Some people are able to make the time to successfully do this. If you are not one of those people, you are better off thinking of achieving your goals the way you would look after a garden. You do a little bit each day rather than attempting a complete landscape in a day then sitting back for the rest of the year.

When you work on your goal over time, over time your goal will manifest.

The one thing you can be certain of is that time will pass, so why not put it to good use? Good writers say if you want to write a book, then you only have to write 20 minutes a day. Over time you'll be a published author. If you want to retrain and learn something new, you may think that you'll be too old once you've finished your study. But how old will you be if you don't go to school?

"Good is the enemy of great."
—JIM COLLINS, AUTHOR

You don't just want to be comfortable – there's no growth in that. This doesn't mean you have to be great in all areas of your life at once as it may lead to stress. The good news is that ordinary effort over time will achieve extraordinary results. Think about the effects of time and how the money you saved from your first part-time job turned into paying for a vacation, the favourite items that started a collection are now worth more than the car and the extra chocolate after dinner became five kilos of undesired weight on the waist.

📖 *Sharpen Up!*

It was the final of the tree-cutting competition and the two woodcutters couldn't be any different. One was very experienced but a bit long in the tooth whereas the other was young, fit and had blown away the other competitors with his brute strength.

The final started and the young woodcutter attacked the trees with his axe. He felled tree after tree and impressed everyone with his constant energy. He noticed that the old woodcutter was pacing himself and would take short breaks every now and then. He didn't stop though and continued to chop every tree as fast as possible. At the end of the competition, the young man stood back looking at all the trees he'd cut down, confident he had won. The smile soon left his face when it became clear that the old woodcutter had cut many more trees than he.

"How is this possible?" asked the young woodcutter. *"I'm stronger than you and I worked harder. Unlike you, I didn't even take a break."*

The old woodcutter smiled and said, *"Yes, you are stronger and yes, you did work harder. But I wasn't taking breaks. I was stopping only to sharpen my axe."*

You need to stop ploughing ahead and make sure you're working smarter, and not just harder. S.U.C.C.E.E.D. is a concept that helps you achieve your success by taking small and doable steps on a regular basis. As the old saying goes, how do you eat an elephant? One mouthful at a time. This process of breaking down your goals is further explored in Chunking (Week 4 Day 4).

REMEMBER:

1. Do a little bit towards your desired outcome each day.

2. Make time, don't try and find it.

3. Turn your important shoulds into musts.

Week 1 Day 3:
Overcoming Internal Barriers

"Problems do not go away. They must be worked through or else they remain, forever a barrier to the growth and development of the spirit."

—M. SCOTT PECK, PSYCHIATRIST & AUTHOR

What stops you from living the life you desire and doing things you've always wanted to do?

From an early age, your parents, teachers, peers and society condition you to believe that experimentation outside their boundaries can be harmful to yourself and to others. Phrases such as *"I don't think you should do that"*, *"that's not how you do it"*, *"do you have permission to do that?"*, *"better check with your mother/father/teacher/ boss first"* probably sound familiar.

William Glasser, psychologist and founder of Choice Theory, calls this *external control psychology*. It's where people spend so much of their time trying to control others, when the only person you can really control is yourself. So focus your attention on yourself.

> **Cliff Says...**
> It's a little known fact that... if you grew up in a relatively positive household you were told NO! more than 148,000 times. Quick question: How many times can you remember being told that you could accomplish anything in your life?

"Freedom lies in being bold."

—ROBERT FROST, POET

Risk taking

A fulfilling life requires an element of risk taking. The risk of exposing something of your individuality, leaving the safety of your comfort zone, making mistakes, learning from new experiences and exposing yourself to unintended consequences. Living a fulfilling life is often a process of overcoming these negative influences that have controlled your behaviour from a young age.

"I've missed more than 9000 shots in my career. I've lost almost 300 games. Twenty-six times, I've been trusted to take the game-winning shot and missed. I've failed over and over and over again in my life. And that is why I succeed."

—MICHAEL JORDAN, BASKETBALL PLAYER

Most of your barriers are not in your conscious awareness but in your unconscious. There are different kinds of barriers but most of them stem from issues of self-esteem and uncertainty about how significant, competent or likable you are. This distorts your view of yourself and as a result you'll avoid doing anything where you may be rejected, criticised or embarrassed. Becoming aware of a particular barrier and working to overcome it is well worth the effort. It requires a detached view of your *self* where you are supportive and non-judgemental of who you are and what you're doing.

> *"Show me someone who hasn't failed, and I'll show you someone who hasn't tried hard enough."*
> —ALBERT EINSTEIN, PHYSICIST

4 Internal barriers

There are four internal barriers in each of the four components of behaviour (Introduction: Self Intelligence):

i. Perceptual – includes stereotyping and assumptions
ii. Emotional – includes fear and jealousy
iii. Thinking – includes irrational beliefs and imagination issues
iv. Acting – includes inadequate communication skills

i) Perceptual barriers

Perceptual barriers are obstacles preventing you from clearly perceiving the situation due to the way your brain learns and filters information (Neurons: Week 2 Day 3). Your mind is a self-organising system that is excellent at forming and identifying patterns from what you sense (see, hear, feel, smell, and taste). You recognise sequences, cycles, shapes, processes, similarities and probabilities based on your knowledge and experience.

While this ability serves you it also gives rise to a common problem in becoming fixated on one particular approach, method, strategy without seeing more appropriate ways of doing things. It's very easy to make assumptions and fall into stereotypical thinking. You'll do things because they make sense at the time and this becomes the way to do things. Circumstances will change but you still do the things you always did because it's what you know.

I Am What I Am

The finance team of a company we worked with didn't believe they were creative. They had stereotyped themselves as being the boring accountants that no other department wanted to work with on projects. They were considered as handbrakes and they didn't like this label.

Within the finance team was one member who had a completely different mindset to the rest. He had read books and done courses... *cont'd over* on creativity and ways of thinking, and was not at all fazed by the others.

The others in the finance team thought he was a loose cannon and maybe too "out there" for them. But this person was always asked for by other divisions requiring a finance person to work on their projects. It wasn't because he was a loose cannon but because he constructively added value to a project by being a team member. He was open to ideas and creatively sought ways to help their projects succeed financially rather than being bottom line focused and over-domineering on the financial aspects.

The irony was, despite being thought a loose cannon by the others, they all wanted what he achieved with other divisions.

If you have an issue that is stopping you achieving something in your life then you need to check that the problem is correctly identified. Inadequate or incorrect information can also obscure problems. When you state or analyse what's holding you back, make sure you look at the issue from various viewpoints and don't limit the problem area too closely by imposing constraints on it. Ask others for a contrasting view.

EXAMPLE: You feel you can't meditate because you don't have the time, you get uncomfortable sitting still or your mind constantly wanders. The problem is you're looking at meditation from a stereotyped viewpoint, sitting cross-legged like a Yogi in front of a candle for an hour. Ultimately, meditating is focusing your attention and quietening the chatter of your mind. So there are many different ways to meditate and there's no time limit on it. You could meditate sitting in a chair, or by going for a walk and focusing your thoughts. You could meditate while sunbathing, while sitting at a traffic light, on the bus, in the shower, or doing the dishes.

ii) Emotional barriers
Fear is the biggest barrier of all and as such we will look at this in more detail in Emotional Barriers (Week 5 Day 2).

Jealousy is another common emotional barrier. Ever been bitten by the green-eyed monster? Of course you have. Don't fret, we all have. We offer you a way to get out of dumpsville when you recognise the dead-end road you're on.

Comparing yourself with others is often the way you judge where you stand. Unfortunately, comparing yourself with others is a great way of bringing doubt and dissatisfaction into your life. It has an adverse effect on your self-image and therefore can inhibit your ability to achieve.

REMEDY: Practise the 'gratitude attitude' (Gratitude: Week 4 Day 1) when you catch yourself comparing your situation with another. Remind yourself that you may only be seeing the positives of their situation and not taking into account the negatives. You are a unique individual with a totally different skill set and motivators to everyone else, so focus your attention on your own talents.

If you are going to compare yourself with others, then compare yourself with those who are less fortunate than you – that sure helps put your life into perspective!

📖 Trip To The Country

One day a wealthy man took his son on a trip to the country with the intention of showing him how poor people can be. They stayed with a very poor family on a rundown farm. After their trip the father asked his son, *"How was the trip to the country?"*

"It was excellent, Dad, a real eye-opener!" came the response. *"I got to see how poor people can be."*

The father asked his son, *"What did you learn?"*

"Well," said the son. *"I learnt that we have a dog at home but they have three dogs, some sheep and a goat. We have a pool in the backyard and they have a creek that just keeps going and going. We have Chinese lanterns in the garden and they have the stars. Our deck allows us to see up to our neighbour's property and they have the whole horizon."*

The father was speechless as his son turned to him and said, *"Thanks, Dad, for showing me how poor we are."*

Abundance vs Scarcity mentality

People who constantly compare themselves with others have a scarcity mentality. They feel there isn't enough to go round and are unable to celebrate other people's successes.

Imagine you're an out-of-work actor who desires to make it to the big time. You've done all the training and are a talented actor. An acting buddy of yours calls you up and tells you that they've just been cast in a feature film that starts shooting next month. How do you react? Can you honestly be pleased and excited for your friend or do your thoughts turn immediately to your own situation?

People with an abundance mentality don't look at life as a competition. They think win-win in all their dealings and are genuinely happy for other people's success.

Another person's victory is not your loss!

REMEDY: Combat this by practising an abundance mentality. When someone tells you their good news, be genuinely happy for them rather than thinking you're missing out. Tell yourself, *"There's enough for everyone. My turn will come."*

Yes, this takes a great deal of emotional maturity but you'll avoid being a slave to envy and enjoy a more positive outlook.

iii) Thinking barriers

Your beliefs and how you see the world can limit your thinking. We'll explore this more in Beliefs (Week 6 Day 1). Your mind's imagination can also cause you issues that result in barriers.

Issues occur because of three main reasons:

1. Your imagination fills in and leaves out details indiscriminately.
2. Your imagination projects your present onto your future.
3. Your imagination fails to realise that events and situations will look different once they've happened.

1. You may not want to do something positive for yourself because you've exaggerated the reasons for not doing it due to a past experience that is stored inaccurately in your memory. Your memory has edited it down to the only negative part and stored that as a representation of the whole experience.

EXAMPLE: You want to join a gym and start to exercise more regularly. However, you think back to the last time you joined and recall how you never went at all. When in actual fact it is your imagination that has taken over and left out all the times you did go and felt great about exercising.

2. You may not bother trying an activity or task that has positive benefits for you because you think your future will be much the same as your present is now. But research shows that human beings greatly underestimate how things will turn out in the future and how they will feel about those things.

EXAMPLE: You've always wanted to learn wind surfing and do it on the weekends. However, you think that it wouldn't really make a big difference in your life so you give it a miss. Your imagination blocks all the exciting experiences and new people you'll meet by thinking it wouldn't have much impact on you.

3. You may not attempt something that is good for you because of how you imagine it will be. However, your brain has the marvellous ability to rationalise things that don't go your way and turn them around so they work for you.

EXAMPLE: There's an exercise in this Challenge you think will have no benefit for you. You don't have to do it to know this, you just use your imagination. However, you give it a try and then find it really resonates with you and wasn't what you expected at all.

> ### Yeah, Right
> We had a workout participant who told the JOLT Challenge trainer after a class they were totally sceptical about the Autogenic Training but went along with it to humour him. As the exercise started, she thought to herself, *"Yeah right, as if this is going to work"* only to find herself saying a few moments later *"Oh my God, this is working!"*

iv) Acting barriers

You are always communicating. You communicate through how you act – more specifically, what you say and do. You need to be aware of how you communicate even when you think you're not, as communication is made up of not only the words you say but also your tone of voice and your physiology (non-verbal communication).

The often bandied around figures for communication – 55% non-verbal, 38% vocal tone and 7% the words you say, are figures that have been taken out of context from a study by Albert Mehrabrian of UCLA. His research was never meant to be applied to normal communication and he himself states there are very few things that can be communicated non-verbally.

> **Cliff Says...**
> *It's a little known fact that...* the figures above came from Albert Mehrabrian's work where volunteers in a laboratory said one word only – *"maybe"*. No real surprise then that the value of this word was only 7%.

Regardless of what the actual percentages may be, all three culminate in your communication. Poor communication can result in misunderstandings and breakdowns in relationships, which in turn create barriers for you. You must take responsibility for how you communicate and understand that:

The response you get is the meaning of your communication

It may not be what you intended but that's how the other person interpreted it.

REMEDY: Be aware of how your communication affects others and resolve any misunderstandings sooner rather than later. Common sense, really – but then again common sense is not common practice!

> **Go Billy!**
> Watch the movie *Billy Elliot* from the perspective of overcoming internal barriers. Which barriers were overcome and what was required to achieve this?

REMEMBER:

1. Your conditioning has created barriers – your job is to identify them and overcome them.

2. You need to take risks in order to have a fulfilling life.

3. Practising the abundance mentality results in an inner peace and happiness.

Week 1 Day 4:
Overcoming External Barriers

*"The bravest are surely those who have the clearest
vision of what is before them, glory and danger
alike, and yet notwithstanding go out to meet it."*
—THUCYDIDES, HISTORIAN

There are two external barriers that can stop you from living a fulfilling life:
  i.   Culture   – includes social pressure
  ii. Environment   – includes physical space

i) Cultural barriers

A culture is an amalgamation of shared values, beliefs and customs. It can be in a family, business or wider social setting. A culture is displayed in the unwritten rules and expectations of behaviour.

Cultural barriers result from the pressure to conform or at least be thought of as normal. If you subscribe to these cultural norms, you may sacrifice living your true desire and settle for second best, third best or even worse. As this becomes a habit you start forgetting what is best for you and end up going with the crowd, never daring to stand up for yourself and what you truly want to do. As a result, you may end up doing a job you don't like, being stuck in a relationship you don't want to be in or living in a city you want to get out of.

*"Two roads diverged in a wood, and I,
I took the one less travelled by,
And that has made all the difference."*
—ROBERT FROST, POET

It can be a scary thing to go against the norm. People can have huge reactions to it. Friends and family may tell you that you're crazy to throw in such a well-paid job, or that you should consider yourself lucky to have such and such a relationship. Allow them to have those reactions, as only you know your truth. People may call you selfish and accuse you of looking out for number one. We've even had a participant report how a friend called them selfish for doing this Challenge!

> **To Fight Or Not To Fight**
> A JOLT Challenge trainer shared learnings that he and his wife had about the different ways they handled conflict. He always wanted to avoid conflict and would go out of his way to do so. Whereas his wife would welcome it as a way of clearing the air and moving through things. When she would bring things up that were potentially confrontational, he would always shut down emotionally and stop communicating. The reason they had such different ways of dealing with conflict was due to the way conflict was handled at home as children.
> In his home, conflict was always avoided and suppressed. In her home, there was always loud and animated discussion about matters with everything out in the open.
> Understanding the impact of this cultural conditioning helped them understand each other better and helped when conflict arose.

Imagine the pressure that may arise from a relationship between two people of different cultures. This occurs usually when the traditional practices of one or both cultures are so strong that they feel any relationships outside their culture will dilute and endanger it. You can easily see the cultural pressure that would build up if a young Indian woman and a young Japanese man from traditional families were in love and wanted to marry.

> **My Big Fat Greek Wedding**
> *My Big Fat Greek Wedding* is a comedy about a Greek-American woman who falls in love with a non-Greek American. The problem is her father is very staunch about Greek culture, values and tradition and tries to dominate her life, right down to who she can marry.

Be positively self-centred

To a certain extent you need to be selfish or as we call it 'positively self-centred'. Being centred on the *self* means that you don't sacrifice your life for someone else's. This stops you living another person's dream or having to live up to other people's standards and expectations. We don't mean selfish or self-centred in the way of having no respect, appreciation or regard for other people but there is a distinct order here. Think of the old flight safety message on aeroplanes – put the oxygen mask on yourself first and then help others. Having this viewpoint doesn't make you any less generous, kind or compassionate a person, but it will give you more confidence when dealing with cultural barriers. It means you're a passionate person who is on purpose. You can also be as generous, kind or compassionate as the next person, they're not mutually exclusive.

The idea of being thought of as selfish can stop you from doing what you want. Yet even one of the world's most caring people was positively self-centred. That's right, we're calling Mother Teresa (positively) self-centred. The reason she did what she did was because that's what gave her life meaning. She wasn't helping the poor, sick people of Calcutta because she thought others would approve of her. She did it because it was what she had to do. It gave her life meaning and a sense of fulfilment that she felt she couldn't have gotten any other way.

> ### Donkey Work
> A father and son were travelling from their village to the big city with their donkey. The man was riding the donkey while the son walked beside it holding the rope. As they neared the city gates, they heard a passerby say, *"Look at the father sitting on the donkey while he makes his son run around him trying to keep up."*
>
> The father, terribly embarrassed, got off the donkey immediately and put his son on the donkey. As they entered the city they heard someone else say, *"Well I never! What is the world coming to when a young boy can sit there all smug like a king, while the father has to walk beside the beast?"*
>
> Shamed to the core, the son asked his father to join him on the donkey. As they both sat there, they heard another passerby call out, *"What you're doing to that poor animal is disgraceful. You expect it to carry both of you? What is the human race coming to?"*
>
> Both father and son got off the donkey and walked beside it. As they turned into a street within the city, they heard derisive laughter and a man called out, *"Look at this, three asses! What's the point of having a donkey if it's not going to do any donkey work?"*
>
> The father and son stopped in the street and looked at each other. The father, patting the donkey said, *"Son, this has been an important lesson. I think it's time we did what we feel is right."*

Being positively self-centred means you are focusing on yourself rather than trying to change others. Keep in mind that when people criticise you, they may be jealous that they don't have what it takes to do what you're doing – not bowing down to the enormous pressure of society but rather choosing to live your own life.

"If each of us sweeps in front of our own steps, the whole world would be clean."
—JOHANN WOLFGANG VON GOETHE, POLYMATH

22

It may be a tough decision, but if you've invested in a path that your parents or friends thought you should do, then what's better – keep that bad investment going or cut your losses and do what's right for you? What's the rest of your life doing something you're not happy with compared with what you've already invested? Only you can answer this.

"The best time to plant a tree is twenty years ago. The second best time is today."

I Rule!

Kevin Spacey's character in the movie *American Beauty* breaks out of his going nowhere routine by quitting his job and starts to do all the things he'd always wanted to do. And of course, the people around him think he is crazy which reflects their values, beliefs and conditioning.

Strawberry Wisdom

Buddha once had a young disciple whose father hated the fact that this young man was wasting his time following this spiritual leader. The more the father thought about it the more enraged he became, until finally he went to Buddha to unleash his fury. He yelled and screamed at Buddha telling him how terrible and wicked he was for ruining his son's life and filling his head with nonsense. Buddha just sat there very quietly not saying anything. Finally the man became quiet and in exasperation asked, *"Why don't you say something?"*

Buddha asked him, *"What happens if a person gives you a plate of strawberries and you don't take it?"*

The man thought for a moment and replied, *"Well, I guess the strawberries stay with the giver."*

Buddha said, *"And so it is with your words, they remain with you."*

A look at great business leaders show that a big part of what they do is for other people. Anita Roddick, founder of the Body Shop once said, *"I love the relationship I have with my franchises. With my employees, who are my most treasured, loved friends. They are my extended family."* Hardly the words of a narcissist who doesn't care about others, yet Anita Roddick did what she loved, and lived her dream.

"Courage is the first of all human qualities because it is a quality which guarantees all the others."

—WINSTON CHURCHILL, POLITICIAN

It takes courage to be yourself. Some spiritual teachers say that's all enlightenment is – being yourself.

ii) Environmental barriers
Environmental barriers arise from the physical environment in which you live and work. It's obvious that you are going to be more effective in an environment where you feel comfortable.

STRENGTHEN YOUR FOUNDATIONS

Some of history's great thinkers have created environments and conditions to stimulate their thinking. The writer Marcel Proust worked in a cork-lined room. The composer Gustav Mahler wrote his music in a tiny cottage in the middle of a meadow. During the roaring twenties many noted writers and artists believed Paris to be the only city worth living in. Charles Dickens turned his bed and writing desk to face north, believing himself to be enabled by the magnetic forces. The philosopher Friedrich Schiller favoured the scent of fermenting apples he kept in a drawer in his desk.

How is your working environment? Is it conducive to maximum output? Often the office layout is decided for you. If you're in an open plan office and you actually prefer a quiet, enclosed space then at the very least let your manager know. You may be able to put up a partition, have a break-out room, a hot desk space or work from home one day of the week.

The same applies to your home environment. If you find you are not able to relax, create a quiet place. Similarly, if you need stimulation for thinking or creating, what will provide this for you? Just like anything, the more you put into your environment to understand what it might need for you, the more you'll get out of it.

You need a multi-sensory environment for optimum performance.

EXAMPLE: A comfortable chair and desk that's set up ergonomically. Perhaps pictures of loved ones, a plant, background music, essential oils, flowers and anything else that provides the right kind of stimulation.

First step

The first step is to identify any areas in your life where you feel blocked. We've provided some methods of overcoming barriers here and you'll find others as you venture forth throughout JOLT Challenge.

REMEMBER:

1. Cultural barriers can arise from your conditioning, a pressure to conform or at least to be thought of as normal.

2. You must be positively self-centred and focused on what you want in life.

3. Make sure your environment is congruent with your desired outcomes and suited to your personal tastes as much as possible.

Week 1 Day 5: Procrastination

"Procrastination is the bad habit of putting off until the day after tomorrow what should have been done the day before yesterday."

—NAPOLEON HILL, AUTHOR

Avoiding fulfilment

The ways to avoid fulfilment in life are many and varied but probably the most common way is procrastination. When you procrastinate, you sabotage yourself. Procrastination is the result of different barriers and people procrastinate for different reasons but ultimately it hurts your performance. Ever noticed how your room gets tidied up, the leaky tap gets fixed and you decide that you should re-catalogue your CDs alphabetically before starting on the important stuff?

People often put it down to a lack of time, but a study on habitual procrastinators found them no different in their ability to estimate time than achievers. So procrastination is not a problem of time management or poor planning. We all have the same amount of time – it's what we do with it that counts.

The good news is – everyone procrastinates. Unfortunately it's only good news because then you're not alone when you procrastinate. There are a variety of reasons why you put things off. It may be because you don't want to do the task, or because you have too many other things on your plate. To be human is to put things off, whether it's big or small things.

Pay attention to the small things before they become big things!

Can procrastination be good for you?

Yes, there is good procrastination. That is when the thing that needs doing is too small to worry about, or the task would be an annoying interruption to the flow of things. If you put off washing your car, and a dirty car doesn't bother you, who cares? Only when your procrastination results in your feeling discouraged and overwhelmed is it time to take action. Good procrastination is, as the saying goes, avoiding majoring in minor things. Sometimes you may have to disappoint people by saying no or delaying their smaller requirements to allow you to achieve what is important to you.

However, this isn't the kind of procrastination that most people deal with. Procrastination on important tasks can be a major problem to your career, relationships, finance and goals. Missed opportunities, stress, resentment, guilt and loss in productivity are just some of the symptoms.

*"Even if you're on the right track, you'll get run over
if you just sit there."*
—WILLIAM PENN, PROPRIETOR AND FOUNDER OF PHILADELPHIA

The Over Achiever
A journalist once asked Mahatma Gandhi's wife Kasturba, how he managed to accomplish so much. Her reply was *"Simple. Gandhi is congruent in regards to his speech, thought and action."*

A woman once asked Gandhi to tell her son to stop eating sugar. Gandhi told her to return with her son, in three weeks' time. Although confused, she did as she was asked. Three weeks later Gandhi looked at the boy and told him, *"Stop eating sugar."*

Later on, the woman asked Gandhi why he didn't tell him that three weeks ago. *"Because,"* Gandhi replied, *"three weeks ago I was eating sugar."*

"Suit the action to the word, the word to the action."
—WILLIAM SHAKESPEARE, THE BARD

Causes of procrastination

So why don't you do some of the things you think you should? One of the main reasons that you avoid doing things is a principle first proposed by Sigmund Freud, one of the world's most famous psychologists. Freud called it the 'pleasure principle'. Simply, it states, the basic motivation for all human behaviour is to seek pleasure and avoid pain.

It is totally natural to avoid pain and conflict. And because facing the truth can be painful, seeking the truth is not always something you do by nature. In creating the life you desire, you need to raise your levels of awareness, objectivity and detachment.

So how does the pleasure principle relate to procrastination? Well, if moving away from pain to pleasure is the basic motivation for all human behaviour, at some level you find pleasure in the inaction and believe that the pain of doing the task far outweighs any satisfaction you find in doing it. When you overcome this barrier, you will see the real pleasure gained from completing the task.

EXAMPLE: You find it a real drag to sit down each morning or evening to think and write in your Journal. Therefore, instead of setting aside time to follow the exercises in this book you watch television or chat on the phone to friends and maybe even take delight in feeling guilty. This is because you have not identified with the pleasure that you will gain by discovering your strengths, identifying your beliefs, and understanding the behaviours that have prevented you fulfilling your desires and potential that will result in setting you in motion on a path of fulfilment.

"Delaying gratification is a process of scheduling the pain and pleasure of life in such a way as to enhance the pleasure by meeting and experiencing the pain first and getting it over with. It is the only decent way to live."

—M. SCOTT PECK, PSYCHIATRIST & AUTHOR

Cliff Says...
It's a little known fact that... 20% of people identify themselves as chronic procrastinators, and it affects all areas of their life. Procrastination is the third most common reason people visit behavioural therapists.

There are many different psychological causes of procrastination, but generally these surround issues of anxiety, low sense of self-worth and a self-defeating mentality.

Here are a few reasons that might apply to you when you're not doing what you want to or know you should be doing:

a) Fear of failure
This is one of the most common fears, and not starting something protects you from failure. As the saying goes, it's only a failure when you fail to learn the lesson. Accept that you can only learn by doing.

b) Perfectomondo
Sure, The Fonz from the TV show *Happy Days* was perfect, but attempting to do things to the level of perfection is just going to cause you pain. If you consider yourself a perfectionist then understand that this view of yourself isn't going to help you, so cut yourself some slack. Lower your sights from "perfection" to "an incredibly high standard".

c) Easy like Sunday morning
You might believe that you shouldn't have to do anything that is demanding or not fun. Think of the long-term benefits and keep in mind, if it was easy then everyone would be doing it.

d) Under pressure
You might subscribe to the belief that if it wasn't for the last minute you wouldn't get anything done. Believing that you do your best work under pressure and right on deadline is a dangerous belief as you become hooked on the rush of adrenaline as you finish just before a client walks through the door, or at the close of business. This becomes a routine for you despite feeling exhausted for days afterwards, the exhaustion being the result of an adrenaline dump. We look at this addictive adrenaline rush in Brain & Body Chemicals (Week 2 Day 4). Know that more time spent on a task means the work is going to be of a higher standard.

e) My way

No one likes being told what to do, even if it's posed as a question and said to be in your best interests.

You might have a little sulk, do as little as possible or find ways to further procrastinate. If it's something that you should do, then you have to put your grown-up pants on and get started. Of course you think your way is the best way. And it may be the case. It may not. Open yourself up to learn other ways of doing things.

Dish It Up

In the movie *The Break Up*, the following dialogue occurs between the characters played by Jennifer Aniston and Vince Vaughn.

> Him: *"Okay, I'll do the dishes."*
> Her: *"I want you to want to do the dishes."*
> Him: *"Why would I want to do the dishes?"*

f) Almost ready

You may believe you'll get started as soon as you have a quiet, tidy room that's painted forest green with a north-facing window, and Mozart's *piano concerto no 2 K 39* playing on a Bose hi-fi system. Accept that you're never going to have the right situation, information and environment all the time. Life gets in the way of the perfect surroundings. All you need are the basic tools to get the job started and things will fall into place once you've started.

So if you're a procrastinator, then you're in good company – pretty much everyone else. Chances are you have some unhelpful beliefs about the thing you're procrastinating about. We look at how to change your beliefs to ones that best serve you in Beliefs (Week 6 Day 1).

> *"It is not because things are difficult that we do not dare, it is because we do not dare that they are difficult."*
> —SENECA THE YOUNGER, PHILOSOPHER & DRAMATIST

REMEMBER:

1. Everyone procrastinates in some form and it's not because of poor time management.

2. Good procrastination is avoiding doing the things that aren't as important.

3. A major cause of procrastination is losing sight of the pleasure/benefits gained from completing a particular task.

Week 1 summary map:

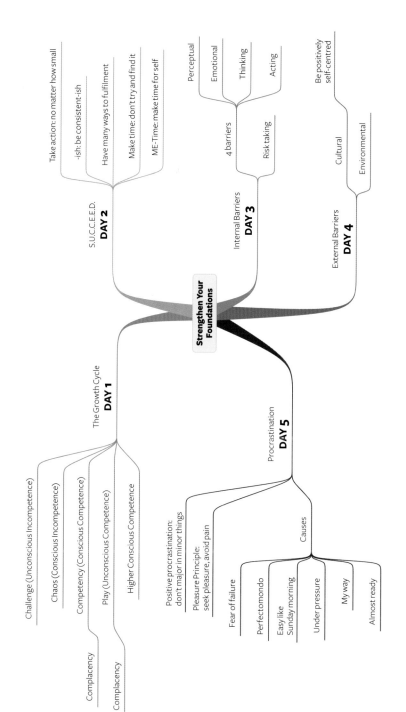

WEEK TWO:

Discover Your Amazing Brain

Purpose

To gain a general understanding of various brain functions, its chemicals and how you can optimise your learning process.

Overview

Day 1: Brain Map
Day 2: Emotional Brain
Day 3: Neurons
Day 4: Brain & Body Chemicals
Day 5: Senses

Benefits

This week's experience in the Challenge guides you to:

- improve your understanding of perception and reinforce that change is possible for you
- change your emotional state at will
- develop your sensory acuity to be more aware of your surroundings
- increase attention and your ability to focus
- bring on relaxation and calmness and diffuse stress
- help to enhance binocular peripheral vision and hand/eye coordination
- boost reading, writing and comprehension skills
- relieve eye strain that comes from staring at a computer all day.

Week 2 Day 1: Brain Map

"The growth of the human mind is still high adventure, in many ways the highest adventure on earth."

—NORMAN COUSINS, POLITICAL JOURNALIST & AUTHOR

Positive change starts in the mind. Therefore it's important to know the mechanics of your mind. We're going to start with your brain.

Your brain is amazing. The extent of your brain's capabilities is actually unknown but it is without a doubt the most complex living structure in the universe. It is constantly learning and organising itself as it reacts to new stimuli whether you're aware of it or not. With the exception of the dolphin, the human brain is six times larger, relative to body size, than any other mammal's.

> **Cliff Says...**
> *It's a little known fact that...* the human brain can process and store in the neighbourhood of one hundred trillion bits of information.

Three ways of looking at your brain

Different ways to view the brain include:

1. Triune brain
2. Brain division
3. Cerebral hemispheres

1. Triune brain

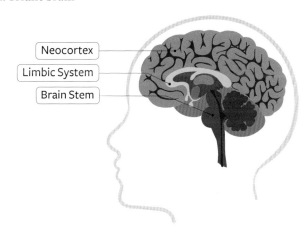

Neocortex

Limbic System

Brain Stem

The triune brain model developed by neuroscientist Paul MacLean at the National Institute of Health in the mid-1970s states that the brain evolved from bottom up – the brain stem (hind brain), the limbic system (midbrain) and the cerebrum or neocortex (forebrain). Keep in mind that despite the different parts to the brain and their ability to work independently, the whole brain actually works together to make the sum greater than the parts.

i) **Brain stem** – regulates basic life functions like breathing, heart rate and various levels of sleep and wakefulness. It's called the reptilian brain because it's the same brain that snakes and lizards have.

The cerebellum, situated behind the brain stem, is included in the first brain. It is responsible for balance, coordinates muscle movements and develops muscle memory. When you walk you probably don't think about consciously stepping with each foot or swinging your arms. This is because movement is being programmed into the cerebellum allowing you to put your conscious attention elsewhere. More recent research shows that the cerebellum is closely connected to the frontal lobe and also plays a part in complex emotional behaviours.

ii) **Limbic system** – the centre for emotions, learning and memory. It's called the mammalian brain because it's the same brain mammals have and explains why dogs hang out with other dogs and not chickens. It regulates temperature control, hormone levels, digestion and the fight or flight response. When a mammal sees something it comes up with limited choices, all starting with the letter F. Should I fight it, flee it, feed on it or … mate it.

The limbic system is also referred to as the emotional brain, which you'll be looking at in more detail in the following chapter. This is the part of your brain that can override your intellect.

iii) **Neocortex** – the part of the brain responsible for thinking, planning, perception, rationality and new learning. Making up around 76% of the mass of the brain, it gives us the ability to have feelings about our feelings, to think about our thinking and is what makes humans different from other animals.

When your boss criticises your work and you get angry it's the limbic system that has kicked in (emotion) and it's the reptilian brain that wants to inflict pain on them (defend yourself). But the neocortex then steps in and tells you it may not be such a good idea (rational thought). It's the limbic system again that generates the bad feeling (emotion) about the experience and burns that memory into your brain circuitry for future reference.

Cliff Says...

It's a little known fact that... chimpanzees have 96% of the same genetic material as humans but lack a developed neocortex. In humans, this part of the brain doesn't develop fully until some time in the early twenties, which may explain some teenagers' behaviour!

What's in a Brain?

A JOLT Challenge participant asked the trainer why they should learn about the brain. The trainer told them a story about going on a road trip with a friend. After stopping for a meal around 8 pm they found the car wouldn't start. The trainer knew nothing about cars and thought they would be spending the night in the vehicle. His friend, however, had a look under the hood, checked the spark plugs and tweaked the starter motor. The car started. The trainer said to his friend, *"I didn't know you were a mechanic."*

The friend replied, *"I'm not. I have only a basic understanding of cars to help get me out of trouble when I need it."*

The trainer told the JOLT Challenge participant that the information in this week wasn't going to make them a brain surgeon. However, it provides enough information to give a deeper awareness. This awareness leads to better choices – the trainer's friend didn't play with all the other parts under the hood but knew where to look first. Better choices lead to fulfilment.

Greater understanding = Deeper awareness = Better choices = Fulfilment

2. Brain division

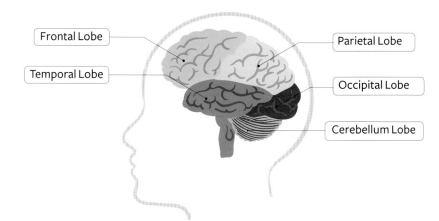

Frontal Lobe

Temporal Lobe

Parietal Lobe

Occipital Lobe

Cerebellum Lobe

The neocortex is divided into four main lobes:

We use the acronym F-TOP to help people remember.

i) **Frontal lobe** – this makes up approximately 38% of the neocortex. When it comes to being human, this is the big kahuna. It is what allows for self-awareness. It is responsible for the overall thinking process including planning, organising, imagining, reasoning and controlling. It is where language processing and movement coordination take place. It is the home of free will and responsible for any conscious choices you make and actions you take. We'll be covering more about the frontal lobe in Neurons (Week 2 Day 3).

ii) **Temporal lobe** – this makes up approximately 22% of the neocortex. Located just above each ear, the temporal lobes are responsible for hearing activity and interpreting speech, pitch, tone, sound and rhythm. It is also responsible for your sense of smell and your sense of balance. The temporal lobes help you associate experiences so you can recognise familiar stimuli.

iii) **Occipital lobe** – this makes up approximately 9% of the neocortex. It's responsible for vision and interpreting shape, colour and movement. It has six different areas that deal specifically with these different functions. One area makes out the shape, another area distinguishes the colour, while a different part can only see moving objects.

iv) **Parietal lobe** – this makes up approximately 25% of the neocortex. Located just above each ear, the parietal lobes are responsible for integrating sensory information from various parts of the body, your sense of taste, and your sense of position in space. It also processes what you feel with your hands and body, interpreting pressure, pain, pleasure and temperature.

> *"If the brain were so simple we could understand it,*
> *we would be so simple we couldn't."*
> —LYALL WATSON, ZOOLOGIST & ANTHROPOLOGIST

3. Cerebral hemispheres

Neuropsychologist Roger Sperry won a Nobel Prize for his work in split-brain research. It shows how your brain has two hemispheres – the right and left – and each side has its own unique and special abilities as listed below. The corpus callosum, made up of 300 million nerve fibres, is the part that links the two hemispheres, allowing them to communicate.

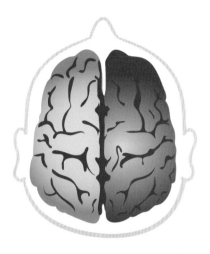

LEFT HEMISPHERE	RIGHT HEMISPHERE
Words	Images
Verbal	Physical
Parts	Whole
Logical	Intuitive
Intellect	Sensory
Structure	Creativity
Analysis	Synthesis
Linear & Sequential	Diffusely & Simultaneous
Either / Or	Both / And
Right / Wrong	Ambiguity
Time	Space
Connects to right side of body	Connects to left side of body

The two sides are not mirror images of each other and because the brain is a complex integrated system, it is a generalisation to say that left side is the logic brain and the right hemisphere is purely your creative brain. This categorisation is more metaphorical than physiologically accurate but it helps to identify different ways of thinking. And while you probably have a dominant side, it is safe to say that if you are only using one side of your brain, you're missing out!

> *"As long as our brain is a mystery, the universe, the reflection of the structure of the brain will also be a mystery."*
>
> —SANTIAGO RAMON Y CAJAL, HISTOLOGIST & PHYSICIAN

Spot the dog

The left hemisphere of your brain sees this picture as a collection of dots (parts) whereas your right hemisphere sees it as a picture of a Dalmatian dog (whole).

Cliff Says...
It's a little known fact that... the left hemisphere of the brain appears to be more dominant than the right for the majority of humans, which may explain why most people are in fact right-handed.

> *"Brain: an apparatus with which we think that we think.*
> *Mind, n: a mysterious form of matter secreted by the brain."*
>
> —AMBROSE BIERCE, JOURNALIST & SATIRIST

Brain waves

Your brain operates at five different frequencies that are commonly called Brain Waves. These frequencies are electrical impulses that fluctuate rhythmically depending on the type of brain activity going on. This activity is influenced by your thoughts, emotions and state of being.

BRAINWAVE FREQUENCIES

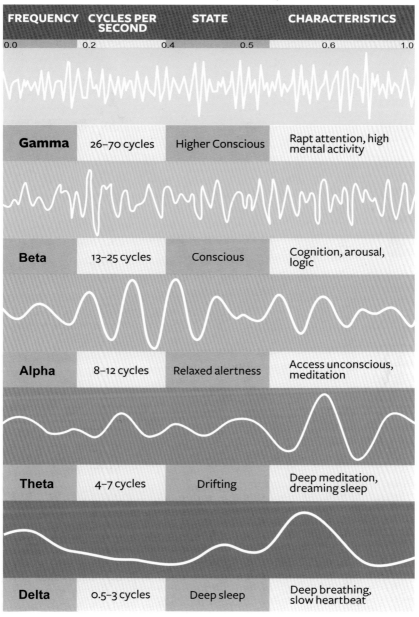

FREQUENCY	CYCLES PER SECOND	STATE	CHARACTERISTICS
Gamma	26–70 cycles	Higher Conscious	Rapt attention, high mental activity
Beta	13–25 cycles	Conscious	Cognition, arousal, logic
Alpha	8–12 cycles	Relaxed alertness	Access unconscious, meditation
Theta	4–7 cycles	Drifting	Deep meditation, dreaming sleep
Delta	0.5–3 cycles	Deep sleep	Deep breathing, slow heartbeat

0.0   0.2   0.4   0.5   0.6   1.0

Gamma is the highest state and its rhythms occur in humans and other mammals following sensory stimuli. The beta state is your normal waking state and some researchers include the gamma state in beta brain waves. The critical voice that lives in your head is more active in the beta state. By slowing the brain down and going into alpha state, you are able to access information stored at an unconscious level (Introduction: Self Intelligence).

"The brain is a world consisting of a number of unexplored continents and great stretches of unknown territory."
—SANTIAGO RAMON Y CAJAL, HISTOLOGIST & PHYSICIAN

Meditation and hypnosis are activities that allow your critical watchdog to take a back seat and let your unconscious mind provide personal insight and guidance. Studies on mediation have shown that it synchronises both the left and right hemisphere and the limbic and neocortex regions of the brain, making it more coherent and allowing it to communicate harmoniously.

Monking Around

In leading science writer Lynne McTaggart's book, *The Intention Experiment*, she tells the tale of the Dalai Lama sending eight of his most seasoned practitioners of meditation to the University of Wisconsin's Laboratory for Affective Neuroscience.

There, they measured the monks' brain waves while they meditated and found that they rapidly shifted from beta to alpha. This was expected and in line with previous research on the brain wave state during meditation.

Then the unexpected happened. The monks' brain waves then went back up to beta and then finally into gamma. This state is considered crucial for achieving heightened awareness and is often linked to moments of intense concentration.

The years of intensive meditation had permanently altered the monks' neural processing giving them the ability to quickly reach a state of heightened perception. This heightened state also activated the part of the brain most associated with happiness meaning that the monks had trained their brains to tap into joy. This probably explains why you don't bump into too many aggressive monks.

Cliff Says...

It's a little known fact that... studies of yogis have shown that they also have achieved gamma or high-frequency beta waves during deep meditation.

You'll be exploring more on the brain waves in Sleep (Week 3 Day 4). At this stage it's hugely beneficial for you to incorporate ways of achieving the alpha state into your daily routine so you can tap into the power of your unconscious mind and enjoy whole brain thinking.

REMEMBER:

1. The full potential of your brain is unknown, so explore it whenever you can.

2. You are a combination of instinct, emotions and logical thought and your behaviour reflects this.

3. There's a lot of power lying in your unconscious mind waiting for you to tap into.

Week 2 Day 2: Emotional Brain

"The heart has its reasons of which reason knows nothing."

—BLAISE PASCAL, MATHEMATICIAN & PHILOSOPHER

The emotional brain is the name given to the limbic system, the part of your brain responsible for emotions, learning and memory. Although recent research shows that emotions can also be stored in the body, our focus in this section is on the more classical locations of emotions. The emotional brain is made up of five major structures in the brain: the hypothalamus, amygdala, hippocampus, thalamus and basal ganglia. While the frontal lobes of the neocortex may add the logic to any decision you make, it is the limbic system that gives the decision emotional sway and is crucial for guiding you on a day-to-day basis.

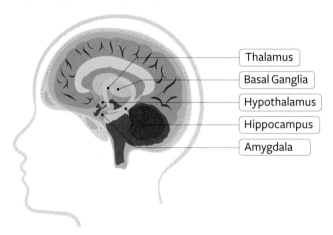

- Thalamus
- Basal Ganglia
- Hypothalamus
- Hippocampus
- Amygdala

People with damage to certain parts of the frontal lobes that connect directly to the limbic system can't decide which they'd rather do – watch their children play sport on the weekend or watch paint dry. Decisions become not only irrational but also neutral as the emotional context is lost. Think of the big decisions in your life – who you married or would like to marry, a house or car you've bought, where you last went for a holiday and you'll find logic and emotion working hand-in-hand.

The limbic system is a series of nerve pathways that is also linked to the autonomic nervous system. The autonomic nervous system regulates certain muscles and glands and is responsible for all your automatic (involuntary) functions, such as your heart beating, your breathing, blood vessel contraction, pupil dilation and other bodily organs.

The autonomic nervous system is divided into two separate parts:

i.   Sympathetic nervous system   – fight or flight response
ii. Parasympathetic nervous system   – rest and relax response

Imagine your ancestors are walking through the woods and come across a bear. They either froze, put their dukes up and showed him who's boss or found somewhere else to be – fast! The fact that you're here means the chances are, they didn't freeze or fight the bear but took flight (sympathetic). Once they were safe, they calmed down and their bodies began to return to normal (parasympathetic).

Hypothalamus

The hypothalamus is the part of the brain that regulates the autonomic nervous system. It is one of the busiest parts of the brain as it also regulates your levels of hunger, thirst, pain, pleasure, sexual arousal, your sleep/wake cycle and more.

Amygdala

The limbic system, like the rest of the brain, is an integrated system and one of the main areas involved with emotions is the amygdala.

The amygdala is responsible for your feelings and their significance, which means without the amygdala you wouldn't be able to recognise or experience any emotion. Life would lose all meaning. The amygdala also identifies danger so it is fundamental for self-preservation. The neuroscientist Joseph LeDoux was the first to discover the role of the amygdala in the emotional brain. His research found that the amygdala controls what we do while the neocortex is still making up its mind (pun definitely intended).

Imagine you're lying in bed at night and you hear a noise in the kitchen. You jump out of bed heart pounding, ready for action before you've even had time to realise that it was just the cat leaping up onto the bench.

This is an example of an emotional hijack. Sensory input comes in and the amygdala stimulates the sympathetic nervous system, your fight or flight response. Your self-preservation mechanisms kick in before logic and reason has a chance to react. This is great in moments of danger and when you're under attack. Unfortunately it's the same system that kicks in no matter how small or trivial the attack may be.

Imagine your significant other rings while you're under stress at work to tell you that the cat is sick. It triggers an abrupt *"I don't care"* response and now you're in the bad books.

Imagine your manager harshly criticises your report in front of you and others. Without thinking, you tell your manager where they can stick that report.

"Delay is the best remedy for anger."

—SENECA, PHILOSOPHER & DRAMATIST

The emotional brain can make a response in the first few milliseconds of perceiving something before you have even consciously become aware of what it is. It's a fast but not always accurate system and is separate from your logical, rational mind. If the amygdala senses a pattern from the incoming sensory data it goes "*oh no, not this again!*" and then it jumps to a conclusion.

Imagine you see a look on your manager's face and you think it's the same look they had last time they criticised you. So you go on the offensive even though they were actually going to praise your good work.

Because of the more complex neural circuitry involved, rational thought and analysis from the frontal lobes kick in after an emotional response. So in non-crisis moments it's wise to follow Seneca's words and delay before taking action on your rapid judgement.

Hippocampus

The other main area involved with emotions is the hippocampus. Its main function is memory and converts short-term memories into long-term memories. The hippocampus remembers things and events, putting those memories into context while the amygdala stores the emotional content of those memories.

Imagine you see a colleague walking towards you. It's the hippocampus that remembers his face, while the amygdala that tells you, you can't stand him.

Our strongest memories are those with a fired-up amygdala giving a stronger emotional content. This is why most people remember where they were or what they were doing when they heard that New Zealand had won its first America's Cup, when the World Trade Center was attacked and when they proposed or were proposed to.

> ### Cliff Says...
> *It's a little known fact that...* hippocampus gets its name from its curved shape resembling a seahorse. In Greek 'hippos' means 'horse' and 'kampi' translates as 'curve'.

Damage to the hippocampus can result in anterograde amnesia, which is the loss of ability to form new long-term memories. Previous memories prior to the damage remain intact. This is the opposite of retrograde amnesia, which is the inability to recall memories of the past, going beyond ordinary forgetfulness.

> ### His Name Rings A Bell
> There have been a number of movies that have used amnesia as the main plot. The Jason Bourne trilogy movies see Matt Damon, suffering retrograde amnesia, trying to find out who he is. The movie *Memento* starring Guy Pearce was based on anterograde amnesia as was the Adam Sandler and Drew Barrymore film *50 First Dates*. And of course, we can't forget Dory, the regal blue tang fish who also suffered anterograde amnesia in *Finding Nemo*.

Short-term Henry
In 1953, Dr William Scoville removed the hippocampus of a 23-year-old man called Henry in an attempt to cure him of epilepsy. It was thought that memory was spread all over the brain due to Karl Lashley's experiments in 1929, where rats could still remember how to perform tasks even with up to 90% of their brain removed or destroyed.

However, it soon became obvious after the surgery that although Henry was having far fewer fits he also couldn't form any new memories. Since the time of the surgery, he couldn't remember anyone he'd met five minutes previously. Although he could learn new skills, such as playing tennis and basketball, he couldn't remember ever learning them. For that he needed his hippocampus. Henry, known as H.M., became the most studied individual in the history of brain research.

Thalamus & basal ganglia
The thalamus and basal ganglia make up the other two areas of the limbic system. The thalamus relays motor impulses from the neocortex through the brain stem and out to the muscles. It receives all incoming information from the sensory organs interpreting pain and temperature. The basal ganglia are a complex bundle of nerves that connect the frontal lobe to the cerebellum. They integrate thoughts and feelings with physical actions.

Cliff Says...
It's a little known fact that... people who have Tourette's syndrome have their basal ganglia firing improperly which results in a lack of coordination between their thoughts and feelings, with their actions.

The harmony of emotion and thought
It's important to realise that emotions and logic go together equally. Living a life of emotion without rational thought would be tumultuous as you react to every new stimulus and get swept up in the current of constantly changing emotions. Life without emotions takes away the richness and beauty of life. Recognise the role that both play in your life, and live your life on a daily basis that harmonises both your head and your heart.

REMEMBER:

1. Non-crisis events can also stimulate your fight or flight response, creating stress.

2. Emotional hijacks are best dealt with by delaying judgement and action until you have the full picture.

3. Emotions and logic go together. The skill is utilising them to get the best result for you.

Week 2 Day 3:   Neurons

"Old minds are like old horses; you must exercise them if you wish to keep them in working order."

—JOHN QUINCY ADAMS, POLITICIAN

The brain has about 100 billion neurons (nerve cells) that can connect to each other creating a neural path with electrical, chemical and hormonal information transmitted along this pathway. Thinking is the process of neural connection. The result of this process is called learning. Understanding your thinking process results in making better choices in life.

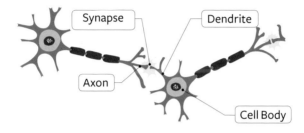

How thinking works

The gap between each neuron is called a synapse. Neurons communicate to each other via chemical messengers called neurotransmitters. Every time we take in some information, think a thought, or remember something, a pulse of energy moves through the jungle of neurons in our brain, mapping a route from cell to cell. That map is what we call a thought. These neural pathways are very malleable and are constantly changing as a direct result of your life experience. You are able to override genetic neural wiring that you are born with. This means there is huge potential for change and growth in your life. It also means you *can* teach an old dog new tricks.

Imagine you have a garden shed in your backyard. The grass has grown waist high and there is no path. So the first time you walk from your house to the shed you have difficulty making it. By walking there once, you have started to create the path by walking over the wild grass. If you keep walking regularly from the house to the shed, soon you will have created a path that you can travel along with ease.

Neurons that fire together, wire together

And so it goes with learning anything in life. Do something once and you're not very good at it. The more you do it, the more solid the connection between the neurons becomes, creating a neural pathway that makes it easier to accomplish the task whether it's tying your shoelaces or performing brain surgery.

> **Cliff Says...**
> *It's a little known fact that...* this type of learning is called Hebbian learning after psychologist Donald Hebb introduced the theory of cell assembly in 1949.

It's this very principle in action that makes changing unwanted behaviours and out-of-date thought patterns so challenging. Because they are repeated, they are laid down firmly in your brain. Fortunately, the reverse is also true.

Neurons that don't fire together, don't wire together

Disrupting the neural connetion be-gins to break down habitual thought, emotional and behavioural patterns. The connections loosen till the dendrites finally break off allowing them to connect with other neurons as in the diagram on the right.

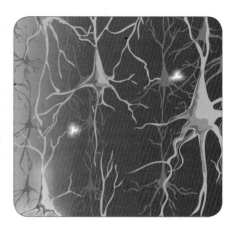

This makes the old adage "Use it or lose it" ring very true.

Patterns

The brain is a self-organising system that creates thought, emotional and behavioural patterns. These patterns can be extremely useful, as you don't want to have to remember who you are every time you wake up and try and figure out how to put your pants on.

The danger is you get used to these well-worn neural pathway patterns and don't even bother to look for another path. There may be a quicker, more effective path to the garden shed from the house. There may be a better destination than the garden shed that you're unaware of because you're not looking for it. Sticking to the same patterns in life can find you stuck in a rut.

> *"The only difference between a rut and a grave is how deep it is."*
> —CHARLES GARFIELD, AUTHOR & PSYCHOLOGIST

Gauge The Rut

The distance between rails in the US railway system is four feet, eight and a half inches (143.51 centimetres). This unusual measurement is used because it's the measurement used on British railways, and British ex-pats built the US railways. If you ask the question why did British railways use this measurement, you get the answer, because the railway lines were based on the tramlines. And the tramlines? They were built by people who used the same tools that had been used for building horse-drawn wagons.

So why did they use this unusual measurement? Because in Britain, that was the average spacing of already established wheel ruts. These old rutted roads existed because Imperial Rome had these roads built to improve travelling long distances and it was the Roman war chariots that created the original ruts. In order to set a consistent standard, it was decreed that all chariots have the same wheel spacing. And what determined the wheel spacing? Well, the war chariots were built to accommodate the rear ends of two horses.

This even impacts space travel. The booster rockets on space shuttles aren't made at Cape Canaveral. They are transported by train and go through a tunnel that is slightly wider than the railway track, which means the booster rockets also have to work in the measurement. So space travel, the most advanced form of transport is determined by a couple of horses' butts. This gives a whole new meaning to the term horse power!

In order to create positive change in your life you need to re-examine current patterns and see if they serve you. If they do, fantastic. If not, it's time to start disrupting old neurons and start firing some new ones.

Frontal lobes

When you visualise positive change in your life, you're firing the frontal lobes in the neocortex. The frontal lobes are the powerhouse of creativity, allowing you to dream up and visualise goals.

It is the size of the frontal lobes in relation to the rest of the neocortex that separates human beings from other species. As you read in Brain Map (Week 2 Day 1), your frontal lobes make up around 38% of your neocortex. Compare that with a cat with 3.5% or a dog with 7% and you can understand why we are at the top of the food chain. Even our closest genetic relative, the chimpanzee's frontal lobe, makes up 14% of their total brain mass.

So when you choose where to put your attention, to focus your mind and concentrate, it is your frontal lobes at work.

Filtering

> *"An intellectual is someone whose mind watches itself."*
> —ALBERT CAMUS, PHILOSOPHER & AUTHOR

Just like a water filter that stops impurities and lets only the good stuff get through, your brain has its own filter system. However it's not always as efficient as a water filter system.

The part of your brain that is responsible for arousal and motivation is called the Reticular Activating System (RAS), which is part of the central nervous system situated at the core of the brain stem and travels up the brain. It is able to impact activity in other areas of the brain including the frontal lobes. It is responsible for the things you notice and pay attention to and is constantly scanning for meaningful information and often discards what it deems as unimportant.

> **Cliff Says...**
> *It's a little known fact that...* your brain responds to tasks that are too simple, the same way it does for ones that are too demanding. It loses its ability to focus.

Your sensory neurons are able to receive around 400 billion pieces of information per second. In order to function effectively and avoid overload, your brain spends a lot of time keeping messages out and is only able to consciously receive and process around 2000 pieces of information per second.

For example, as you read these words you probably aren't paying too much attention to the noises outside the room, the things you can see in your periphery, the smell of your deodorant, the remaining tastes in your mouth of your food or the tension levels in your left calf muscle right now.

Information goes through different types of filters. You delete, distort or generalise information according to how you see the world. If you believe clowns are evil due to a bad childhood experience then when one shows up at a child's birthday party, you may think to yourself, the kids need to be protected from their dangerous ways, deleting what specifically is dangerous about clowns. You may distort his genuine smile for a menacing sneer and generalise that all clowns are evil and end up pouncing on the clown. You've filtered the information according to your beliefs and now will never be invited back to any more children's parties.

This also explains how two people can have completely different points of view on the same subject – the glass may be half full or half empty. Your filter system will influence your perception (understanding) and perspectives (viewpoint) just as a new experience may in turn impact your filter system.

Your beliefs, values, and emotions help decide what information gets priority in your consciousness and memory. The bigger the emotional experience, the higher up in the priority queue it goes. For example, if a fire broke out around you right now, you'd probably lower the piece of information that you need to finish reading this sentence and deal with what's important – your survival.

Just like a water filter system, your brain filter system can become clogged and not work to its optimum, allowing worthless thoughts (*"I'm not good enough"*) to get into your consciousness and worthy thoughts (*"I can do this"*) to be blocked.

You need to monitor your filter system just as a water filter system needs to be checked up on and changed periodically. Are negative thoughts sneaking through into your system? Do you need to clear the debris and allow only quality thoughts to enable your system to run effectively?

"Watch your thoughts, they become words.
Watch your words; they become actions.
Watch your actions; they become habits.
Watch your habits; they become character.
Watch your character; it becomes your destiny."

—ATTRIBUTED TO FRANK OUTLAW, UNKNOWN

REMEMBER:

1. Your brain is incredibly malleable which means you can always learn if you desire to.

2. It's challenging to break old habits but it can be done with practice.

3. Watching the quality of your thoughts is as important as drawing breath.

Week 2 Day 4:
Brain & Body Chemicals

"The living body is the best pharmacy ever devised. The dosage is always right and given on time; side effects are minimal or non-existent."

—DEEPAK CHOPRA, DOCTOR & WRITER

The human body is a 24/7 pharmaceutical shop. Brain chemicals are neurotransmitters that cross the synapse enabling neurons to communicate with each other. Your brain and body's chemical balance are constantly changing and the main areas that impact your biochemistry are the way you think, the food you eat, the quality of your sleep and exercise and the way you manage your stress.

There are three main chemicals that help get you the 'happy high' by naturally raising your energy – adrenaline, serotonin and dopamine. While they allow you to feel happy, serotonin and dopamine also play a key role in the restructuring of your brain.

Adrenaline

Adrenaline (aka epinephrine) is one of the body's big chemicals and the impact on the body when it's released into the bloodstream is usually immediate. Adrenaline is the chemical that gives you that natural rush as your sympathetic nervous system  (Emotional Brain: Week 2 Day 2) is activated. Historically it's the chemical that has aided our race's survival as it kicks in the fight or flight response to danger.

In more modern times adrenaline still helps you in threatening situations, but is also the chemical that gets you through all those busy times throughout your day. It is more of a short-term way of raising your energy and if you stay too long on the adrenaline rush then you risk burnout.

The trap is that the adrenaline rush can be very addictive as everything seems to move faster, you're more productive and nothing can slow you down when you are "on". However you crash badly when you come down from this high. The best way to minimise the crash is to have plenty of the brain chemical serotonin stockpiled and ready to kick in when you no longer need to be "on".

Serotonin

Serotonin is one of the oldest transmitters of all and is the happy chemical that gives you feelings of calmness and bliss. It helps regulate appetite, sleep, memory and learning, temperature regulation, mood, behaviour, cardiovascular function and muscle contraction so it's a pretty darn important chemical to have lots of!

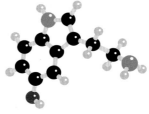

When you're sad, serotonin levels are low and if they remain low it may lead to chronic depression. It is serotonin that antidepressants such as Prozac keep boosted in the system, as serotonin gives you a long-term high. Unlike the adrenaline high, this is the high that you can sustain over time and should strive for.

Ways of increasing serotonin levels include doing non-stressful exercise like going for a walk, going to bed and getting up at set hours (yes, even on weekends), taking time out for yourself, getting a massage, and going on a relaxing vacation.

> 🍺 *Cliff Says...*
>
> *It's a little known fact that...* Donatella Marazziti, a professor of psychiatry at the University of Pisa, compared the serotonin levels of three groups – people who recently had fallen in love, people suffering from obsessive-compulsive disorder (OCD) and people free from both passion and mental illness. Serotonin levels were 40% lower in both the lovers and OCD subjects compared with the control group. Hmmm, could love and mental illness be one and the same?

Dopamine

"To find pleasure and avoid pain – that's what drives human evolution."

—CANDACE PERT, NEUROSCIENTIST

Dopamine, a chemical relative to serotonin, is responsible for feelings of pleasure. It regulates two systems – the brain's reward mechanism (motivation) and movement control, thus it controls your 'get up and go' both literally and metaphorically. The reward mechanism is actually a misleading term, as it's not the reward that stimulates the neurons but the *expectation* of the reward.

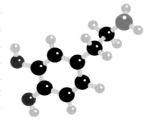

Imagine someone bets you fifty dollars you can't win over a particular customer at work. But, you do. It's not the actual fifty dollars that makes you happy. Sure, the money is nice but the pleasure comes from the anticipation of meeting your colleague and letting them know you won.

Dopamine controls arousal levels and plays a key role in learning, desire and how you learn to make choices that lead to good outcomes, while avoiding bad ones. When you reach a deadline and feel good about it – that's dopamine going through your system. When you get that warm feeling when you see the one you love or would like to love – that's dopamine. That feeling you have after watching a Hollywood movie with a happy ending – yep, your good friend dopamine again.

You'll be finding out more about dopamine, its effect on desire and the dark side of this chemical in Desire (Week 5 Day 5).

Melatonin

Melatonin is produced in your brain during times of darkness and production stops when there's artificial or natural light allowing serotonin to kick back into action. Serotonin is required for voluntary muscle contraction so if it were still in your system at night you'd physically act out your dreams, which is one way of scaring away any potential life partners. How much melatonin your body produces is dependent on how much natural 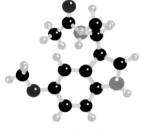 light you get during the day. The more natural light you get during the day, the more melatonin you produce at night. Your melatonin level is at its highest at 3 am.

Cortisol

Cortisol is the other body chemical along with adrenaline that gets released into your system when you come under stress. A little bit of cortisol isn't bad for you as it helps regulate blood pressure, can heighten memory function, lower sensitivity to pain and help maintain homeostasis (body balance).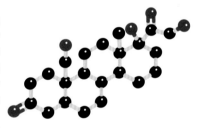

The problem is today's unhealthy culture of compulsive productivity keeps your sympathetic nervous system constantly activated, which keeps cortisol in your system resulting in wear and tear on your body and mind – ie: you're constantly stressed.

Having high levels of cortisol in your bloodstream constantly can impact on you in a number of ways. You can become more tense and more susceptible to suffering from anxiety, fear and guilt, and/or become more on edge. It lowers your immunity, raises your blood pressure and creates blood sugar imbalances which contribute to the low feeling you get after a stressful event.

You need to make particular activities that are proven to keep stress down a regular part of your routine. These activities include exercise, journalling, massage, autogenic training, and breathing exercises. You'll explore these more in Stress Alignment (Week 7 Day 1).

Are you just a drug?

"To think is to practise brain chemistry."
—DEEPAK CHOPRA, DOCTOR & AUTHOR

You probably like to think of yourself as an intelligent person with hopes, dreams and ambitions rather than a mere combination of chemicals. Take heart, although your chemical balance is the foundation of your thoughts and feelings, none of the chemicals are sufficient enough to create an emotion by itself. The chemicals are just part of an intricate and complex process that makes you up. Sure, they're an important part, but you are more than your brain structure and the chemicals within.

> **Cliff Says...**
> *It's a little known fact that...* it is these brain chemicals that many of the illegal recreational drugs affect. Cocaine increases and sustains dopamine in the system by blocking the agents that normally get rid of excess dopamine.

So save yourself some money and make the healthier choice – create ways of getting your long-term high the natural way.

REMEMBER:

1. The adrenaline rush is addictive and although it feels good, overuse leads to burnout.

2. You need lots of serotonin to feel good long term and enjoy the feeling of bliss in life.

3. The expectation of something pleasant is a powerful motivator, so that's one reason it's important to have stated goals in life to work towards.

Week 2 Day 5:   Senses

> *"The average human looks without seeing, listens without hearing, touches without feeling, eats without tasting, moves without physical awareness, inhales without awareness of odour or fragrance and talks without thinking."*
>
> —LEONARDO DA VINCI, POLYMATH

Take 5

Let's not be average! Leonardo da Vinci engaged in a rigorous regime of exercises to develop his sensory skills. This is because all the senses have an important role to play in your thinking both directly and indirectly. The brain takes in information through your five senses and helps you form an understanding of yourself and the world you live in – your reality.

Traditionally there are five senses referred to as VAKOG – Visual (see), Auditory (hear), Kinaesthetic (touch/movement), Olfactory (smell) and Gustatory (taste). If you can see dead people then you have a refined sixth sense and need to give Bruce Willis a call.

SENSE	DESCRIPTION	FUNCTION
Visual	Sight	receives light energy
Auditory	Sound	receives sound wave energy
Kinaesthetic	Proprioception (body awareness)	receives mechanical energy
	Vestibular (balance)	receives mechanical energy
	Tactile (touch)	receives thermal and physical energy
Olfactory	Smell	receives chemical energy
Gustatory	Taste	receives chemical energy

Your brain's sensory receptors transform each type of energy into electrochemical energy in order for it to understand the various forms of energy it receives. The brain doesn't just filter and store this sensory input, it also associates it with other events, which is how we learn. There are different parts of the brain that are responsible for processing each sense (Brain Map: Week 2 Day 1). Researchers have found that by stimulating different parts of the brain, patients have been able to taste Thai green curry or hear birds singing.

Heightened sensory acuity not only involves developing skills in sensing external information, it also includes refining the same sense internally as the following chart highlights:

Sense	Area	Function
Visual	Internal	images you see inside your head
	External	images you see with your eyes
Auditory	Internal	sounds & dialogue you hear inside your head
	External	sounds & dialogue you hear

Cliff Says...

It's a little known fact that... synaesthesia is when the brain's wires are crossed giving people the ability to sense one or more forms of energy with a sensory system other than the one typically used. They may be able to feel shapes, smell noises, see flavours, hear colours etc. It affects about one in every 2000 people, with coloured hearing being the most common quality. The writer Goethe saw musical notes in colour and novelist Anthony Burgess described the oboe as *"silver green lemon juice"* and a flute as *"light brown and cold veal gravy"*.

So let's take a brief look at each of your senses.

Sight

"The eye is the window of the human body through which it feels its way and enjoys the beauty of the world."

—LEONARDO DA VINCI, POLYMATH

It is through the eyes that the majority of your world is perceived. Your eyes provide input regarding such things as colour, light, body language, and facial expressions. When properly received and analysed by your brain, it allows you to, amongst other things sense danger, find your way around, recognise loved ones and appreciate visual art.

When a visual signal hits your retina, it travels across five more synapses to get from the occipital cortex at the back of your brain to the frontal cortex. As it travels across these synapses, the visual image becomes more and more complex and richer in detail. This explains why, for a split second, you think you've seen someone you know when it's actually a stranger.

Sound

"God gave man two ears, but only one mouth, that he might hear twice as much as he speaks."

—EPICTETUS, PHILOSOPHER

You use your ears to hear voices, music and nature, to process information and sense danger. A person whose senses are well integrated can stand in the centre of a party surrounded by music, talking, plates and glasses clinking and still carry on a conversation with the person sitting across the table. Their brain simply filters out the unnecessary information, and focuses on the words the individual speaker is saying.

You probably don't think of sound as influencing you beyond communication and entertainment; however, sound and frequencies can significantly affect the way you think and behave. Don Campbell who popularised the 'Mozart effect' – that classical music has a positive impact on your brain and learning – identified a diverse list of the musical effects on human behaviour:

- Improve concentration
- Enhance intuitive leaps
- Form mental pictures
- Recognise variations among objects
- Change perception of space
- Slow and equalise brain waves

There is more space within the tones in slow music than in fast music, making the environment feel lighter, spacious and more elegant. It can reduce feelings of restriction and confinement. Heart and breathing rates respond to musical variables such as frequency, tempo and volume, tending to speed up or slow down to match the rhythm of a sound. The faster the music, the faster the heart will beat and vice versa. A lower heartbeat reduces physical tension and calms the mind, a state suited to effective creative thinking.

Touch

"The body becomes the battlefield for the war games of the mind."

—BRIAN LUKE SEAWARD, AUTHOR

You only have two eyes, two ears, and one nose, but your body is covered with very sensitive touch receptors. Through them you get information about hot and cold, hard and soft, smooth and rough, pain and pleasure. When a person's brain is receiving and analysing this information from the tactile system correctly, they will quickly remove their hand from a hot stove, put mittens on when going out into the snow, and smile when receiving a caress from a loved one.

Neuroscientist Candace Pert highlights in her book *Molecules of Emotion*, how your body is your unconscious mind. Your body stores memories, both positive and negative ones. Touch is a sense that can help with healing both your mind and body. Imagine how good a massage would feel right now or just a good old-fashioned hug from a loved one.

Smell

"Smell is a potent wizard that transports us across thousands of miles and all the years we have lived."
—HELEN KELLER, AUTHOR & ACTIVIST

Although the human sense of smell is able to distinguish at least 10,000 separate odours, most people have a limited vocabulary when it comes to describing smells. It either smells good or bad. You are often surrounded by fragrant scents, from perfume and flowers and the delicious smells of freshly baked bread, to the pungent odours of cleaning agents, diesel fumes or cigarette smoke. Smells may be acrid, amber, camphor, citrus, floral, fresh, foul, fungal, grassy, honey, minty, musky, musty, powdery, resinous, rose, rotten, spicy, sulphuric, sweet or synthetic, to name a few.

Your sense of smell is used to bring you pleasure, enhance your ability to taste food, and warn you of danger. However, as with the other senses, the sense of smell can cause frustration for a person whose brain is not able to properly analyse, screen out, or respond to the information it receives.

Smell is the oldest and considered the most powerful sense, as it is only one synapse away from the nose to the amygdala in the limbic system (Emotional Brain: Week 2 Day 2). As a result of this, smell is strongly linked to memory.

> **30 Year Flashback**
> A JOLT Challenge participant shared a story of a recent time when he walked into a shop and smelt the perfume on a sales assistant. He was immediately transported back thirty years to his primary school where his teacher wore the same perfume.
> He hadn't smelt it or thought of his teacher for all those years yet his brain had linked that smell with that person.

There are links between foul odour and ill health. Aromatherapy is a way to use smell to affect the brain. Aromatherapy works by using various odours to achieve specific therapeutic results through the limbic system. The odours of essential oils trigger limbic responses that affect the person physically, mentally and emotionally. The oils affect the brain depending on the oil's chemical constituents and memories associated with that odour.

Oils recommended for stimulating the mind and body are:

Basil	clears, stimulates and invigorates the mind
Lemon	good for clear decision making and overcoming procrastination
Rosemary	stimulates the body for exercise, and the mind for memory

Oils recommended for calming the mind and body are:

Bergamot	calms the nervous system and is emotionally uplifting
Frankincense	deeply calming on an emotional and spiritual level
Lavender	calms the mind and relieves nervous tension
Marjoram	induces deep relaxation and calms emotions
Neroli	releases stress and induces relaxation

Taste

 "Everyone eats and drinks but few appreciate taste."
—KUNG FU TSU (CONFUCIUS), PHILOSOPHER

Despite having approximately 10,000 taste buds, you have only five distinct tastes. They are sweet, sour, bitter, salty and umami also known as savoury. Although the weakest of the five senses, taste often brings you pleasure. You probably have the tendency to eat the things that taste good. However, taste can also warn you of danger. You know that milk may be sour or food may be rotten based on the way it tastes.

> **Cliff Says...**
> *It's a little known fact that...* in 1908 Japanese researcher Kikunae Ikeda first discovered Umami as a taste while researching the strong taste in seaweed broth. This led to him discovering monosodium glutamate (MSG) that we'll look at in Brain Nutrition (Week 3 Day 1).

"The strong man is the one who is able to intercept at will the communication between the senses and the mind."
—NAPOLEON BONAPARTE, MILITARY & POLITICAL LEADER

> **Chocolate Anyone?**
> Watch the movie *Chocolat* in regards to the impact your different senses can have on you. The movie characterises people by their sense of taste. Could you be characterised the same way?

Anchors

Any internal or external stimulus that triggers a certain response is called an anchor. Anchors are very useful for changing your emotional state. You can turn anything into an anchor. A picture of a loved one on your desk, the sounds of nature, a comfortable chair, the smell of coffee, the taste of a cold drink on a hot day. You can use anchoring to raise or relax your energy.

Cliff Says...
It's a little known fact that... 2004 Olympic gold medalist Sarah Ulmer uses certain music (auditory external) as an anchor to get herself in the right mindset for peak performance.

Much-needed Vacation
In the movie *Collateral* starring Tom Cruise and Jamie Foxx, Foxx plays a taxi driver who has a picture of a tropical island resort stuck on his car's visor. He tells a passenger that every time things get too stressful he looks at the picture and goes there on holiday in his mind. This is an example of a visual external anchor.

Perception & perspective

Perceiving is taking in the raw energy and information about the world through your senses, which forms your perception and understanding. Your perspective is determined by your values and beliefs on the information that you perceive, also known as your point of view.

Developing your sensory acuity means you're developing your perception ability. This greatly aids in mastering your emotions and improving your creativity and decision-making skills. Why? Because with greater awareness you can take in more information, and consequently you can make better-informed decisions about what you want to do in regards to your health, wealth and relationships.

Quantum physics has provided a profoundly interesting and important insight into the nature of reality:

Actuality and potentiality are equally real

The essential difference between actuality (what exists) and potentiality (what could exist) is a matter of perspective.

Imagine you drive a partially restored 1959 Ford Anglia that, to everyone else, is an old rust bucket that should be allowed to die, whereas you see the car in its finished state and know it will grace the cover of the *Classic Cars* magazine.

Imagine you get given a new project to work on. To everyone it's the short straw, but once you get started, you can see the potential benefits for you from working on such a project.

Where Are You From?

A taxi driver was waiting for customers at the airport, as a woman approached and got into the car. She asked the taxi driver what the people were like in this city. The taxi driver asked the customer how people were, in her city.

"They're friendly, willing to help and always have something nice to say," said the customer.

"Well, you're in luck," said the taxi driver, "that's how they are here in this city too."

Later that day the taxi driver was back at the airport when another customer approached and asked how the people are in this city. The taxi driver again asked how the customer found people in his city back home.

"They are unfriendly to the point of surliness and will take advantage of you if given the chance," said the customer.

"Well," said the taxi driver as he put the customer's luggage into the boot of the car, "unfortunately, you'll find the people of this city the same."

"We don't see things as they are, we see things as we are."
—ANAÏS NIN, AUTHOR

The Truth

Watch the movies *Rashamon* and *One Night at McCool's* to see how difficult it is to get to the truth when people hold different perspectives.

Thinking should be a partnership between our sensations and knowledge. Deepak Chopra, doctor and author, warns that you use your senses as the ultimate measure of reality; however, your senses do not provide you with a reliable test for reality. The senses filter out information, creating one version of the world where reality is purely a matter of perspective.

"The senses do not deceive us, but the judgement does."
—JOHANN WOLFGANG VON GOETHE, POLYMATH

In the image on the opposite page, the spots between the black squares do not exist; they are constructs of your mind. You can make a few disappear by focusing on a few but not all of them for any length of time. The optical illusion's power means you can't trust your perceptions without further thought. In order to make the best decisions you need to use your mind to penetrate the depths that your senses alone can't perceive. Sensory misinterpretation is the result of what you *think* you see or hear, rather than what you *actually* see or hear.

EXAMPLE: An optical illusion

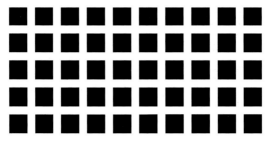

"The intellect can intuit nothing, the senses can think nothing. Only through their union can knowledge arise."
—IMMANUEL KANT, PHILOSOPHER

What you actually perceive is your current version of the truth. Remember a time when you made a bad mistake. Remember the reasons you had at the time for making that decision. They were probably good ones, but in hindsight and *with more information* you'd probably make different choices now. Recent studies show high correlations between acute sensory perception skills and mental insight, so it's wise to develop your sensory acuity.

REMEMBER:

1. Your senses are the vehicle for your brain to receive information, and your beliefs will influence your perspective.

2. You can use your senses to alter your emotional state.

3. You can't always trust your senses, as reality is merely a matter of perspective.

Week 2 summary map:

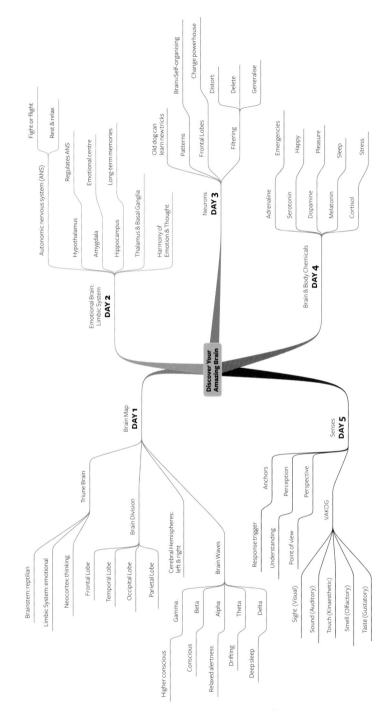

WEEK THREE:

Maximise Your Energy

Purpose

To optimise your mental and physical well-being through keeping your mind and body healthy.

Overview

Day 1: Brain Nutrition
Day 2: Water
Day 3: Breathing
Day 4: Sleep
Day 5: Exercise

Benefits

This week's experience in the Challenge guides you to:

- enjoy more energy and a higher quality of life
- raise your energy and improve blood circulation
- harmonise the dominance of the brain hemispheres to improve its overall function
- calm the mind and your nervous system
- improve blood quality to help remove toxins
- improve your nervous system, build healthy lungs and strengthen your heart
- reduce muscle tension and alleviate stress
- increase your physical awareness
- improve the quality of your sleep
- boost your immune system the natural way
- sharpen your ability to focus and concentrate
- increase reaction speed and mental agility.

Week 3 Day 1:   Brain Nutrition

"One must eat to live, not live to eat."

—MOLIÈRE, PLAYWRIGHT

The starting point for a healthy brain is a healthy body. The goal is to achieve what Juvenal the Roman poet wrote when he answered the question of what you should ask for in life: *"mens sana in corpore sano"* (a sound mind in a sound body).

 key elements

While there is a huge amount of (often conflicting) information available on nutrition, the focus here is on brain nutrition only. The three key elements to boost your brainpower, keep your brain healthy and your mental processes operating effectively are:

1. High-quality food

2. Water

3. Oxygen

Your brain uses 20–25% of the total energy you consume to power your 100 billion brain cells. Because a malfunctioning brain can take the rest of the body down with it, the brain gets first choice of the available nutrients.

There is a relationship between what you eat and how you think, act and learn. Ultimately the body's performance is determined by the foods you eat. You require a minimum quantity of calories, fatty acids, vitamins and minerals to perform; however, some foods will increase your brain power. So by eating the right food, you can enhance mental capabilities, aid concentration, tune sensorimotor skills, keep motivated, improve memory, speed up reaction times, defuse stress, prevent brain aging, boost IQ, and improve your mood. Skilful use of nutrition, botanicals and supplements in your diet can significantly increase your brainpower.

Nutrients are required to enable the whole brain circuitry to function properly. If the neurons (brain cells), myelin sheath (neuron protective covering) and neurotransmitters (brain chemicals) are deficient in nutrients, then like a defective electrical wire, the circuit misfires.

Food for thoughts: How the brain uses nutrients

- The brain uses carbohydrates for energy and omega-3 fatty acids for forming its cell structure.
- Proteins provide amino acids from which neurotransmitters are made and therefore affect brain performance.

- Neurotransmitters are manufactured, released and assisted by folic acid, vitamins B6 and B12.

Omega-3

Fats make up 60% of the brain and the nerves that run every system in the body. The wrong fats make it hard for blood to transport oxygen to brain cells and send messages throughout the brain. Lack of omega-3 fats in your diet can lead to depression, poor memory, learning disabilities, and many more mental disorders.

Omega-3 foods include fish such as salmon, cod, fish oil, flax seeds, cauliflower, cabbage, Brussels sprouts, walnuts, cooked soy beans, tofu, scallops and kiwifruit.

Antioxidants

Antioxidants are naturally produced in the body to protect against free radicals, which attack and damage body cells. In the modern world there are numerous new sources of artificially produced free radicals like radiation, smoke, food additives, hydrogenated vegetable oils and fats. The best way to protect the brain is to eliminate sources of free radicals and start taking antioxidants to fortify your body against the damage that the free radicals are causing in your body.

Foods high in antioxidants are prunes, blueberries, strawberries, colourful fruits and vegetables, dark chocolate and tea.

Phytochemicals

Phyto comes from the Greek word for plant. Phytochemicals refer to the rapidly expanding list of biologically potent chemicals found in various fruit and vegetables. It is a type of antioxidant, and their importance to good health can be illustrated by the fact that people who eat a lot of fruit and vegetables are 80% less likely to develop certain cancers. Phytochemicals have a beneficial effect on blood vessels, vascular and artery efficiency, prevent DNA damage and help lower cholesterol.

Phytochemical-rich foods include: berries, grapes, broccoli, cabbage, tomatoes, garlic, green tea and turmeric.

Vitamins and minerals

Vitamins and minerals are essential for the growth and functioning of the brain. The B complex vitamins (B1, B3, B6, B12) play a vital role from manufacturing neurotransmitters to producing energy. Minerals are also critical to mental functioning and performance. Sodium, potassium and calcium are important in the thinking process and they facilitate the transmission of messages while magnesium is needed for brain energy.

The best way to ensure you get the right supply of vitamins and minerals is to eat a variety of fresh vegetables and fruits.

**An easy way of getting the right variety of food
is to eat different natural colours**

Choline

Choline is a chemical building block of every cell. Its purpose is to provide nutrition to the myelin sheaths, which protect your brain cells. Without adequate supplies of choline the brain cannot adequately store new information. A lack of choline is considered to be a significant cause of Alzheimer's disease.

Choline-rich foods include: wheat germ, peanuts, liver, ham, lamb and whole wheat flour.

Fibre

While fibre is not directly involved in brain function, it does influence how other nutrients affect the brain. Putting the right food in helps, but it's important to get it out too. Clearing out the system will lead to improved mental performance.

Fibre-rich foods are beans, lentils, wheat bran, oats, grapefruit, apples and raisins.

In general, you should aim to have a wide variety of such foods, thereby maximising the antioxidants that are available in your body cells to 'quench' free radicals. They should have lots of fibre and be low in saturated animal fats. You need a broad range of minerals and trace elements, which function as enzyme co-factors in the multitude of chemical reactions occurring in each of your 50 trillion body cells. Likewise you need all the essential (as in, you cannot make them so you must obtain them through the food you eat) vitamins, amino acids and fatty acids. All these provide support for enzyme pathways and optimise the ability of your cells to generate energy and sustain and repair themselves.

It's all in the... timing

It makes a big difference to your mental performance if protein is eaten before carbohydrates or vice versa. This is because of two competing amino acids, the building blocks of protein biosynthesis, tyrosine and tryptophan. It depends upon which one gets to the brain first to exert its biochemical effects.

Tyrosine

Tyrosine produces the chemicals dopamine and norepinephrine, both central to sharp thinking, recall and general alertness. This will cause the brain to stay at peak performance for hours and the body is able to make tyrosine if required.

Tyrosine is found in meat, poultry, seafood, beans, almonds, avocados, seaweed and bananas.

Tryptophan

Tryptophan is an essential amino acid and it must be obtained from the diet. If tryptophan gets to the brain first it causes the release of serotonin and melatonin which induces sleep, slows down reaction time and causes a drop in IQ. Although protein contains higher levels, carbohydrates containing tryptophan get to the brain more effectively.

Tryptophan is found in dairy products, bananas, spinach, spirulina and sunflower seeds.

If you need lots of mental acuity in the morning, start the day with a low-calorie, high-protein breakfast and keep the carbohydrates in limited supply. In the late afternoon and evening when you need to wind down, the time is right for some complex carbohydrates.

The timing of the carbohydrate and protein intake is the key to what effect the meal will have on your brainpower and energy levels. Barry Sears, author of *Enter the Zone*, recommends a 40% carbohydrate, 30% protein and 30% fat balance for every meal to stay energetic and healthy.

T. Colin Campbell, author of *The China Study*, which covers the results from the most comprehensive study on nutrition ever done, recommends a whole foods, plant based diet. He states that while animal protein stimulates physical growth in humans, it's not the healthiest choice in the long run.

Remember:

The key is to experiment and discover what works best for you

Warning zones – things to go easy on

Caffeine

Caffeine is the number one drug used to boost energy levels and fight against sleepiness.

It can be found in coffee, tea, cola, chocolate and most energy drinks. Caffeine is addictive and affects your system similarly to amphetamines and cocaine. However, 200–400 mg per day (2–4 cups of coffee) has been shown to be relatively harmless. The key is when to drink it. The best time to have caffeine is when you wake up. Avoid using it as a replacement for sleep. A little nap or just closing your eyes for a few minutes is a much better and healthier alternative for a pick-me-up. Other alternatives include eating licorice or having green tea.

Caffeine, like most addictive substances, often traps you in a vicious cycle.

You drink it, you get an increase of adrenaline, you feel more energetic, you get an increase of dopamine, you feel better, you feel you can stay up later so you have less sleep, you are more tired the next day, so you need more caffeine, due to the chemical acclimatisation you get less increase per cup, so you increase the dosage and so on it goes.

If you want to lessen your caffeine intake then do this gradually over 3–4 days rather than just going cold turkey.

Alcohol

Alcohol is a depressant so it's all about moderation. A little bit of alcohol (eg: a glass of wine with dinner) can relax the blood vessels and lower the risk of heart disease, plus red wine is rich in antioxidants. However, it is fair to say that alcohol doesn't help you become a peak mental performer. In small doses it increases dopamine and serotonin but the effects don't usually last long, and if a small dose becomes a large dose you'll find yourself slurring your words, telling the same story over and over again and having an inflated view of your dancing ability.

Sugar

Your brain depends on a normal range of blood sugar called glucose, which perks up memory, concentration and learning abilities. Too little can cause brain malfunction, too much will impair performance and memory, and accelerate mental decline. When you are engaged in mental activity you need more blood sugars. The types of carbohydrate you eat greatly affect how quickly the sugars are released in your blood. The best sugars for the brain are low glycaemic index (GI) starches and fruit sugars. They take longer to break down providing a time-release source of steady energy rather than a sudden burst.

Simple carbohydrates from processed flour products and sugary foods enter the bloodstream quickly. This results in the pancreas releasing insulin to regain balance. The trouble is that insulin is a hormone that tells the body to not only store fat but also not to release any. So you experience a sudden surge of energy then a sudden drop followed by the body looking to store the excess carbohydrate as fat.

The 'sugar surge' causes wild fluctuations in performance and mood through neurotransmitter imbalance, resulting in irritability and poor concentration. Research published in 2003 showed kids breakfasting on fizzy drinks, sugary snacks and cereals performed at an average 70-year-olds' level, in tests of memory and attention. Eating too much sugar over a long period of time will ultimately lead to brain damage.

 Danger zones – things to avoid

Nicotine

"To cease smoking is the easiest thing I ever did. I ought to know as I've done it a thousand times."

—MARK TWAIN, AUTHOR

Nicotine? No. Sorry, but if you smoke you're massively reducing your mental performance abilities. Your body can tolerate low levels of caffeine and alcohol but nicotine is plain nasty to your brain because it starves the brain of oxygen and blocks the arteries that enable oxygen-rich blood to circulate.

Aspartame (additive code – 950, 951)

There is a lot of controversy surrounding aspartame, the artificial sweetener found in many foods and beverages. In the United States, aspartame accounts for over 75% of the adverse reactions to food additives reported to the Food and Drug Administration. Aspartame has been linked to a range of health concerns including headaches/migraines, dizziness, seizures, nausea, weight gain, depression, fatigue, insomnia and heart palpitations to name a few. There's a reason why people call aspartame 'sweet poison'. A smart diet doesn't include aspartame.

Aspartame is found in many sugar-free foods, sugar-free chewing gums, diet soft drinks, fizzy vitamin supplements and sugar replacements such as NutraSweet and Equal.

MSG (additive code – E621)

MSG (monosodium glutamate) is a food additive that enhances the flavour in food. MSG is helpful as it replaces the loss of taste in many low-fat, no-fat foods. However, MSG is made up of 78% free glutamic acid which is considered neurotoxic, meaning it kills neurons in your brain. An obvious clue that MSG is dangerous is the fact that many restaurants and companies advertise that their food and products are MSG-free. If MSG and aspartame are bad for you then why is it legal? Well, there's a lot of controversy involving lobby groups, big business dollars and conflict of interest research that has seen both these toxins slip through. If you consume either MSG or aspartame then we encourage you to do your own research and make an informed decision.

MSG can go under different names and is always in the following: hydrolyzed vegetable protein, plant protein extract, yeast extract and corn oil. Malt extract, stock, flavouring and spices often contain MSG. Read your food labels carefully as a healthy diet doesn't include MSG.

REMEMBER:

1. High-quality food, water and oxygen are essential to maximising your brain power.

2. More protein in the morning and more carbohydrates in the afternoon.

3. Caffeine and alcohol are okay in small doses but nicotine, aspartame and MSG have no place in a smart diet.

Week 3 Day 2:   Water

"Water is life's matter and matrix, mother and medium. There is no life without water."

—ALBERT SZENT-GYORGYI, PHYSIOLOGIST

Water is ranked second only to oxygen as being essential for life. You can live for only a few days without it. Water is the most abundant substance on the earth and in the body. It makes up 60–70% of body weight and is important in numerous bodily processes and functions.

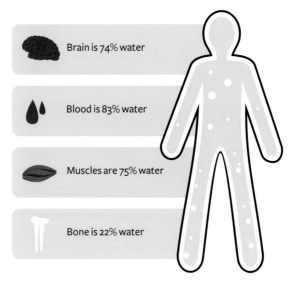

Brain is 74% water

Blood is 83% water

Muscles are 75% water

Bone is 22% water

Water, water everywhere...

"Thousands have lived without love, not one without water."

—W.H. AUDEN, POET

Our bodily systems are electrical so every physiological function depends on water. Having 4–5% less than the recommended daily amount of water can affect your mental and physical performance by up to 20–30%.

When water is pure and free of contaminants a steady dose of water a day will:
- improve your energy
- increase your mental & physical performance
- remove toxins and waste products from your body

- keep skin healthy and glowing
- help you lose weight
- reduce headaches and dizziness
- allow for proper digestion
- help to keep you more alkaline

Water provides the hydration necessary to conduct electrical impulses throughout the body that carry messages from the brain to the muscles and feedback to the brain. It protects organs and tissues, and is necessary for your body to digest and absorb vitamins and nutrients. Water is essential for concentration and mental alertness so drinking water acts as a brain boost by improving concentration and mental and physical coordination.

... and not a drop to drink

You lose water through urination, respiration, and by sweating. If you become dehydrated, every part of your body suffers, your blood is literally thicker, and your body has to work much harder for it to circulate. As a result, the brain becomes less active, it's hard to concentrate and your body feels tired. Poor hydration is often the root of fatigue problems.

Just Water Please

In the movie *Wild Hogs*, the four main characters on their trip across America run out of gas going through a desert. William H. Macy's know-it-all character almost gets himself killed by the others when he points out how their blood is thickening and their hearts are having to work much harder.

Thirst is an obvious sign of dehydration and many physicians say you need water long before you feel thirsty. What is dangerous about this is that when you are very dehydrated you don't feel thirsty as your body has lost the ability to detect dehydration. Symptoms of mild dehydration include chronic pains in joints and muscles, lower back pain, headaches, nausea and constipation. Yellow or amber-coloured urine may indicate that you are not getting enough water. Long-term dehydration has been linked to asthma and allergies, and heartburn, hypertension and headaches, poor muscle tone, and inefficiencies in digestion, metabolism, and organ function.

When you are physically active or sweat, more water is lost. If you don't or can't drink, that's when the body will begin to squeeze water from its own tissues, including the brain and the skin. This can cause a headache and is why skin can look ragged and dry. Drinking water will soothe headaches and revive skin tone. Diuretics such as caffeine and alcohol create the urge to drink more because they create a salt/water imbalance that results in you feeling thirsty. If you keep drinking more caffeine and alcohol, you're creating a vicious cycle for yourself. Drinking lots of water before you go to bed after a night out on the town is a well-known way to avoid hangovers.

Water and diet

"I believe that water is the only drink for a wise man."
—HENRY DAVID THOREAU, PHILOSOPHER

If you are dieting, water will not only aid proper digestion, but also prevent overeating. The sensations of thirst and hunger are generated simultaneously to indicate the brain's need for water. If you're not getting plenty of water, you'll likely eat more to satisfy your body's urge for water. When you feel hungry, try drinking a few glasses of water first. You may not be as hungry as you think. It's also important to remember that when the body is dehydrated, fat cells get rubbery and cannot be easily metabolised. This means that it's harder to lose weight when you don't drink your water.

What kind of water?

There are pros and cons with each of the different kinds of water on offer: tap water, bottled water and filtered water. Blind taste tests have shown that most people can't even tell the difference between the different types of water. One test screened on TV had 75% of the tested subjects actually prefer the taste of tap water over bottled water.

In 1999 the National Resources Defense Council in America published the results of a four-year study in which 1000 samples of 103 brands of bottled water were tested. It was found that an estimated 25% or more of bottled water is really just tap water in a bottle. One particular brand which was advertised as *"pure, glacier water"* actually got its water from a town's water supply. With bottled water costing more per litre than petrol, it's not hard to make a case for the cheaper and more convenient filtered tap water.

> **Cliff Says...**
> *It's a little known fact that...* in New Zealand, tap water supplies can contain sediment, sulphur, giardia, chlorine and dissolved aluminium.

Since water filters can remove dangerous contaminants from water while keeping the healthy mineral deposits, we recommend investing in a water filter system for your house or kitchen bench top at the very least.

How much water should you drink?

You've probably heard the eight glasses a day rule. Dr Heinz Vatlin, professor emeritus of physiology at Dartmouth Medical School, published a report in the *American Journal of Physiology* in 2002 stating there's no scientific evidence to back up this generally accepted notion. The standard eight glasses a day rule doesn't take into account different body sizes or the active from the sedentary lifestyles. The little research on how much water you should drink states that if you have no medical conditions you should aim to drink one standard 250 ml glass for each 10 kg

MAXIMISE YOUR ENERGY

③

of body weight. So if you're 70 kg, that's 7 glasses of water. In addition, if you drink tea, coffee or sodas (all of which contain caffeine, a diuretic that causes the body to lose water), it may pay to add an extra glass of water for each cup of coffee you drink and two for each alcoholic drink.

Notice how it affects you and cut back or increase your water intake until you find what works best for you. Don't be surprised that your bathroom visits increase in the first week or so when you start drinking the appropriate daily amount of water. It's just your kidneys adjusting to the water intake. Your body will thank you for it. Many people who have followed this guideline have noticed that once they start drinking more water, they begin to notice how thirsty they are.

You are naturally thirsty/dehydrated in the morning. Help your body flush out the toxins it has been processing all night and take advantage of this thirst to get a start on your daily water requirements by drinking a glass of water or two first thing.

> **Cliff Says...**
> *It's a little known fact that...* losing as little as 1–2% of your body weight can result in dehydration. Many fad 'lose weight fast' diets are just helping you lose water rather than excess fat.

Don't wait until you're thirsty to have a drink – you're probably already dehydrated if you feel thirsty. Spread your water intake out throughout the day, and to stop night-time visits to the bathroom, drink most of your quota before 6 pm. The closer to body temperature the water is, the easier it is for your body to take it where it needs to go. Very cold water can over-stimulate the kidneys.

You can also liven up ordinary water first thing in the morning with a squirt of lime or lemon juice to increase the flush of toxins from your body. However, be aware that drinking juice is not the same as drinking water. Most juices are high in sugar (natural or otherwise) and don't do the same job as good old water.

REMEMBER:

1. Waiting till you're thirsty to drink water can be a sign that you're already dehydrated.

2. Drink water when you feel hungry during the day – chances are you're thirsty.

3. Drink 250 ml per 10 kg of your body weight.

Week 3 Day 3: Breathing

"Breath is the bridge which connects life to consciousness, which unites your body to your thoughts."

—THICH NHAT HANH, BUDDHIST MONK

Oxygen is a vital nutrient for your body. It is essential for the integrity of the brain, nerves, glands and internal organs. You can do without food for weeks and without water for days, but without oxygen, you'll die within a few minutes.

Oxygen's role

As you breathe, you not only take in oxygen but also remove carbon dioxide from your body. The carbon dioxide levels in the blood regulate the blood supply to the brain and other tissues. The oxygen that is inhaled purifies your blood by removing poisonous waste products circulating throughout your blood system. Experts estimate that proper breathing helps your body eliminate toxins 15 times faster than poor, shallow breathing does.

For a long time, lack of oxygen has been considered a major cause of cancer. Research done in Germany in 1947 showed that when oxygen was withdrawn, normal body cells could turn into cancer cells.

Shiver Me Timbers!

In the opening scenes of *Pirates of the Caribbean*, Keira Knightley's character Elizabeth climbs to the top of the fort parapets wearing a corset. She is breathless, faints and falls over the parapet. Johnny Depp has to remove her corset to resuscitate her.

When your sympathetic nervous system is activated – the fight or flight response – your breathing automatically becomes more rapid in order to lower carbon dioxide levels. This change in body chemistry means that your muscles are able to contract more strongly and you are better suited to fight or run. However, you aren't designed to stay in this state for long. Breathing rapidly lowers blood carbon dioxide levels so it reduces the blood supply and consequently the oxygen supply to the brain and the heart.

Controlling your breath

Controlling your breathing patterns not only rejuvenates your whole mind and body, it also counters the effects of stress. In stressful situations, good breathing technique is often the first thing to fail and becomes irregular, which just adds to the stress and general deterioration of performance. One of the major secrets of vitality and rejuvenation is a purified bloodstream. The quickest and most effective way to purify the bloodstream is by taking in extra supplies of oxygen from the air you breathe. By purifying the bloodstream every part of the body benefits, as well as the mind, thereby increasing your performance.

When we are relaxed, our breathing is slow and regular, with the length of time breathing out equal to or longer than the time spent breathing in. Although we breathe automatically, breathing can be under our conscious control, and relaxation techniques that use controlled breathing are extremely useful in managing stress and neck and shoulder tension. Your respiratory rhythms often reflect the state of your unconscious mind.

> *"For breath is life, and if you breathe well you will live long on earth."*
>
> —SANSKRIT PROVERB

About one third of the oxygen absorbed goes to your brain and the more oxygen you receive the better the brain function will be. Insufficient oxygen supply results in mental sluggishness, depression and, eventually, a decline in vision and hearing.

Cliff Says...

It's a little known fact that... production of the brain chemical serotonin is dependent upon a good oxygen supply to the brain, which you achieve by breathing slowly.

The elderly and those people with clogged arteries (which prevent the blood effectively circulating) get irritated very quickly. Becoming senile and vague is often because of the reduction of oxygen to the brain. An acute circulation blockage deprives the heart of oxygen resulting in heart attacks. If this occurs to the brain, the result is a stroke.

EXAMPLE: Try performing a difficult mental exercise such as a calculation when you are out of breath. You won't be able to concentrate until your breathing has settled down. Short breaths tend to result in short attention spans. Deep full breaths will enable you to speak in longer more complex sentences and form deeper thoughts.

> *"A healthy mind has an easy breath."*
>
> —SOMEBODY WISE

Increasing your oxygen

Increasing the oxygen flow to your brain will accomplish two things:

i. Activate areas of your brain that are inefficient through lack of blood
ii. Slow down the degeneration of brain cells

Yogis realised the importance of an adequate oxygen supply thousands of years ago. They developed and perfected various breathing techniques. Breathing exercises are crucial for people with sedentary lifestyles. If you sit in an office all day your brain can easily become oxygen starved because your body is not performing the physical activities it was designed for. This oxygen starvation leads to feeling tired, irritable and nervous, plus you are likely to have poor sleeping patterns which result in a bad start to the following day, thus keeping the cycle going. This weakens your immune system, making you more susceptible to catching colds and other diseases.

> *"If I had to limit my advice on healthier living to just one tip, it would be simply to learn how to breathe correctly."*
>
> —ANDREW WEIL, DOCTOR

Cliff Says...
It's a little known fact that... the Greeks used the same word 'phren' to describe both the breath and the mind. They felt that the two were interrelated.

Diaphragmatic breathing

The value of proper breathing is often underestimated, but it is crucial to building and maintaining good health. It triggers a whole chain of physiological reactions, spanning each of the billions of cells that make up your body.

The act of breathing is much more than just inhaling and exhaling air. Everyone can do that but not everyone is good at breathing. You enter the world as a good breather. Observe any baby and you'll see that when they inhale and exhale, it is not the chest that is rising and falling, but the *stomach*. Or to be precise, it is the diaphragm, the muscle between the chest and the abdominal muscles. When the diaphragm is contracted it is forced down causing the abdomen to expand. This negative pressure within the chest forces air into the lungs bringing the oxygen needed to nourish all the cells into your body. This is what we mean by diaphragmatic breathing, also known as abdominal breathing.

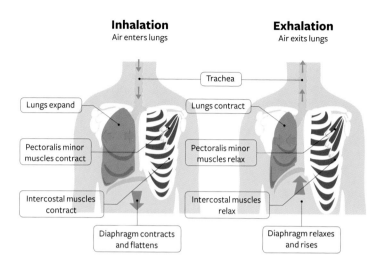

Inhalation
Air enters lungs

Exhalation
Air exits lungs

Trachea

Lungs expand

Lungs contract

Pectoralis minor muscles contract

Pectoralis minor muscles relax

Intercostal muscles contract

Intercostal muscles relax

Diaphragm contracts and flattens

Diaphragm relaxes and rises

Good diaphragmatic breathing leads to improved stamina in athletic activity and protects you from disease. But most of all it is an excellent tool to stimulate the relaxation response that results in less tension and an overall sense of well-being.

Unfortunately, over time, stress causes your chest and stomach muscles to tighten up and your breathing rate to quicken. Your breathing becomes shallow, and you begin to breathe in the chest, rather than the stomach. Most people become 'thoracic breathers', using only the middle and upper parts of their lungs. If you are like most people, your upper chest expands as you inhale and contracts as you exhale. Over the years, you have learned to hold your stomach in, especially if you spend a lot of time at the beach.

Are you shallow?

Research shows that many people's normal breathing patterns are too shallow, too quick, not taking in sufficient oxygen and eliminating too much carbon dioxide. Modern science agrees with the ancient yogis on the subject of shallow breathing. An editorial in the *Journal of the Royal Society of Medicine* suggests that fast, shallow breathing can cause fatigue, sleep disorders, anxiety, stomach upsets, heartburn, gas, muscle cramps, dizziness, visual problems, chest pain and heart palpitations. Scientists have also found that a lot of people who believe they have heart disease are really suffering from improper breathing.

The major reason your breathing is fast and shallow is a result of the modern lifestyle. You, like everyone, are probably in a hurry most of the time. Your movements and breathing follow your rushed life and this stress makes you breathe more quickly and less deeply. Negative emotional states caused by the busyness of life also affect the rate of your breathing. Sedentary work reduces your physical activity so there is less opportunity to breathe deeply, and a shallow breathing habit is born.

> **Cliff Says...**
> *It's a little known fact that...* people who practise yoga have higher carbon dioxide concentrations in their blood than non-practitoners and people who are anxious. This means that the brains of people who practise yoga have a better oxygen supply.

Add another to the list

The shift from diaphragmatic (abdominal) breathing to thoracic breathing isn't just a part of growing older. Many experts believe that it is simply a bad habit. Evidence shows that by breaking the habit, and returning to good breathing patterns like that of an infant, you can help rid yourself of everyday complaints like headaches and fatigue. So, like everything, the first step is self-awareness. Observe how you breathe, then take action to practise good breathing habits. Using and learning proper breathing techniques is one of the most beneficial things that can be done for both short- and long-term physical and emotional health.

Posture

Your posture plays an important part in not only your breathing but general well-being. Good posture is when you have a spine with a normal curve in your low back so your head isn't poking forward and your shoulders aren't rounded. Good posture supports and protects major organs, allows you to maximise use of your five senses, and positively affects your mental health.

EXAMPLE: Be aware of your posture when you sit at the computer. When your head is thrust forwards and the shoulders are elevated, tension is created in your jaw, head and throughout your body. This posture will create a poor breathing pattern and consequently reduced brain effectiveness due to reduced oxygen. If you make sure that you have a normal curve in your lower back you are more likely to breathe better abdominally.

> **Cliff Says...**
> *It's a little known fact that...* ex-All Black rugby great Grant Fox used to practise slow diaphragmatic breathing to help him focus and relax when he was goal kicking.

Fashion victim

Not even your breathing escapes fashion trends. Society's emphasis on having flat stomachs today encourages people to hold their stomach muscle area tense. Unfortunately, this can prevent effective breathing patterns, restricting the capacity of the lungs to the chest area.

Adverse reactions to life events can also cause poor breathing patterns and lead to dizzy spells, asthma, and musculoskeletal problems. Breathing retraining, exercise and self-massage techniques will help with breathing problems.

By a nose

Indeed, your nose has it! The first rule for correct breathing is that you should breathe through your nose. Yes, yes, this may seem obvious and the best things are, but still many people breathe principally through their mouth.

There are three very good reasons to breathe through the nose:

i. Your breathing must slow down because you are breathing through two small holes instead of one big one.

ii. Breathing through your nose increases the oxygen concentration in your blood by 10%!

iii. The nose has various defence mechanisms to make sure that pure, warm air enters the lungs as the air is hygienically filtered and warmed by your nasal passages.

An exception to the rule is when you're exercising. The mouth acts as an overflow when volumes are too great for the nose alone. However, the nose is still breathing while you're exercising.

Top 10 reasons to breathe deeply

1. Improves blood quality due to increased oxygenation in the lungs helping to remove toxins.

2. Increases efficiency of digestion and assimilation and oxygenation of food.

3. Improves nervous system, including the brain, spinal cord, nerve centres and nerves.

4. Rejuvenates glands, especially the pituitary and pineal glands.

5. Rejuvenates skin. The skin becomes smoother and a reduction of facial wrinkles occurs.

6. Massages abdominal muscles and the heart, and stimulates upper body blood circulation.

7. Builds healthy powerful lungs, and is good insurance against respiratory problems.

8. Makes an efficient, stronger heart, and reduces its workload, blood pressure and heart disease.

9. Burns up excess fat more efficiently and feeds starving tissues and glands when underweight.

10. Improves the body's lymphatic drainage.

"Breathing control gives man strength, vitality, inspiration, and magic powers."

—CHUANG TZU, PHILOSOPHER

Breathing exercises have been practised for thousands of years in the East. The West began studying the effectiveness and importance of them several years ago. We now have sufficient research to verify the usefulness of these techniques for calming the mind and body and inducing a heightened sense of awareness.

REMEMBER:

1. Diaphragmatic (abdominal) breathing is essential for good health.

2. Breathe through your nose rather than your mouth.

3. Good posture – keeping your sternum up and back straight allows for proper breathing.

Week 3 Day 4:   Sleep

"Rest: the sweet sauce of labour."

—PLUTARCH, HISTORIAN

Like mind and body, sleep and exercise are two sides of the same coin. You can't affect one without affecting the other. If you have a poor night's sleep you will lack energy throughout the day. If you are active throughout the day you will sleep soundly at night.

Why sleep?

There are three theories for why you sleep. One is that sleep is a time for your body to rest, heal and a return to homeostasis (balance). The other theory is that sleep is the result of an internal timing mechanism and that human beings are programmed to sleep at night due to evolution and the safety that night provides. Another is, it's the time to encode memories from the day. Chances are, all theories are right.

"Sleep is the most undervalued contributor to optimal health and performance."

—KEITH HUMPHREYS, PSYCHIATRIST

Your brain doesn't turn off when you sleep as it processes information from the day's events. We're not alone here. Studies have shown that rats who run through mazes during the day, re-run through these mazes in their mind when they sleep. The most active part of your brain when you're dreaming is the limbic system – your emotional brain – which explains why many dreams are emotionally charged.

Getting quality sleep is essential for boosting your immune system and getting the most out of life. Growth hormones are released while you sleep helping you get the benefits from any physical workouts, and it keeps your appetite in check.

> **Cliff Says...**
> *It's a little known fact that...* chronic lack of sleep increases ghrelin and decreases leptin, the hormones which regulate your hunger and appetite respectively. An increase of ghrelin makes you feel hungry even when you're not and decreased leptin levels keep you eating even though you don't need the calories.

The two elements that are key to quality sleep are the chemical melatonin, and your circadian rhythm (your 24-hour body clock).

We discussed melatonin in Brain & Body Chemicals (Week 2 Day 4). It's produced in your brain and the quantity is determined by the amount of sunlight you get. You want sunlight not just for vitamin D, but also because it raises your body temperature. Why is this important? It's all about the rhythm.

You've got rhythm

Most people's body clocks run just over 24 hours and most cells in your body carry the circadian rhythm gene. Your circadian rhythm is temperature compensated, which means that when your body temperature drops it's a signal for you to go to sleep and when it rises it's time to be active. So the more sunlight you get means you can be more active during the day and will sleep deeper at night.

On average, the highest point of sleepiness comes in the middle of the night, reaches the lowest point at awakening, and again increases slightly mid-afternoon.

Your circadian rhythm, which is genetically predetermined, will tell you whether you're an early bird or a night owl. However, you can if you wish reset your body clock to a limited extent. Early birds can keep their room dark in the morning and get more light in the afternoon. If night owls get more light in the morning, in a few days they'll find they will cope better with early morning starts. The basic rhythm of the day is universal, the only difference being that it starts a bit quicker for early birds than the night owls.

Daily rhythm

Of course, the following diagram is only a guideline. You will discover your own inner rhythm by experimenting with your daily routine.

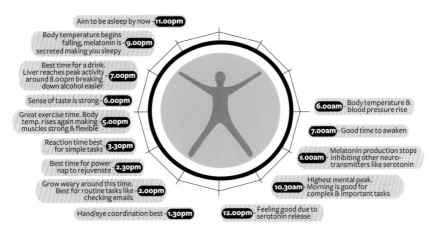

Cliff Says...

It's a little known fact that... shift workers, and especially night shift workers, suffer more health issues and accidents on the job compared with non-shift workers. These health issues include insomnia, fatigue, high blood pressure, heart disease and ulcers, with some studies showing links to breast cancer.

So you need a regular time to go to bed and get up, and yes, that includes weekends! Parents know this and set this routine for their children all week long. They know if they disrupt the child's sleeping pattern there is mood and behaviour change in their little darling. Yet, unfortunately most adults don't follow this good practice for themselves.

There are plenty of myths on getting quality sleep, and catching up on sleep over the weekend is one of them. There's a reason you're tired with the 'Monday Morning Blues' – you've thrown your body clock out trying to catch up on sleep over the weekend.

I Can't Get No Sleep
To see the effects of no sleep, watch Al Pacino in the movie *Insomnia*. He plays a guilt-ridden detective stuck in an Alaskan summer where it's daytime 24/7.

The Sleep Cycle

Sleep has its own cycles that go from higher brain wave frequencies to lower frequencies and back again. This continues until we wake up. Each cycle is about 60-90 minutes. Your sleep gets deeper as your brain waves slow. Ever received a phone call in the middle of the night and felt like a zombie? That's probably because the caller caught you in the middle of the theta or delta stage of sleep. Conversely, ever woken up in the middle of the night and felt fresh as a daisy and couldn't get back to sleep? You've probably just finished a sleep cycle.

The first period of the delta stage (deep sleep) is the longest and this gets shorter throughout the night, whereas the REM sleep starts off short and gets longer over the course of your sleep.

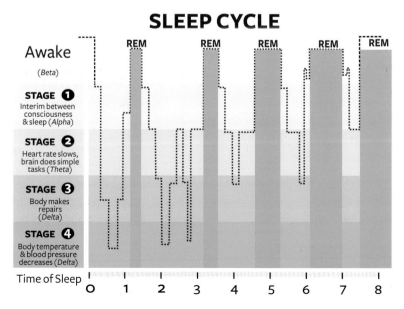

SLEEP CYCLE

Awake *(Beta)*

STAGE ❶ Interim between consciousness & sleep *(Alpha)*

STAGE ❷ Heart rate slows, brain does simple tasks *(Theta)*

STAGE ❸ Body makes repairs *(Delta)*

STAGE ❹ Body temperature & blood pressure decreases *(Delta)*

Time of Sleep   0   1   2   3   4   5   6   7   8

REM   REM   REM   REM   REM

MAXIMISE YOUR ENERGY

83

REM sleep (rapid eye movement)

REM sleep still has scientists unclear whether its purpose is to maintain mental health, maintain normal levels of motivation, or process memories. Your physiological responses and cerebral activity in REM sleep is very similar to when you're awake. That's why 80% of people who wake up in REM sleep can recall their dreams (and why they seem so real), while only 7% can from non-REM sleep. The last few hours of the sleep cycle for most people is REM sleep, so it's not restorative.

> **Cliff Says...**
> *It's a little known fact that...* in 1965 Randy Gardner set the world record at the time for consecutive wakefulness by staying awake for 11 days. His first sleep after setting the record was 14 hours and then he was straight back into his normal eight-hour routine. He did not have to catch up on all the lost sleep.

Power naps – you know you want one!

So what do you do when you're tired and want a sleep? Be a napster! No, we don't mean become a music-sharing website. We mean have a 10–20 minute nap that will rejuvenate you. This is the better alternative to catching up on sleep over the weekend.

"Personally, I enjoy working about 18 hours a day. Besides the short catnaps I take each day, I average about four to five hours of sleep per night."
—THOMAS EDISON, INVENTOR

Now you don't have to have only four to five hours' sleep like Thomas Edison but you can follow his philosophy of catnaps. Call it a catnap, micro sleep, power nap, siesta, whatever you like but you are chemically designed to have a nap around mid-afternoon when your body temperature drops. Research shows that power naps have recuperative powers out of proportion with their brevity. One NASA study showed that a 26-minute nap improved a pilot's performance by more than 34%.

Unless you're in Spain, the modern working lifestyle makes power napping difficult but if you're feeling lethargic, then 5–10 minutes of shuteye (even if it's actually just shutting your eyes) at your desk after lunch will work wonders for you, much better than a coffee! Any more than 20 minutes of power napping and your brain waves start slowing down into theta and delta stages and you'll feel even worse than before you started napping. If you can get away with sleeping at your desk for 20 minutes, let us know as we want to work where you work!

Another nifty trick that works well for people is that you do a 5–10 minute self-hypnosis session where you suggest to yourself that you've had a refreshing six-hour sleep. People have stated it's just like having the real thing.

> **Cliff Says...**
> *It's a little known fact that...* in recent years it has been shown that regular short daytime naps relieve brain fatigue and paradoxically night-time sleep. A study in Okinawa, Japan, showed that after four weeks of taking short afternoon naps and an evening walk, participants' mental and physical health improved. In towns that implemented similar activities medical costs for the elderly dropped by 70%.

If you like to nap then you're in good company. Famous napsters include Napoleon, Thomas Edison, Albert Einstein, Winston Churchill, J. F. Kennedy and Bill Gates.

Bad news

A series of large-scale studies done in the USA and Japan have shattered the myth that adults need eight hours of sleep a night. The study followed 104,010 people for 10 years and the healthiest and fewest deaths occurred among people sleeping between five and seven hours per night. The key is to tune into your own circadian rhythm.

We can hear you screaming *"Nooooo! I need my eight hours of shuteye. If I don't get it I feel terrible."* What actually makes you feel terrible may be the combination of inconsistent times of going to bed and waking up, sleeping in the REM stage where the brain is active for long periods of time, or being woken up at a deep stage of the sleep cycle. You can thrive on approximately six hours of sleep with a bit of practice. Some rhythms are different, some people can thrive on less and some may need a bit more. Your brain and body is hugely adaptive and it has taken people as little as one to three weeks to master it but the results are worth it.

> **Cliff Says...**
> *It's a little known fact that...* most people sleep over 200,000 hours in their lifetime. That's a third of their life asleep. If you were to live to 70 years old, you would have slept more than 23 of those years away.

Reducing two hours of sleep a day gives you 14 more hours in a week to spend on doing things that are important to you. The good thing is that there would be fewer interruptions and demands on your time as most people would be asleep! You've effectively cheated time by giving yourself an extra month in the year.

Studies show that those who learn to sleep less are not missing out on quality restorative sleep and in fact they improve their sleep efficiency. You may find that by eating well and getting adequate exercise you require less sleep anyway.

Be wary of mis-information and your own set beliefs about sleep. Make an informed decision by designing and trialling your own sleep-reduction program. Experiment until you find your natural circadian rhythm.

REMEMBER:

1. You CAN flourish and give yourself the gift of time by getting into the habit of sleeping five to seven hours a night.

2. The key is to go to bed and get up at the same time each day.

3. Maximum of 20-minute naps, activity and getting sunlight are all ways of improving your sleeping habits.

Week 3 Day 5:   Exercise

"Those who think they have no time for bodily exercise will sooner or later have to find time for illness."

—EDWARD STANLEY, POLITICIAN

Exercise benefits

Let's start this section off with a no-brainer: physical exercise can improve both your mental and physical health. You know that, we know that. There's a lot of information and mis-information about exercise but pretty much everyone agrees that exercise can:

- prevent diseases such as arthritis, depression, diabetes, obesity
- strengthen your heart
- lower blood pressure
- alleviate stress
- help you sleep better
- increase your ability to deal with pressure and changes in your mood
- enhance your digestive system
- reduce bad cholesterol
- improve your sex life
- help you relax more easily and increase your ability to focus
- increase energy and improve both your strength and fitness.

"The only exercise some people get is jumping to conclusions, running down their friends, side-stepping responsibility, and pushing their luck!"

—ANON

Human beings are made for movement and in years gone by we had enough activity in our daily lives that it wasn't required to schedule time simply to exercise our bodies. However, with today's sedentary lifestyle reigning supreme, it's important that we do physical exercise daily.

The two main types of physical exercise are aerobic and anaerobic.

Aerobic

- Improves cardiovascular (heart and lung) endurance
- Increases numbers of red blood cells which, in turn, aids the transport of oxygen around the body
- Uses a mixture of carbohydrate and fat for fuel
- Elevates metabolism for at least two hours after exercise

More oxygen is required for prolonged activities so aerobic exercise tends to be of a lower intensity in comparison with anaerobic exercise.

EXAMPLES: Jogging, dancing, cycling, aerobic classes, skipping, swimming, walking.

Anaerobic
- Increases muscle strength and power
- Uses carbohydrate for fuel
- Prepares muscles for quick bursts of speed
- Evens out blood sugar levels
- Increases your metabolism by adding more muscle tissue
- Increases your BMR (Basal Metabolic Rate) i.e. the amount of energy you expend at rest
- Improves bone strength and density

Anaerobic means 'without oxygen' and therefore it can't last long. It uses muscles at high intensity for a short period of time.

EXAMPLES: Weight lifting, sprinting, any rapid burst of hard exercise.

Improving bone strength and density is especially important for women, as they are at risk of osteoporosis as they age. Weight training helps bones absorb calcium better and strengthens connective tissue, which increases joint stability.

Many women fear that if they lift weights they will become muscle bound or put on weight. These fears are unfounded as women only produce a fraction of the testosterone men do (it varies between 6 and 25%), so they will not get the same increases in muscle mass that a man would. And stay off the scales too. You may be in better shape but weigh the same. This is due to losing some fat and putting on some muscle. The best guide to use is to pay attention to how your clothes fit you. If they're getting looser, you know you're on the right track regardless of what the scales tell you.

> **Cliff Says...**
> *It's a little known fact that...* women's upper body strength is typically low relative to a man's. All things being equal, women have 72% of the lower body strength of men but only 57% of the upper body strength.

Flexibility
Flexibility is improved by stretching your muscles and tendons, which increases your joints' range of motion. Every animal stretches and so should you! Stretching has a number of health benefits that include:
- increased muscle and tendon length
- improved range of movement in the joints

- increased blood circulation
- reduced muscle tension
- helping prevent injuries
- alleviated stress
- increased energy levels
- better body balance.

There are different types of stretching techniques and you should talk to a qualified instructor to customise a stretching routine that suits you. However, you can't go wrong if you gradually stretch each major muscle group for 30 seconds each.

Types	Description	When to use
Ballistic	Bouncing in the stretch	NOT RECOMMENDED!
Dynamic	Fast and controlled movement	As a warm-up
PNF/ Isometric	Contract then relax stretching	Only after dynamic stretches or a workout
Static	Gradual stretching	As a warm-down or as a workout by itself

If you are performing high-intensity anaerobic exercise such as weight training then stretching beforehand is NOT recommended. Stretching prior to heavy lifting (relative to the individual) reduces strength in the associated muscle groups. It is better to perform 'warm-up' sets of a light to moderate load before heavy lifting, as this will prepare your body for exercise and not decrease performance.

Getting fit

> *"If it weren't for the fact that the TV set and the refrigerator are so far apart, some of us wouldn't get any exercise at all."*
>
> —JOEY ADAMS, COMEDIAN

If you want to get fit then just going for a leisurely stroll won't do it for you. Sure, it will improve your health and increase your serotonin levels but improving your fitness requires you to increase your heart rate and use muscles that you wouldn't normally use.

We're not here to tell you which exercise program you should do as there are many options available to you. We're here to tell you that you should choose one that you like. Not one that other people recommend for you but one that you enjoy and is aligned to your health goals. If you enjoy swimming then swim. If it's jogging, then jog. If it's chasing buffalo on foot across the American plains then we say go get 'em Crazy Horse. If you enjoy the exercise then the chances of you doing it every day is greatly improved. Another important point is to ensure there's variety in your life when it comes to exercise. Go for a swim one day and chase the buffalo the next. This stops you getting bored with it all.

"Many people treat their bodies as if they were rented from Hertz – something they are using to get around in but nothing they genuinely care about understanding."

—CHUNGLIANG AL HUANG, MARTIAL ARTIST AND AUTHOR

Popular culture has had a major influence on what exercise was considered trendy. In the 1980s it was big muscles and we saw people like Arnold Schwarzenegger and Sylvester Stallone all beefed up taking on the world. Then came the aerobics revolution and soon everyone was jumping up and down to music. The next phase was to combine the two and currently we are enjoying a psychophysical understanding taken from Eastern traditions like Yoga, Qi-Gong, martial arts and bodywork techniques like Pilates and Alexander technique. The benefits of cross training are becoming more desirable as it is becoming recognised that the body *and* mind can be strong and flexible with more and more people now seeking a harmonious mind, body, spirit connection.

When to exercise

"I exercise every morning without fail. One eyelid goes up and the other follows."

—PETE POSTLETHWAITE, ACTOR

Exercise, just like sunlight, causes an increase in body temperature. Therefore exercising in the early morning is better for you as the increase in your body temperature delays the energy drop in the afternoon giving you greater energy levels when you need it. Conversely, ensure you exercise no later than four hours before you want to go to sleep, as the raise in body temperature will make it difficult for you to get to sleep.

There are different theories on when the best time to exercise is but obviously you have to do what best suits you. Some theories say to exercise in the morning before breakfast as you'll burn more fat due to your low blood sugar levels. The reasoning behind this theory is that you'll eat up more calories in the morning on an empty stomach than at any other time.

However, while this is technically true, there are other factors that need to be considered.

If you eat prior to exercise, you are able to perform longer and at a higher intensity level because your cells aren't being starved of glucose. This means that your total calorie output will be much higher and as a result, you will burn more fat.

The important thing to remember is that fat loss isn't about burning as much fat as you can via exercise. It's about total calorie expenditure, ie: energy in vs energy out. As a general guide, if you're doing an aerobic workout eat some carbohydrates (fruits, vegetables, grains) two hours before your workout. If you work out first thing in the morning, at the very least have a banana 30 minutes prior.

If you're doing an anaerobic workout have protein (eggs, meat, soy products, dairy products) two hours prior. If you're a morning exerciser, then have a protein shake before heading to the gym.

Always eat after a workout – especially protein as it helps rebuild muscles.

The best advice we can give you is to pay attention to your body and do best by what it tells you.

How long should you exercise for? Thirty minutes a day is a good guideline. But every day need not be a strenuous workout, as even a 30-minute walk has a positive impact on your health. Look for other activities that can be deemed as exercise. Activities such as gardening, coaching a sports team, walking up stairs rather than taking the elevator and rearranging the furniture are all forms of exercise.

Exercise and your biochemistry

"The value of exercise has less to do with building muscles or burning calories than it has to do with getting your heart to pump faster and more efficiently and thereby increase blood flow to nourish and cleanse your brain and all your organs."
—CANDACE PERT, NEUROSCIENTIST

Exercise has a big effect on your biochemistry by:
- helping produce more melatonin enabling you to sleep better
- increasing serotonin levels which gives you that warm, happy feeling
- releasing endorphins, the body's natural painkiller
- breaking down cortisol, which is also known as the stress hormone as it causes exactly that if it stays in your system for too long
- forming new neurons.

Exercise the black dog

"Whenever I get the urge to exercise I lie down until it goes away."
—WINSTON CHURCHILL, POLITICIAN

Winston Churchill was famous for saying his elixir of life was *"no sports, just whisky and cigars"* yet he was plagued by deep depression, which he called his black dog, always by his side. Exercise can raise the spirits even in people who suffer from deep depression, as it releases the happiness chemical serotonin.

> *"For the mind's sake, it's necessary to exercise the body."*
>
> —JEAN JACQUES ROUSSEAU, PHILOSOPHER

③

Mental exercise

Can you stay mentally sharp as you get older or are you destined to lose your marbles as a natural result of living to a ripe old age? Well, the good news is that a decline in mental abilities associated with aging, such as memory loss, sluggish thinking and lack of creative thinking is not inevitable if the brain remains challenged.

Your mental exercise regimen should include developing abilities like perception, long- and short-term memory, creativity, logic, and verbal abilities. Things like playing board games, doing crosswords and Sudoku, doing mental arithmetic and memorising shopping lists and phone numbers are all ways of keeping your brain mentally sharp and enhancing your cognitive functions.

As discussed in Neurons (Week 2 Day 3), the old adage "Use it or lose it is" true for mental fitness as well as physical fitness.

Sex

And now it's time for sex. Figuratively speaking. What would you choose between: running 75 miles or having sex three times a week for a year? Choose carefully now because they both burn 7500 calories. If you choose the run, then you're probably single. If you're not single, you may soon be! There have been a number of studies to show that sex can be good for your mental and physical health. Unfortunately we missed out in partaking in all this research.

Sex can:

- increase your energy
- lower your cholesterol
- alleviate stress and ward off depression
- strengthen muscle and bones
- boost self-esteem.

Sex can give you a good workout depending on how vigorous you are of course. Your heart and breathing rate increases and different muscle groups like your arms, legs, buttocks and stomach muscles are engaged. Testosterone levels are also increased and it's thought that this hormone plays an active part in strengthening your muscles and bones.

> **Cliff Says...**
> *It's a little known fact that...* an active sex life may help you live longer. David Weeks, a clinical neuropsychologist, studied 3500 people of different ages (18 years to 102 years old). The study showed that sex actually slows the aging process.

The thing that impresses us most about this study is that 102-year-olds are having sex. Sex requires some stamina so people who are physically fit are more likely to have a more satisfying sex life than those who'd rather sit on the couch and watch re-runs of *Friends*. So being fit may enhance your sex life but having sex may enhance your fitness because it improves muscle tone, cardiovascular fitness and mental health.

> *"Remember, if you smoke after sex you're doing it too fast."*
> —WOODY ALLEN, COMEDIAN

Sex for her

For women, sex releases oxytocin, a hormone that increases feelings of affection and is responsible for social bonding and the nurturing instinct. Women who maintain levels of oxytocin during sad events in their lives are less likely to suffer from anxiety issues. Sex also acts as a beauty treatment for women as the hormone oestrogen is produced, making your hair shiny and your skin smooth.

Sex for him

Men who have sex at least three times each week have a decreased risk of developing prostate problems and have a lower risk of heart attack.

Sex is good for you on many levels and definitely has a place in your exercise regime!

> *"Good sex is like good bridge. If you don't have a good partner, you'd better have a good hand."*
> —MAE WEST, ACTRESS

REMEMBER:

1. Find a variety of exercises and activities that you enjoy doing.

2. Exercise for 30 minutes a day at a time that best suits your chosen activity.

3. The "Use it or lose it" adage applies to physical, mental and sexual activity.

Week 3 summary map:

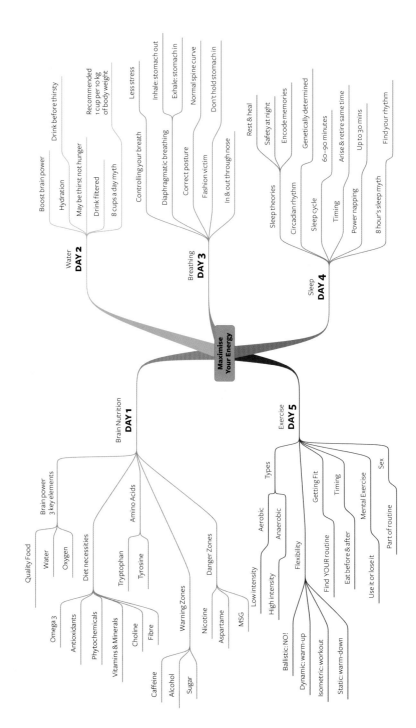

Maximise
Your Energy

Water
DAY 2
- Boost brain power
- Hydration
  - Drink before thirsty
  - May be thirst not hunger
  - Recommended 1 cup per 10 kg of body weight
- Drink filtered
- 8 cups a day myth

Breathing
DAY 3
- Less stress
- Controlling your breath
- Diaphragmatic breathing
  - Inhale: stomach out
  - Exhale: stomach in
- Correct posture
  - Normal spine curve
- Fashion victim
  - Don't hold stomach in
- In & out through nose

Sleep
DAY 4
- Sleep theories
  - Rest & heal
  - Safety at night
  - Encode memories
- Circadian rhythm
  - Genetically determined
- Sleep cycle
  - 60–90 minutes
- Timing
  - Arise & retire same time
- Power napping
  - Up to 30 mins
- 8 hour's sleep myth
  - Find your rhythm

Brain Nutrition
DAY 1
- Quality Food
  - Brain power 3 key elements
    - Water
    - Oxygen
  - Diet necessities
    - Omega 3
    - Antioxidants
    - Phytochemicals
    - Vitamins & Minerals
    - Choline
    - Fibre
  - Amino Acids
    - Tryptophan
    - Tyrosine
  - Warning Zones
    - Caffeine
    - Alcohol
    - Sugar
  - Danger Zones
    - Nicotine
    - Aspartame
    - MSG

Exercise
DAY 5
- Types
  - Aerobic
    - Low intensity
  - Anaerobic
    - High intensity
- Flexibility
  - Ballistic: NO!
  - Dynamic: warm-up
  - Isometric: workout
  - Static: warm-down
- Getting Fit
  - Find YOUR routine
- Timing
  - Eat before & after
- Mental Exercise
  - Use it or lose it
- Sex
  - Part of routine

Action Your Success Strategies

Purpose

To understand key success strategies allowing you to create your reality and have a clear vision of your desired future.

Overview

Day 1: Gratitude
Day 2: Intention
Day 3: Visualisation
Day 4: Chunking
Day 5: Modelling

Benefits

This week's experience in the Challenge guides you to:

- create positivity within and around you
- increase your confidence and boost your self-esteem
- experiment with different ways to achieve your desired level of fulfilment
- shift yourself into a positive mental state and enjoy a sense of inner peace
- build rapport easily with people
- increase mental agility
- manage time more easily
- bring structure to your days
- take on new perspectives.

Week 4 Day 1:   Gratitude

"Gratitude is not only the greatest of virtues, but the parent of all others."

—CICERO, POLITICIAN & ORATOR

Gratitude is an emotion where you feel a sense of appreciation towards someone or something. It is your gateway to happiness and transports you from living in your past or future, right into the present. Research shows that feelings of gratitude promote emotional well-being.

Many philosophers, spiritual teachers and major religions promote being grateful. Your parents and grandparents no doubt told you to be grateful – especially around dinner time when you didn't want to eat your Brussels sprouts and were reminded about the starving kids in Africa.

Science says...

Results of a University of Texas study indicated that a group who did daily gratitude exercises reported higher levels of alertness, enthusiasm, determination, optimism and energy than those who did not. Additionally, the people in the gratitude group experienced less depression and stress, were more likely to help others, exercised more regularly and made more progress towards personal goals. Those who feel grateful are also more likely to feel loved, and gratitude encouraged a positive cycle of reciprocal kindness among people, since one act of gratitude encourages another.

"If the only prayer you said in your whole life was, 'thank you', that would suffice."

—MEISTER ECKHART, PHILOSOPHER

It doesn't matter what your faith is and whether you do or don't believe in a divine being at all. It is better to be grateful for what you have in life and enjoy the positive results that flow from this mindset.

> **Cliff Says...**
> *It's a little known fact that...* in a study of organ recipients, patients who kept gratitude journals scored better on all measures of health than those who just kept routine notes.

"Gratitude is heaven itself."

—WILLIAM BLAKE, POET

An Economic Fishing Plan

A boat docked in Maketu, a tiny NZ village on the Bay of Plenty coast.

An American tourist complimented the Maori fisherman on the quality of his fish and asked how long it took him to catch them.

"Not very long," answered Tama.

"But then, why don't you stay out longer and catch more?" asked the American.

Tama explained that his small catch was sufficient to meet his needs and those of his family. The American asked, *"But what do you do with the rest of your time?"*

"I sleep late, fish a little, play with my children and take a moe (sleep) with my wife. In the evenings I go into town to see my friends, have a few drinks, play the guitar, and sing a few songs. I have a full life."

The American interrupted, *"I have an MBA from Harvard and I can help you. You should start fishing longer every day. You can sell the extra fish you catch. With the extra revenue, you can buy a bigger boat. With the extra money the larger boat will bring, you can buy a second one and a third one and so on until you have an entire fleet of trawlers. Instead of selling your fish to a middleman, you can negotiate directly with the processing plants and maybe even open your own plant. You can leave this little village and move to Rotorua, Hamilton, or even Auckland. From there you can direct your huge enterprise."*

"How long would that take?" asked Tama.

"Twenty, perhaps twenty-five years," replied the American.

"And after that?" asked Tama.

"Afterwards? That's when it gets really interesting," answered the American laughing. *"When your business gets really big, you start selling stocks and make millions."*

"Millions? Really? And after that?"

"After that you'll be able to retire, live in a tiny village near the coast, sleep late, play with your children, catch a few fish, take a moe and spend your evenings drinking and enjoying your friends."

The law of attraction

Being grateful creates a positive energy within you. Ultimately, everything is energy. The universe itself is one big ball of energy. The law of attraction is a law based on the scientific theory of energy and entanglement (we're all connected and from the same source). When you break down what you're made up of, your material self, you find that it's energy.

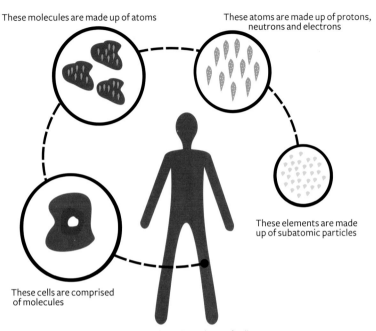

These molecules are made up of atoms

These atoms are made up of protons, neutrons and electrons

These elements are made up of subatomic particles

These cells are comprised of molecules

Your human tissue is made up of cells

When you break down the subatomic particles and get right down to the source – you find what Einstein and other scientists found – there's nothing to you but invisible, fast, vibrating energy and information. This energy and information moves far too fast for your senses to process it so you see the clusters of energy and information as solid objects like chairs, people, cars.

So, ultimately, you are made up of the same energy as everything else that exists in the universe. Your thoughts are energy that have their own measurable frequency. Energy can be influenced and directed and that's what the law of attraction is about.

> *"All we are is the result of what we have thought."*
> —BUDDHA, SPIRITUAL TEACHER

The law of attraction states your environment is an extension of your mind and that you attract what you think about. Basically, like attracts like. If you think about the things you don't want, then you attract more of those things.

EXAMPLE: If you think, "I don't want more time pressure", bingo – you'll find more things being heaped onto your already busy plate.

> *"What you resist, persists."*
> —CARL JUNG, PSYCHIATRIST

So, the key is to think of what you want or are intending to create, as if it's already happening, even if you don't have it yet.

Ssshhh
The movie *The Secret* explores the law of attraction. Of course many people would argue that it ain't no secret but rather a clever marketing ploy. Nonetheless – the law of attraction works.

Having an attitude of gratitude helps you put your focus on what you have rather than what you don't have. If you don't feel grateful then just pretend! If others say you aren't being genuine, you can always explain that you're working on being a more grateful person. This is the old "fake it till you make it" ploy at work.

> *"Who does not thank for little will not thank for much."*
>
> —ESTONIAN PROVERB

Plus the Hat
A grandmother was walking with her little grandson along a beautiful beach. The grandson, the apple of his grandma's eye, would run ahead, play with some shells and bring them back to his grandmother. As he ran ahead, a freak wave came from the sea, picked up the grandson and took him out to sea.

The grandmother could only stand there in shock. Then she got angry. She raged against God, she raged against the heavens about the injustice of taking her sweet boy. She raged with a force never seen before.

Suddenly, another freak wave appeared and the grandson reappeared on the beach unharmed. The grandmother turned to the sky, shook her fist and said, *"He was wearing a hat!"*

Things to be grateful for
What could you be grateful about? Let's look at it from **The Big** **3** point of view.

1. Health
This could include being grateful for:
- the gift of life today
- your heart that keeps beating
- the quality of air you breathe
- your organs which do a great job every moment, keeping you fit and well
- having mobility and dexterity skills
- your thoughts and emotions
- your mistakes and hardships that have helped define you.

2. Wealth

This could include being grateful for:

- your job – your income, the challenges, the successes, the failures, the learning
- your skills – all the different things you're able to do
- your knowledge – all the different things you know and have experienced
- your material possessions – your house, car, bike, TV, books, furniture
- your holidays – trips to the beach, the mountains.

3. Relationships

This could include being grateful for:

- your partner/spouse/significant other
- your family
- your family of origin
- your friends
- your colleagues
- past relationships.

This is by no means a complete list – just a starting point.

"Gratitude is the heart's memory."

—FRENCH PROVERB

 Grateful for Gratitude

An overseas friend of a JOLT Challenge trainer was stressed to the point of constantly bursting into tears. Her husband and her father weren't getting along in the new family business. It was a startup company so it had its own pressures that came with that and she felt caught in the middle between the two important men in her life. She was also feeling guilty about the time she was spending away from her toddler resulting in her being strung out, which didn't help matters.

The JOLT Challenge trainer took her through the exercise in the JOLT Challenge Journal where she wrote over two pages of things she was grateful for. She reported a transformation both emotionally and mentally. She instantly gained a clearer perspective on matters and was able to sort the issues out and celebrate the things in her life.

And the credit goes to...

Who are you thankful to? It doesn't matter. No matter what your religious and spiritual beliefs or lack thereof, you can be grateful. You can be thankful to God, the Universe, your Creator, your Higher Self, Spirit, life itself or the postman. It really doesn't matter what label you put on it, as long as you're comfortable with it. Just acknowledge and be thankful for whatever you have and receive.

You don't even have to understand the law of attraction to be grateful. Just as most people don't understand how electricity works but still use it on a daily basis to achieve their desired outcome, so too can you use the law of attraction and have an attitude of gratitude.

> *"What this power is I cannot say, all I know is that it exists."*
>
> —ALEXANDER GRAHAM BELL, INVENTOR

Make gratitude a part of who you are, a part of your identity. Embrace the things you have and allow yourself to open up to receive more of what you desire.

REMEMBER:

1. Being grateful positively impacts on your happiness and health.

2. Your thoughts are energy that attract whatever you think about.

3. Who you are grateful to may be irrelevant, the act of being grateful is paramount.

Week 4 Day 2:   Intention

"Intention is a power that's present everywhere as a field of energy."

—WAYNE DYER, AUTHOR

Setting your intention

Setting your intention is a strategy to tap into the power of intent, a force that exists within you. The act of daily setting your intention recognises that you create your own reality. It's about setting your intention for each day, detaching from it and allowing it to manifest. Often you get in the way of your own success by over-analysing something, which leads to you not taking action at all. This is called 'analysis paralysis'. The opposite, being impulsive, also prevents you from acting on your intentions.

When you set your intention, you send out a message of energy of what you want. Your brain by its sheer design and connection to the universe will start looking for ways to make it happen, often at an unconscious level.

You've probably experienced it for yourself. Ever thought about someone you hadn't heard from for a while and then they called? Ever desperately needed cash for some bills and then you came into some money out of the blue? Ever left a job without another lined up and then a friend just happens to mention they have a connection with a certain company that results in you securing your dream job?

Coincidence? Perhaps. Remember though, that 'to coincide' means to agree perfectly. The prefix 'co' means 'with' or 'together', suggesting a relationship. 'Incidence' comes from 'incident', meaning an event, so coincidence is actually two events that are meant to go together. Maybe when those coincidences occur it's actually evidence of your brain and the universe conspiring to help you get what you need.

"Every coincidence is a message, a clue about a particular facet of our lives that requires attention."

—DEEPAK CHOPRA, DOCTOR & AUTHOR

Science says...

Robert Jahn and Brenda Dunne from Princeton University have conducted over 2.5 million trials that demonstrated how human intention can influence electronic devices. Subjects are asked to set their intention to a particular number over another number (eg: to get more ones than zeros) on a random number generator. These results were replicated by sixty-eight independent investigators and the US National Research Council also stated that the trials could not be explained by chance.

"When you realise there is nothing lacking, the whole world belongs to you."

—LAO TZU, PHILOSOPHER

3 Ways of setting your intention

You can use intention setting in three ways:

1. **Make Your Day** – short-term setting
2. **Make Your Future** – mid-term setting
3. **Make Your Life** – long-term setting

1. Make Your Day

You may think that being able to create your reality is a wonderful thing and you'd be right. But what it also means is that where you are right now in your life journey, you've created. All the good things and bad things that have happened in your life, you've created. This means you are responsible for where you are right now in life. Feel free to read that last sentence again – it's a big one.

As the old saying goes, there are 3 types of people in the world:

i. Those that make things happen
ii. Those that let things happen
iii. Those who ask, "*what happened?*"

Choose to be the first type. Consciously make your day every day. Take responsibility for all the things that happen in your life. It's incredibly empowering. The alternative is to be a victim who blames others for your own situation.

What about when bad things happen to you – overdue bills, carpet stains, family illnesses – did you create that too? What about extreme events such as being crashed into, mugged, raped, shot, murdered – did you create that? The answer is yes and no. No, you're not wholly responsible for other people's actions and events that are out of your control (eg: you didn't create the rainy day). However, you are responsible for your own thoughts, actions and reactions. Keeping in mind that responsibility is *response–ability*, meaning your ability to respond to the events that occur to you, whether they're good or bad. How you choose to respond to the events in your life keeps you in category 1. You make things happen by choosing what those events mean to you. We cover this further in Choice (Week 6 Day 5).

> *"The whole universe is the movement of energy and information."*
>
> —DEEPAK CHOPRA, DOCTOR & AUTHOR

Setting your intention is a strategy for putting positive energy out into the universe. The key is active focus on the positive. Not what's missing in your life, not what you don't want, not even what you do want but rather what you intend to create.

If you focus on the negative, or reasons why you don't have what you want, you'll keep getting more of that. Thinking about what you don't have makes you ungrateful, wallowing in self-pity, and self-pity is a thief who will rob you of your fulfilment in life.

Even if you focus on what you do want, then you will remain in a state of wanting. What you have to do is to think from the end. Imagine you have *already received* what you want. Cultivate and practise that thinking and behaviour, keep focused and it will manifest for you, provided that it is ecologically (considered on all levels) sound and congruent with your actions.

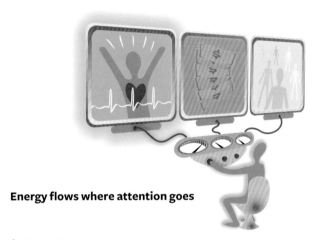

Energy flows where attention goes

2. Make Your Future

In this instance, rather than focusing on what you want to happen each day, you are focusing on the achievement of a particular goal. Intention setting ties in closely with visualisation and mental rehearsing (Visualisation: Week 4 Day 3).

Imagine you want to become a better singer. You can set your intention to focus on hitting high notes and sounding melodious.

No magic wand

Setting your intention isn't a magic wand. You can't just set your intention and then expect it to magically appear. Your mind and body must be congruent.

EXAMPLE: If you set your intention to be the next Olympic 100 metre champion, then you'd want to be in the current top 10 to start with. Just having a lapsed membership of an athletic club makes this an ecologically unsound intention. So if you are in the top 10 you will want to mentally rehearse yourself crossing the finishing line, hearing the voices of the crowd, and feeling the ribbon break across your chest.

Your environment is an extension of your mind

Dance Like a Butterfly...

Muhammad Ali was a master of intention. He used every trick under the sun to create his desired reality. He used affirmations like *"I am the greatest"*, he used visualisation, mental rehearsal and rhymes like:

"You think the world was surprised when Nixon resigned?
Just wait till I whip George Foreman's behind."

Before his third fight against Joe Frazier in Manila, Singapore, in 1975, Ali dubbed Frazier "the gorilla" and carried a little rubber gorilla with him that he would take out and throw punches at for the cameras.

In what is considered by many to be one of the most brutal boxing matches in history, Ali was able to come from, as he described it, *"the closest to dying"* he had ever been to win the fight.

Knockout in the 8th!

Watch *When We Were Kings,* the documentary on Muhammad Ali's boxing match with George Foreman in Zaire in 1974 and see the master of setting intention in action.

3. Make Your Life

The principles and theory of Make Your Life are the same as Make Your Day but this is where you focus on the life you want to live as a whole. It's bringing the positive future you want into the here and now. What kind of life do you want to live? How do you want to live your life on a daily basis?

Intention setting checklist

To set your intention requires an initial focus and detachment. It's important that once you set your intention, you then let it go. Letting go doesn't mean you give up on your intention but rather, you don't remain fixated on it. You surrender the outcome to the universe, God, the greater mind, Spirit, the source, consciousness – to whomever or whatever you choose. This focuses your attention.

The following is a **5** step guide to setting your intention:

Step 1. Ensure you're in a relaxed, positive state
Step 2. Mentally list things you're grateful for
Step 3. State your intention – keep it concise and specific
Step 4. Visualise and mentally rehearse your intention as if it's already achieved
Step 5. Detach from the outcome

Call it karma, call it cause and effect, call it uncanny coincidences, call it whatever you like, but setting your intention focuses your attention on the path before you, and that can only be a positive thing.

REMEMBER:

1. Make your day by setting your intention rather than letting events just happen.

2. Your brain is set up to look for things that you want in your life.

3. Think positively rather than about what's missing in your life.

Week 4 Day 3:   Visualisation

"Whatever the mind of man can conceive, it can achieve."
—W. CLEMENT STONE, BUSINESSMAN & PHILANTHROPIST

Everything that has been and will be created has to be created in the mind first. The chair you're sitting on, the clothes you're wearing, the book you're reading – everything started off as an idea first.

The power of visualisation can affect you mentally, emotionally and physically. It is a potent form of self-empowerment as it exploits the mind/body connection. Tapping into this strategy can help you define and achieve your goals, develop a positive attitude, raise energy levels, increase confidence, improve the memory, ward off disease, and many other aspects of self-development.

What exactly does *visualisation* mean? It means creating the reality in your mind before creating it in your environment. Don't get stuck on the idea that visualisation is just seeing an image. It's using all your senses. Some people see images clearly while others see rough shapes lacking detail, some think about it or become aware of a feeling or impression.

If you think you can't visualise, just answer this question – what is the colour of your house? You would have had to conjure up the image of your house in your mind's eye to answer that question, which is basically what you're doing when you visualise. There is no right or wrong way to visualise. You will quickly come to find which way works best for you.

Visualisation vs Mental rehearsal

Although often the two terms are used interchangeably, they are different. The difference is, visualisation is a dissociated activity and mental rehearsal is an associated one. When you visualise, you're like an observer on the outside who sees yourself doing the action. When you mentally rehearse, you see everything from your perspective, as if looking out from your own eyes. It puts you in that moment.

Imagine you're visualising kicking a football. You see yourself standing in front of the ball, the whole field, the clothes and boots you're wearing and where the goalposts are. If you were doing a mental rehearsal of kicking a football, then the only way you'd know what colour your boots are would be to look down at them.

Mental rehearsal has proven to be a superior tool to use when it comes to doing an activity that you want to master. It is used by many professional athletes to train their mind and body for peak performance. They do this by imagining themselves actually doing their performance. They use all their senses, especially their kinaesthetic sense where they feel their bodies engaged in the activity and feel the emotions when they succeed.

To be effective, you must mentally rehearse in real time, no speeding up or slowing

ACTION YOUR SUCCESS STRATEGIES

107

down as you want to be firing the same neuromuscular pattern when it's time to do the real thing. And a good thing is, unlike with physical practice, you don't get tired when you mentally rehearse.

Visualisation   **Mental Rehearsal**

And it's not just restricted to sports. When you mentally rehearse you actually strengthen the ability of your mind to deal with whatever it is you're imagining.

Imagine you have a presentation to deliver. You can practise seeing the presentation from start to finish in your mind. Run through how you open your presentation, how you stand confidently, speak with authority and hear the applause and positive comments after you've finished.

Visualisation, due to it being a disassociated action, is better suited for reflecting on a past experience and seeing what you can learn from it. It's a useful tool to put some distance between you and the memory especially if it's an emotionally charged one.

Imagine you've had an argument with your significant other. When you replay the situation in your head, you can reflect on what you said and did and see yourself responding in a different way in future.

So both visualisation and mental rehearsal are excellent tools for you to manifest your desired reality. Practise with both and use whichever works best for you.

> **A Tiger Cub on the Golf Course**
> Tiger Woods says his greatest gift is his imagination and recalls how his father taught him his first lesson in visualisation when he was a toddler. His father would ask him if he could see the picture of the hole and then instructed him to putt to the picture.

Science says...

Psychologist Alan Richardson conducted an experiment with three groups of participants. All three groups were selected at random and had no experience in visualisation. They all threw free throws on a basketball court on day one and were told to report back twenty days later to repeat the test. The first group had to practise throwing free throws every day for those twenty days. The second group was only allowed to visualise throwing free throws and the third group did nothing in between the two testing days.

When they reported back and threw free throws twenty days later, the first group that had practised improved by 24%. *The second group that only visualised throwing basketballs improved by 23%.* The third group that wasn't allowed to practise or visualise did not improve at all.

Richardson noted that the most effective visualisation was when the visualiser used their senses and felt the basketball in their hands, heard it bounce off the backboard and saw it going through the hoop.

> *"Unless we can visualise something we are unable to think about it."*
>
> —E.M. FORSTER, NOVELIST

Cliff Says...
It's a little known fact that... a study of volunteers found that those who worked out increased strength by 30% and those who put themselves through an imaginary workout increased strength by 16%. So you can get that burn from the couch!

Why visualisation is so powerful

Your brain isn't able to tell the difference between what's real and what's imagined so visualising something is a powerful way to create your reality.

Experience that now. Look up from this book and at something that's in the room around you – it may be a pen, light switch, the cover of the book itself. Best not to look at a switched-on light bulb. Look at it for 5 seconds. Now close your eyes and imagine that object now. The same parts of your brain are working.

You can use visualisation to change your self-perception. People who succeed in life think and behave in ways that make it more likely for them to succeed. This is why it's crucial you develop and maintain a positive self-image.

Cliff Says...
It's a little known fact that... Nikola Tesla, the inventor of AC electricity, the radio, the electric car, wireless communication, and speaker of eight languages trained his powers of visualisation from a young age. He found that as a result of doing so he didn't need models, drawings or experiments when it came to his inventions as he could picture creating them all in his mind.

Visualisation strengthens the law of attraction to work in your favour and will start to act as a magnet, drawing more of the things you want into your experience.

"Success often comes to those who have the aptitude to see way down the road."
— LAING BURNS, JR., UNKNOWN

A word of warning
There are books and DVDs out there today that say, have positive thoughts, visualise your desire and it will manifest. Um... no. While it's partly right, having positive thoughts and visualisation are not enough by themselves to achieve success. You still have to get off your butt and put the effort in. Visualisation isn't a substitute for action. Combine visualisation with positive action.
Remember:
Your thoughts and actions have to be congruent

There is a real desire for many people to cut corners to get instant results. The tools in the JOLT Challenge Journal are to help you achieve your desired level of success but you've got to do the work. This will shape who you are and what you get out of life. Besides, keep in mind; it's the journey, not the destination that's more important.

6 of the Best
The following six tips are the best guidelines that will get you mastering visualisation and mental rehearsal in no time. If you follow these tips then you can't go wrong.

1. Sit or lie down
You'll need a quiet place with no distractions. That means turning off your cell phone. You can sit or lie down, whatever is more comfortable for you. Make sure you're wearing comfortable clothes or have at least loosened your clothing. You may find it comfortable to cross your hands and feet.

2. Relax
You want to have your brain waves in the alpha state, as you'll be more creative and open to positive suggestion. Unless of course, you're a Buddhist monk, then you'll have no problem getting into the gamma state. When it comes to mentally rehearsing an activity, you want to re-create the state you'll be in so, depending on the activity, a state of relaxed alertness may be preferred.

3. Close your eyes
You'll be using your mind's eye to visualise or mentally rehearse so close your eyes to minimise distractions.

4. Be positive

Visualise with a positive attitude and feel positive emotions. Reframe all negative images and problems into positive ones and solutions. Use positive affirmations to replace all negative self-talk.

5. Present tense

Picture yourself with the goal achieved or the problem already being solved. Remember, your brain can't tell the difference between what it sees and what it thinks it sees.

6. Intensify

The visualisations that have the greatest effect are those that are strong and clear. To intensify your mental rehearsals, do the following:

- *Use your senses*
  Visualisation involves more than seeing. Flesh out the visualisation with realistic detail by using the sensations of hearing, touch, movement, smell, taste, temperature and colour when conjuring up the images. Then magnify all the images to make them bigger, brighter and louder to help you achieve a peak state.

- *Use your emotions*
  Let the happiness flow through you. Feel the power, glory, sense of satisfaction that comes with achieving your success. Intensify these emotions.

- *Add action and depth*
  Have the mental rehearsal more like a movie than a picture. Static images aren't as powerful as ones that are moving and have depth. Create a foreground, middle ground and background.

When you finish your visualisation or mental rehearsal you should be a changed person. You will have mentally achieved those things you have rehearsed. Remember that patience and practice is required for maximum benefit. Incorporate a little bit of visualisation or mental rehearsal into your morning routine.

REMEMBER:

1. Visualisation (dissociated) and mental rehearsal (associated) can help you in many ways including achieving goals and reaching peak performance.

2. Visualisation and mental rehearsal is almost as good as physical practice itself.

3. It only takes a little bit of practice to become proficient at visualisation and mental rehearsal and the benefits far outweigh the effort exerted.

Week 4 Day 4:   Chunking

> *"The secret of getting ahead is getting started. The secret of getting started is breaking your complex tasks into small manageable tasks, and then starting on the first one."*
>
> —MARK TWAIN, AUTHOR

Chunking refers to a strategy for making more efficient use of information by organising it into groups. The idea was first put forward in 1956 by Harvard psychologist George A. Miller. He published an article entitled *The Magical Number Seven, Plus or Minus Two*. His research showed that the conscious mind can only cope with five to nine pieces of information at one time giving us the phrase 7 +/– 2.

This is why phone numbers and credit card numbers are usually chunked together in fewer than 7 digits. That's why there are many books titled 7 habits, 7 secrets, 7 laws, 7 ways etc. You can chunk up or down. You do both of these things anyway but you'll have a tendency to spend more time doing one than the other. Be aware of the difference between the two. Think of it this way – are you predominantly a big picture person (chunked up) or detail person (chunked down)?

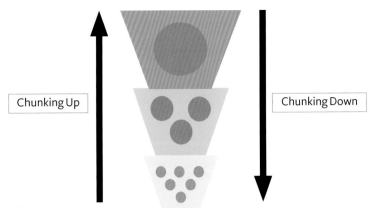

Chunking Up   Chunking Down

Chunking up

Chunking up means moving from the specific to the general, going from small details to larger ones.

i) When you want to inspire yourself or others you need to communicate in a chunked-up style. This applies whether it's verbal or written.

EXAMPLE: When trying to inspire a team to put in more effort, you need to communicate the *why* rather than the *what*. Reiterating the what is the detail (chunked down) and although it tells them what to do it doesn't inspire them. The *why* is the vision, the outcome and inspires people to do the *what*.

ii) Chunking up can help you put things into perspective.

By asking, *"what is this part of?"* you get the bigger picture of a certain area, topic or reason for doing something. This is a great tool to use when faced with menial tasks. Doing the paperwork doesn't seem so bad when you take into account it's part of your overall success.

When defining your goals and outcomes you can ask yourself, *"If I get this, what else would I get?"*

It helps you understand your own and other people's behaviour. You can gain clarity if you chunk up to *"what is this an example of?"* or *"how does this fit into the overall scheme of things?"*

Imagine you are upset about something a colleague has said about you. You can then ask yourself, *"Does what they say about me really matter in my career at work or even in the overall scheme of my life?"* Chunking up enables you to put it into a different perspective.

iii) Chunking up helps put information into an order that you can cope with.

EXAMPLE: Your to-do list may look like this:
- Clear old emails
- Prepare for client meeting
- Organise meeting schedule and prepare notes
- Bank cheques
- Spend time with the kids
- Finish reading the business book
- Follow up outstanding invoices
- Wash the car
- Touch base with marketing department
- Forecast budget for next quarter
- Organise neighbourhood watch meeting
- Write proposal for next project
- Spend time looking at investment opportunities
- Call back prospective clients
- Tidy up garden
- Send thank-you letters
- Record the late-night news

Yikes – good luck! Your to-do list may be overwhelming to the point where you start to wonder, what's the point, as things keep getting added to it faster than you can do it all. This feeling of powerlessness may lead to procrastination and as a result you put off many of the important tasks and just focus on the quick and easy ones. This creates its own vicious cycle.

Of course, keep in mind that you're not supposed to have an empty to-do list – life is supposed to be full!

Chunking is a great strategy to use to make your activities feel manageable. The tasks still have to be done, but it no longer looks overwhelming and helps to keep you in a positive state while you get through them all.

Go through your list and look for items that can be grouped together in categories.

You may create the following chunked-up categories based on the above list:
1. Home people activities
2. Home activities
3. Work activities
4. Work people activities

So that now your to-do list looks more like:

1 – Home people activities
- Spend time with the kids
- Organise neighbourhood watch meeting

2 – Home activities
- Wash the car
- Spend time looking at investment opportunities
- Tidy up garden
- Record the late-night news

3 – Work activities
- Clear old emails
- Prepare for client meeting
- Organise meeting schedule and prepare notes
- Bank cheques
- Finish reading the business book
- Follow up outstanding invoices
- Forecast budget for next quarter
- Write proposal for the next project

4 – Work people activities
- Touch base with marketing department
- Send thank-you letters
- Call back prospective clients

Now your to-do list has gone from an overwhelming 17-point list to a more manageable 4-category list that is within the 7 +/– 2 so you can keep track of it.

Cut to the Chase

One of our JOLT Challenge workout participants shared a story about how knowing the difference between chunking up and down got her a promotion.

As part of a team working on a major project that was past its deadline, they had to give a progress report to the CEO. The team leader started going into all the detail of what went wrong and what they were doing to rectify it. Sitting back from the presentation she sensed the CEO's frustration was in the team leader's delivery rather than the message itself. So she spoke up and added in two simple sentences summing up where they were at, and when they will get to where they wanted to be.

She believes the CEO's response, *"finally, someone who speaks my language"* and leaving the room satisfied played no small part in her getting a promotion eight weeks later.

Chunking down

"Confront the difficult when it is still easy.
Accomplish the great task by a series of small acts."

—TAO TE CHING

Chunking down means moving from the general to the specific, going from the bigger picture to the detail.

i) When you want to find out more information or be more convincing in getting a point across, then you'll need to chunk down to finer detail.

Imagine your boss has told you that she wants you to put more effort into the project. She communicates the why (vision), but doesn't tell you what you need to do differently. Chunking down breaks the whole into parts and helps with specifics.

You may ask questions like:

- What exactly is it you'd like me to do differently?
- What part of the project is most important?
- What resources can I use to speed things up?

ii) Chunking down helps you bring those distant and seemingly unachievable goals into your reality making them more real.

EXAMPLE: You want to save $5000 for a holiday but this appears to be impossible in your current financial reality. Chunking down results in you asking questions like:

- What specifically do I have to do to achieve this goal?
- What prevents me from achieving this goal?
- What are 5 things I can do to save money?

- What are 3 things I can do to make more money?
- How much does my dream holiday actually cost?

iii) Chunking down allows you to defeat procrastination and helps you design a plan for you to achieve goals.

Imagine you want to go to the gym early in the morning before work but can't get out of bed.

Rather than thinking *"I've got to go the gym"*, chunk down the whole act of going to the gym into small achievable steps.

When the alarm goes off at 6 am say to yourself, *"I've got to wake up, sit up and get out of bed."*

Once you're out, say to yourself, *"I've got to get into my gym gear."*

Chunk the whole process down enabling you to build momentum for your desired activity.

The chunked-down process may look like this:
- Wake up and sit up
- Get out of bed
- Get into gym gear
- Get into the car
- Go to the gym

By chunking the desire to go to the gym into simple steps, you've achieved your outcome. Remember the 7 +/– 2 rule – only chunk down to a maximum of five to nine steps.

Look at the current strategies you're using for communication, goals, managing emotions, daily living and consider how chunking up or down may positively influence them.

REMEMBER:

1. The conscious mind can only cope with about five to nine pieces of information at one time.

2. Chunking up means moving from small details to seeing the big picture.

3. Chunking down means moving from general details to small, specific details.

Week 4 Day 5:   Modelling

> "If I have seen further it is by standing on the
> shoulders of giants."
>
> —ISAAC NEWTON, PHYSICIST & MATHEMATICIAN

Modelling is a success strategy for helping us to evolve, and no, we're not talking about how you stroll down the catwalk. Modelling is a way of learning that has been around pretty much forever but has been consciously analysed as a process in more recent times. Modelling is about identifying people who are successful in the way you would like to be successful and studying and practising the way they do it. So yes, basically it's a fancy way of saying 'copying'.

Natural modelling expert
The good news is, you're already an expert at this strategy as you've been using it for years. You learnt to walk by watching others and then doing it. You learnt to talk by copying the sounds you heard and then repeating them. You went to school and copied the smart kids' answers and probably got in a whole lot of trouble for that one. The classroom is where modelling probably died off for you only to be brought back when you got into the working world where this time you were told it's okay to copy successful people.

> **Cliff Says...**
> It's a little known fact that... in 1961 psychologist Albert Bandura conducted the Bobo Doll experiment. Children were exposed to adults modelling violent and non-violent behaviour to an inflatable toy doll. The results showed that children exposed to such behaviour were more likely to act agressively than those who weren't.

Many famous athletes, musicians, actors, artists, successful business and community leaders have studied others and their strategies in an effort to improve their own abilities in their area. Many people read biographies and autobiographies of successful people to see what they thought and what actions they took to make them successful. Actor Johnny Depp modelled his character Captain Jack Sparrow in *Pirates of the Caribbean* on rock star Keith Richards. Jason Alexander who played George Costanza in the TV show *Seinfeld* modelled his character on Woody Allen. Anthony Hopkins modelled his character Hannibal Lecter on a snake – "*have the lambsss ssstopped ssscreaming?*"

Modelling in business
You can see the modelling process in action in most industries today. Successful

companies have no qualms about basing their ideas on those of others.

EXAMPLE: Sony PlayStation copied Nintendo and made improvements in the console gaming industry. Microsoft modelled their Xbox product on both of these products.

Modelling is not a new concept, it's been around ever since there was someone or something to learn from. The Japanese, after World War II, managed to rebuild a flailing economy into a hugely robust economy. They did this by taking specific products manufactured elsewhere, deconstructing them and re-creating them with their own improvements. The Japanese applied the 'Kaizen' process – where there is 'continuous improvement' on productivity.

EXAMPLE: The Japanese car industry now dominates US companies like Ford, GM and Chrysler who have been losing market share to Japanese companies such as Toyota in the US market for three decades. Ironically, the 'Kaizen' process was implemented in Japan by the American management consultant W. Edwards Deming.

Modelling is more than just deconstructing products (reverse engineering) or observing actions; it involves a more holistic view that may include analysing behaviour, skills, thinking strategy, beliefs, values, attitude, relationships and the environment.

Modelling provides you with a foundation of experience and knowledge, but it is up to you what you do with that knowledge. The more successful people who use modelling understand the knowledge and then modify it to suit their own endeavours. You can never actually become that person as you always come with your own innate talent and life experiences.

Two forms of modelling
The two most common forms of modelling are:
  i.   Sensory Modelling   – This will involve analysing behaviour that can be seen or heard.
  ii.   Conceptual Modelling   – Analysing a person's thinking process through the language use.

EXAMPLE: If you were to model a golfer, the sensory modelling process is to analyse behaviour, posture, grip, swing, rhythm, etc. Whereas with conceptual modelling, you find out about their beliefs, strategies and mindset, such as how they focus on each swing, how they talk to themself after a bad shot, etc.

It is natural to see things you like in other people and then take on those habits, beliefs and actions to help you achieve your own goals.

> ### A Great Talent
> In the movie *The Talented Mr. Ripley,* Matt Damon's character Tom Ripley is an expert at modelling himself on other people. He murders Jude Law's wealthy Dickie Greenleaf character and starts to live his life as him. It's fair to suggest that this is taking the concept of modelling to the extreme. We don't recommend this.

Wherever you want success in **The Big 3** (Health, Wealth & Relationships) in your life, you can use Modelling.

You can model:
- health strategies
- leadership skills
- dietary habits
- sales skills
- loving relationships
- problem-solving thinking styles
- wealth-creation strategies
- parenting strategies

and more!

> *"There's no secret about success. Did you ever know a successful man who didn't tell you about it?"*
>
> —KIN HUBBARD, CARTOONIST

Modelling requires you to research the person, and the best place to start is to ask questions to identify the critical success factors that you need to emulate.

EXAMPLE: If you want to achieve financial success, pick someone you respect and would want to model yourself on and find the answers to the following questions:
- How do they allocate their time?
- What books and magazines do they read?
- What are their key values?
- What drives them?
- What is their definition of success?
- Who do they surround themselves with?

SHU HA RI

SHU HA RI is a Japanese term for the cycle of learning. It is the Eastern equivalent of "you have got to know the rules before you can break them" and it's applicable to all areas of life.

守破離

SHU = Follow the rules   **HA** = Break the rules   **RI** = Transcend the rules

SHU:
The first stage is you must follow the principles that create success. This is achieved through repetition of the experiences and success strategies.

HA:
The second stage is once you understand, have assimilated and can act out these principles then, and only then, can you can break them.

RI:
The third stage is for you to transcend the elements that make up success and to make them your own so they suit your character, situation, experiences and desired outcomes.

Your definition of success and fulfilment will differ from the next person's definition. Therefore there is no cookie-cutter model for success. However, there are principles for reaching your desired level of fulfilment.

Be aware not to compare yourself with the person you're modelling. Constantly comparing yourself to others is a journey with unhappiness via the envy or feeling inferior path, so use modelling as a way to learn. Modelling is a fun strategy to put into action that often results in illuminating insights into how people achieved their success plus insight into your own thoughts and beliefs.

REMEMBER:

1. Modelling is identifying and studying people who have succeeded in the area you want to achieve in and doing what they do to see how it works for you.

2. You're already an expert at this strategy as you've been doing it for years.

3. Modelling is a fun, insightful strategy that benefits you in the pursuit of your goals.

Week 4 summary map:

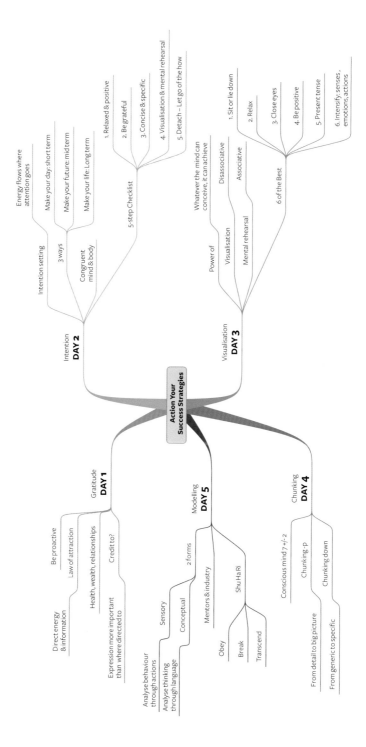

Action Your Success Strategies

Intention – DAY 2

- Intention setting
  - Energy flows where attention goes
  - 3 ways
    - Make your day: short term
    - Make your future: mid term
    - Make your life: Long term
- Congruent mind & body
- 5-step Checklist
  1. Relaxed & positive
  2. Be grateful
  3. Concise & specific
  4. Visualisation & mental rehearsal
  5. Detach – Let go of the how

Visualisation – DAY 3

- Power of
  - Whatever the mind can conceive, it can achieve
  - Visualisation
    - Disassociative
    - Associative
  - Mental rehearsal
- 6 of the Best
  1. Sit or lie down
  2. Relax
  3. Close eyes
  4. Be positive
  5. Present tense
  6. Intensify; senses, emotions, actions

Gratitude – DAY 1

- Direct energy & information
  - Be proactive
  - Law of attraction
- Health, wealth, relationships
- Expression more important than where directed to
  - Credit to?

Modelling – DAY 5

- Analyse behaviour through actions
- Analyse thinking through language
- 2 forms
  - Sensory
  - Conceptual
- Mentors & industry
- Shu Ha Ri
  - Obey
  - Break
  - Transcend

Chunking – DAY 4

- Conscious mind 7 +/- 2
- Chunking-p
- Chunking down
  - From detail to big picture
  - From generic to specific

Master Your Emotions

Purpose

To understand and know how to manage your emotions

Overview

Day 1: Emotions
Day 2: Emotional Barriers
Day 3: Happiness
Day 4: Optimism
Day 5: Desire

Benefits

This week's experience in the Challenge guides you to:

- know how to overcome your fears
- positively affect your biochemistry naturally and increase your happiness
- develop a more positive outlook
- tune in to what you truly desire in life
- help turn negative emotions and experiences into positive ones
- improve your emotional intelligence
- increase your sense of control over your emotions
- experience fresh perspectives on matters that are dragging you down.

Week 5 Day 1: Emotions

"Our feelings are our most genuine paths to knowledge."

—AUDRE LORDE, POET

Emotions vs Feelings

First we need to clarify that emotions and feelings are not quite the same thing despite people using the words interchangeably. Leading science journalist Stefan Klein in his book *The Science of Happiness* draws a distinction between the two, which is feelings are emotions that you're conscious of. Emotions are unconscious and an automatic response of the body to a certain situation.

Most people are unaware of the depth of their emotions on a day-to-day basis but they can be read from the reactions of the body. Emotions are hard-wired into your body and when you are conscious of these emotions they then become feelings. Feelings are more private and exist in the brain. Emotions predate human beings and while we are not the only creatures on the planet that experience emotions, because of our ability to think about emotions, feelings are something that are unique to us.

Emotions are energy in motion and they guide and inform you, provided of course you become aware of them. The challenge is being able to understand the message that your emotions bring. You may react to emotions in different ways – you may act out the emotion, you may suppress it, you may deny it or you may be one of the very few who actually listen to it and get the message.

Because you feel your feelings, that makes all of your emotions valid, whether you label them as being positive or negative. However, that doesn't make an emotion you're feeling "true", as you may be experiencing a variety of emotions.

Imagine you are reprimanded by your manager. You feel embarrassed by this treatment. You also feel angry because you think it's unreasonable. You feel guilt because you know there was a bit of accuracy. You are also disappointed in yourself for letting things go downhill.

So what do you really feel? Embarrassment? Anger? Guilt? Disappointment? Which emotion is "true"? They are all valid but the most intense one and the one that sticks with you longest is probably the one you felt at the end. Why? Research by Nobel Prize winning social psychologist Daniel Kahneman shows that the brain stores the memory of the feeling only at its most intense and in its final moments.

Imagine you're relaxing on the couch enjoying doing nothing for 20 minutes. Then the telephone rings interrupting you and you become annoyed. You've forgotten the 20 blissful minutes and now can only focus on the interrupted second.

Get the message!

While it's important to know which emotions you are feeling, it's even more important to stop criticising yourself for having emotions. Instead, unconditionally accept yourself as a human being who emotes. If you look for the message from your emotions you will understand that there are no "negative" emotions but they are simply a sign for you to take action.

EXAMPLE: If you feel guilt about something you've done, then your emotions are telling you that you have violated one of your own personal values. Rather than wallow in the guilt, accept the message and take action to align your behaviour with what's important to you so you avoid repeating that behaviour.

EXAMPLE: If you feel angry, then you're receiving a strong message that your standards haven't been met. Often you feel angry with yourself. Good. Get the message! What is your anger telling you? What do you have to do differently now? How do you get back into a harmonious state? Feelings aren't good or bad, but rather feedback to foster learning. When you feel something, therefore, ask yourself, "*What can I learn from this?*"

Your response to your emotions helps you get off the treadmill of life and start moving forward.

> *"All great discoveries are made by people whose feelings run ahead of their thinking."*
> —C. H. OAKHURST, UNKNOWN

Certain negative emotions are responsible for your survival and growth. So it's healthy to feel negative emotions, such as anger, grief, regret, displeasure. It's when these emotions turn into depression, shame or despair and stick around long term that they become unhelpful.

Heaven & Hell

A Zen monk was very still, meditating when he was approached by a great warrior. The warrior asked the monk to teach him the difference between heaven and hell. The monk looked the warrior up and down and said scornfully, *"I could never teach such a fool."*

This was a great insult to the warrior who drew his sword and said, *"I'll kill you right here on the spot."* To which the monk replied, *"Now that is hell."*

The great warrior realising that the monk had risked his life to teach him, fell to his knees and begged the monk to forgive him. To which the monk replied, *"Now that is heaven."*

Emotions come about through a three-way process that includes perceiving, moving and thinking. This gives rise to three ways of mastering your emotions.

Imagine you have a presentation to do tomorrow and you're feeling very anxious.

Your options for controlling this angst include:

i. **Biochemically** – you could alter the physiological state of your body by taking certain drugs to calm you down, or drinking chamomile tea instead of coffee

ii. **Physically** – you could do relaxation exercises eg: yoga, visualisation that stimulates your sensorimotor system (responsible for perceiving and moving)

iii. **Neurologically** – you could shift your focus by using reason and/or imagine calming thoughts.

JOLT Challenge focuses on the second and third methods of mastering your emotions (sorry, no drugs), but by doing these two methods you will be creating a biochemical response in your brain anyway. (Yay, natural drugs!)

> *"Your feelings not only keep you alive; they also aid you to survive happily."*
>
> —ALBERT ELLIS, PSYCHOLOGIST

There are many different types of emotions, far too many to list them all here. But all emotions share a basic duality – positive or negative, empowering or disempowering. Below is a list of your six primary (basic) emotions followed by some secondary (variation) ones.

PRIMARY	SECONDARY
Love	Affection, Caring, Compassion, Desire, Longing, Lust, Passion, Tenderness
Happiness	Cheerfulness, Contentment, Enjoyment, Excitement, Joy, Pride, Zeal
Anger	Annoyance, Disgust, Envy, Frustration, Fury, Hate, Irritation, Jealousy, Rage
Sadness	Disappointment, Dismay, Embarrassment, Guilt, Loneliness, Shame
Fear	Anxiety, Distress, Dread, Nervousness, Panic, Shock, Terror, Worry
Surprise	Amazement, Astonishment, Astounded, Nonplussed, Stupefied, Wonderment

There's Always Room

Watch the movie *Hotel Rwanda* with someone and take note of all the different emotions you feel as you watch the movie. Write them down as you experience them. Share the different emotions with the other person. Which emotions were the dominant ones? Discuss why.

Emotional addictions

In Neurons (Week 2 Day 3) you read how the brain creates emotional, thought and behavioural patterns, and through repetition, hard-wires these patterns into an automatic response.

EXAMPLE: You get frustrated and grumpy sitting in traffic most mornings on the way to work. You know what stress lies ahead of you when you hop into the car, yet you allow this grumpiness to become an automatic emotional pattern first thing in the morning.

In Brain & Body Chemicals (Week 2 Day 4) you read how your body has the ability to make its own chemicals.

EXAMPLE: Endorphins aka the 'runner's high' is the body's natural painkiller. Endorphin is made up of the two words 'endogenous morphine' meaning morphine produced within the body.

When these two elements combine, and they do on a daily basis, it can lead to an emotional addiction. Candace Pert in her ground-breaking book *Molecules of Emotion* explains how neurons (Week 2 Day 3), your nerve cells, have receptors on them scanning for chemicals. Emotions produce chemicals that enter these cells and change them accordingly. If you keep repeating that emotion then your cells not only expect it, they demand it.

Imagine you have a bad experience. It could be anything like losing your job, your relationship breaking up, losing money in a bad investment. You tell someone about it and they give you sympathy or even help you solve the problem. You now feel better. You now repeat that process by looking for the negative view on events so that other people can make you feel better by helping you. And voilà, a victim mentality is born.

This is not conscious of course. The victim will say that bad things always happen to them or that they're just unlucky. They don't know their cells are craving that emotion and creating that behaviour.

> **Cliff Says...**
> *It's a little known fact that...* many drug addicts have a pre-planned relapse, so they can go back to rehab and get more of that good encouragement that the "real world" doesn't provide.

Think of people you may know who are hooked on power, adrenaline junkies, people who drag other people down, people who stay in abusive relationships, and you have an idea of the extent that emotional addictions can play in your day-to-day life.

An addiction is something that you can't stop, whether it's an addiction to a substance or a process. Addictions provide you with the release of chemicals that make you feel good (Brain & Body Chemicals: Week 2 Day 4). You can be addicted to helping other people, addicted to your job that fulfils and satisfies you. Some addictions do less harm than others and in fact, being addicted to a pursuit may make you a world champion or help you have a successful career. But because addictions involve obsessive-compulsive striving, it can often end up in misery. The person who is addicted to their BlackBerry isn't dangerous to themselves or anyone else but some aspect of their life is being neglected as a result of this addiction, whether it's their work or family life. All addictions, even the seemingly harmless ones, require ecology (holistic) checks from time to time to ensure that they are not disrupting other areas of your life. The first step is to be aware of the addictions or habits that don't serve you and then break them.

Remember the good news:

The neurons that don't fire together, don't wire together

So the more you change set emotional, thought and behavioural patterns, the easier it gets to change the unwanted ones.

 What the Bleep
The fascinating and highly recommended movie *What The Bleep Do We Know?* makes quantum physics friendly and goes into detail about the science behind emotional addictions.

Emotional Intelligence

> *"Anyone can get angry, but to get angry at the right person, for the right reason, in the right way and to the right degree is difficult."*
>
> —ARISTOTLE, PHILOSOPHER

An important part of mastering your emotions and breaking any emotional addictions is to know which emotion you are experiencing. Often people simplify the way they are feeling to the primary emotions without digging a little deeper. Therefore you need to expand your emotional vocabulary so you can aptly recognise how you're feeling. Be curious about it. Next time you feel a strong emotion, think about which emotion it is.

Imagine you hear that a work colleague says some spiteful things about you behind your back.

You may get upset and/or angry. You can recognise the emotion that you're experiencing and acknowledge that. If you have trouble letting it go then it's healthy to find yourself thinking, *"Isn't that interesting that a smart person like me would continue to stay upset over a colleague speaking about me that way."*

Now you're thinking about the feeling rather than criticising yourself for not letting it go. Often it's not the situation that keeps upsetting you but rather, what you keep telling yourself about it. Your failure to let go, to refute their opinion in your own mind, to take a positive viewpoint or reframe the situation keeps you feeling those unhealthy emotions.

Another approach is to ask yourself these three questions:

1. Could you let it go?
2. Would you let it go?
3. When will you let it go?

This doesn't mean not to be concerned what others say about you. You should care about your behaviour and its impact on others, as it teaches you many things about yourself and gives you opportunities for personal fulfilment. However, you don't need to feel overly concerned about what others say and you certainly don't have to accept anyone's negative opinion of you.

A word of warning here: only spend time mastering *your* emotions. Please do not waste your time and effort trying to change or control other people's emotions and behaviour. That's a pathway to pain and frustration for it's just not going to happen. They are the only ones who can do that. You can only take responsibility for *your* emotions and behaviour.

> *"As long as you still live, you are the master of your emotional fate, the captain of your soul. Poor conditions may block and defeat your ends. Sometimes they can even kill you. But they cannot fully defeat you. Only you can defeat yourself."*
>
> —ALBERT ELLIS, PSYCHOLOGIST

REMEMBER:

1. Your emotions provide you with guidance and give meaning to your life.

2. You can control your emotions by what you do and think.

3. Understanding your emotions leads to a happier life.

Week 5 Day 2:
Emotional Barriers

> *"There can be no transforming of darkness into light and of apathy into movement without emotion."*
>
> —CARL JUNG, PSYCHIATRIST

Humanist psychologists agree you create your life in response to a basic inner desire to grow and fulfil yourself. So what stops you from achieving this?

As we highlighted in Overcoming Internal Barriers (Week 1 Day 3), emotional barriers create the big obstacles stopping you from achieving your desired level of success.

As you've previously read, all emotions act as a guide. It's when you don't get the message they bring, that those negative emotions become a barrier.

Anger

> *"Anger is an acid that can do more harm to the vessel in which it is stored than to anything on which it is poured."*
>
> —MARK TWAIN, AUTHOR

We're not saying anger is bad, in fact in some scenarios it's a life saver. But when you have regular outbursts or when you take it to the extreme, it can ruin relationships and stop you from moving forward in life. Anger can range from a slight irritation to full-blown rage, and is often a default emotion when people don't get their way or feel frustrated. The challenge is to be aware of the emotional addiction to anger and look deeper for the reason why you're angry. That's when you develop your emotional intelligence. If you think anger may be a serious problem that stops you achieving fulfilment then we recommend getting professional help.

> ### Two Dragons
> A disciple was wondering how conflict became such a destructive force, and asked his master to teach him to avoid falling victim to its power.
>
> The old master looked at his disciple and said, *"It is like two dragons engaged in combat; one is full of anger, fear and hatred, while the other is full of love, forgiveness and peace."*
>
> *"Who will win?"* asked the disciple.
>
> The old master replied, *"Only the one I feed."*

Getting Sacked!
Watch the movie *Any Given Sunday* from the perspective of dealing with anger. Can you identify in any way with any of the decisions different characters make?

Fear

The main emotion that inhibits your thinking and action is fear. Fear may create barriers that are temporary states, possibly caused by problems with your boss, or co-workers, financial strains or difficulties with your family relationships. Other emotional barriers can be long-term states of insecurity and anxiety which arise from fear.

There are of course very real and rational fears. If you're about to do your first parachute jump, then you better have some concern for your safety and listen to the instructions. Even riding a bicycle in the inner city, you better have a healthy dose of caution as cars go zipping by. If you don't, then your time on this planet will be short-lived. But this is not the needless or exaggerated fear that immobilises you. This is the healthy and necessary fear that aids your survival.

Cliff Says...
It's a little known fact that... scientists say newborn infants have only two fears – the fear of falling and the fear of loud noises, and even these are learnt in the womb and the first few days of life.

Dealing with fear

If fears are learnt behaviours then this means your natural state is fearless. Karen Horney, the famed psychoanalyst, said there are three ways of dealing with fear:

1. **Move away from fear**
   Denying fear just represses it, meaning it never goes away
2. **Fight fear**
   This deals with the symptoms, but not the cause of fear
3. **Move towards fear**
   You come to understand and overcome the fear

Number three is the most effective way of dealing with fear. You need to be aware of which fears are creating barriers for you. And rather than fight these fears or hope they go away, come to understand them. Observe them, see what you can learn from them, note how they make you feel and watch them dissipate as you acknowledge them and connect to your natural state.

Fear is possibly the single reason why people do not reach their potential. The fear that stops you from achieving your success is usually one of the following:

   i.   **Fear of the unknown**
  ii.   **Fear of failure/rejection**
 iii.   **Fear of judgement/criticism**

Fear of the unknown

> *"Don't be afraid to go out on a limb. That's where the fruit is."*
>
> —H. JACKSON BROWNE, AUTHOR

Fear of not knowing how things are going to turn out is a major emotional barrier. Almost all fears come under this banner as fear rises when you focus on what could happen. Taking action when you don't know how it will end up is deemed a major risk. It means that you have to be vulnerable and open to failure. The opposite of fear is boredom, and boredom is hell on earth; to be free of risk is to be a slave to boredom.

> *"Do the thing you fear, and the death of fear is certain."*
>
> —RALPH WALDO EMERSON, AUTHOR & PHILOSOPHER

Now it's easy to say, take on this attitude, but to incorporate it into your life takes practice. You've probably spent at least twelve years going through an education system that tends to emphasise the idea that there is only one right answer and one way of doing things. This right answer receives reward, wrong answers receive punishment. Your brain is trained to look for the "right" way of doing things.

However, like all good things, it starts with having the right mindset. You must learn to embrace the unknown. To gleefully step off the cliff and then worry about finding your parachute. Now obviously this is a metaphor and is contextual.

EXAMPLE: If you're about to enter into a new business partnership then it pays to be cautious, and to make sure you do due diligence to minimise any potential risk factors. If you're someone who doesn't show any caution, be sure to contact us as we have some time-share real estate in Queensland we'd like to sell you.

Joking aside, too often people err on the cautious side and miss out on all the beautiful fruits of life.

> *"I've lived through many terrible things in my life, some of which have actually happened."*
>
> —MARK TWAIN, AUTHOR

The Caged Bird

There was a bird that sat in a cage. It had done so for quite some time. It would sit in its cage and look through the bars and out the window to the world outside. It could see other birds flying free in the open air. The bird often wondered how it would feel to stretch its wings, to feel the rush of air as it soared up into the clear sky and to circle and swoop to its heart's content. The bird would get quite excited by this notion and would shiver as the thrill of this possibility surged through its body.

One morning, the owner of the caged bird accidentally left the door of the cage open. The bird noticed that the window was also open just enough for it to squeeze through. The bird looked at all the other birds outside flying, soaring and sweeping. It felt a tremor of excitement and began to think about how good it would be to be flying free in the open air. It still hadn't moved when the owner returned and closed the door of the cage.

You no doubt have personal stories and examples of people you know who have embraced the unknown and come out on top. Ending a relationship without having another one to enter, quitting a job without another one lined up, going on a holiday to a place without an itinerary are all examples of embracing the unknown with a high impact on your life.

Of course there are low-impact levels of embracing the unknown. Going to a new restaurant, reading a magazine you've never read before, or striking up a conversation with the person at the checkout counter. Remember:

As is the microcosm, so is the macrocosm

Start bringing in low-impact levels of embracing the unknown into your life on a regular basis. See where the new experiences and insights take you and enjoy the ride. We'll be exploring this in greater detail in Pattern Disruption (Week 8 Day 4).

Fear of failure/rejection

> *"Failure is the vehicle that drives you to success."*
> —WADE JACKSON, ACTOR & AUTHOR

You must make mistakes (think of them as mis-takes) in order to learn. It is this learning that will take you to your success in life. Your most painful times actually carry the biggest learnings for you. The fear of rejection is linked to the fear of failure because you feel you may not be accepted as a worthy person. An important thing to remember is that failure has nothing to do with your value as a person.

A catchy phrase to tell yourself when you're looking for that silver lining is:

Imagine you give a poor presentation at work. This is only failure if you take nothing from what the experience has given you. It may be telling you that you need to spend more time preparing your presentation, that you need to get coaching or that there's a particular area you have to focus on to improve.

> *"One of the reasons people stop learning is that they become less and less willing to risk failure."*
> —JOHN GARDNER, AUTHOR

This doesn't mean that you have to see everything through rose-coloured glasses or that you shouldn't feel negative emotions. That's all part of being human, but failure is a judgement call and only exists if you believe it exists. And you can change your beliefs. What's the value in thinking of yourself as a failure? There's none. Instead, look for the feedback the experience is giving you. The key question is, *"What do I want to do differently?"*

Don't identity yourself with failure!

> *"Failure is an event, not a person."*
> —ZIG ZIGLAR, SALES COACH & AUTHOR

Imagine your partner leaves you for another. Are you a failure? No. Look for what that's telling you. Yes we know, the feedback may be incredibly painful, but opening yourself up to learning is better than lying around the house drinking a bottle of tequila a day swearing you'll never enter another relationship for as long as you live.

Success is a very poor teacher. Once you succeed, you may feel a pressure to only reach this level and therefore everything else below ultimate success is deemed a failure. Success is the goal, but working with failure is your life.

One great way to overcome fear of failure is by reframing what you are looking to do as an experiment. When you experiment you know things may not turn out 100% and if they don't, you look at what went wrong. Your second attempt then incorporates the learnings from the first.

Life is one big experiment!

Fear of judgement/criticism

The fear of being criticised by your seniors, peers or juniors is also a great immobiliser. No one wants to look foolish or inept so it's much better for our ego to play it safe. But at what cost? At the cost of doing something you truly desire to do? At the cost of following your passion and being who you want to be? These are fairly hefty prices to pay for not going against the grain and breaking social conformity.

> **Cliff Says...**
> *It's a little known fact that...* Steve Jobs and Steve Wozniak the founders of Apple Computers took their idea of a personal computer to Atari but were rejected. They then went to Hewlett-Packard and were told they weren't needed. So in the end they decided to do it themselves.

Everybody judges and judging definitely has its place in life. If you judge an alley as being too dangerous to walk down at night then it's a judgement that's probably saving your life, or at least your shoes. However, as discussed in the Emotional Brain (Week 2 Day 2), often you judge before you have all the information. As a general rule, it's better to delay judgement and just perceive, taking in more information to make a better-informed decision.

The fear of judgement was previously explored under cultural blocks in Overcoming External Barriers (Week 1 Day 4). The fear of being isolated from the community or loved ones, or the thought of not being approved of by others can restrict your behaviour.

Vulnerability is strength

Accept the fact that you're going to make mistakes and look foolish from time to time. Acknowledge that you don't know everything. If you do this you will gain respect and the hearts of people. Why? Because this is a fear we all share. As soon as you bring it out into the open you'll find that people relax and open up to you. As you shed this fear you will become freer in mind and body. You may think if people really knew you, they wouldn't like you, but it's a fact that:

Self-revelation breeds intimacy

The mind/body connection is in action here. As you take the action and follow your own path, your self-esteem increases. As your self-esteem increases you tend to be freer with your thoughts and action. It doesn't matter which one comes first as long as you get the ball rolling.

> *"Fear is only as deep as the mind allows."*
> —JAPANESE PROVERB

It's just my imagination...

The Temptations sang about their imagination running away with them, and that's where fear lives, in your imagination, in your mind. Fear is simply a state of mind and you currently have the ability to control your mind. By re-educating your mind, fear can be accepted as a fact of life rather than a barrier. If you knew you could handle anything that came your way you would have nothing to fear.

Letting it go

> *"We are not doomed to repeat our past unless we choose to do so."*
> —WILLIAM GLASSER, PSYCHOLOGIST

A big part of the success of Cognitive Behaviour Therapy (CBT) is the idea that revisiting painful events in your past can contribute little or nothing to what you need to do now. It's accepted that what happened in the past has a great deal to do with where you are today but going back to those events isn't going to help you now. What you need to do is accept those events that were painful, change the meaning of those events so it becomes a lesson for you, and look at what you can do now *in the present* in order to create a happier and enriching future for yourself.

While this rationalisation process works for many people, other therapies such as regressional hypnotherapy find it helpful to go back into the past to become conscious of the emotions and meanings stored at an unconscious level and then help rationalise and see a new meaning of past events.

> *"To be wronged is nothing unless you continue to remember it."*
> —KUNG FU TZU (CONFUCIUS), PHILOSOPHER

The Color Purple

Watch *The Color Purple* and see how the character played by Whoopi Goldberg overcomes her fear.

Secondary gain

Many people actually hold on to problems because they get some kind of benefit from doing so. This is called secondary gain. They may say they want the problem to go but their actions are incongruent with what they say as they don't want to lose those benefits. To identify any potential secondary gain with any issues facing you, ask yourself *"what do I get when I have this problem?"* and list both good and bad points. Being honest with yourself is crucial to develop your Self Intelligence.

> ### Don't Stand So Close To Me
> A JOLT Challenge workout participant shared how in her early twenties she used to surround herself with people of dubious character. She would regularly be stalked by different people and had a lot of drama in her life.
>
> Looking back she realised that she would put herself in those situations and welcome that drama into her life as it gave her attention. Although she'd protest at the time that life was hard for her, she loved the attention she got from it.
>
> Now, a little bit older and a little bit wiser, she gets attention from positive things in her life.

There are other barriers that may limit you such as your belief system, the choices you make and the quality of your inner voice. We delve into these areas in Explore your Behaviour: Week 6.

REMEMBER:

1. To make mistakes is human – it is the most effective way to learn.

2. Adopt the attitude: There is no failure, only feedback. So keep experimenting.

3. Fear is purely a state of mind and you are in control of it.

Week 5 Day 3:   Happiness

*"Happiness is the meaning and the purpose of life,
the whole aim and end of human existence."*

—ARISTOTLE, PHILOSOPHER

The purpose of everything you want, wish, do, achieve, and have goals for, ultimately
is to make you feel one emotion – happiness. You may want a passionate relationship, a million dollars, a house by the sea or a fit firm body. Why? Because of the way
you think these things will make you feel, right? Because if you have these things then
you will feel and be happy, right?

Wrong! This is the great illusion. There are plenty of people who have all of life's
luxuries but have happiness successfully eluding them. Why? Because happiness
doesn't actually come from owning material possessions, having a great relationship, or successful children and being in the best shape of your life.

Identifying happiness

We're not saying these things aren't great to strive for and achieve, of course they are,
but they don't make you happy. What that striving does is actually keep economies
growing. It has nothing to do with your happiness but instead keeps society stable.
Society needs people to produce, procure and consume, otherwise it would be
bankrupt.

But don't make the mistake of identifying material wealth as a sign of happiness.
Why do people who appear to have it all commit suicide or get depressed? Why are
there people who have very little to show for themselves but are grateful, generous
and live full, happy lives? Because they understand that happiness comes from
within. This is very important so we'll repeat this a different way: happiness comes
from within you, biologically (physically) and psychologically (mentally).

> ### Hard Rock
> A quarryman was hard at work breaking rocks in the hot sun. As he broke
> away some rock he found a lamp. As he opened it, out came a genie who promised
> to grant him a wish. The quarryman said, *"Breaking rocks is not the life for me. I'd
> like to be rich. If I had money then I would be happy."* The genie granted him his
> wish and indeed he was happy.
>
> One day the quarryman was lazing around in his mansion up on the hill when
> he heard noise coming from the streets. He got up and saw the King's procession
> moving through the streets. He saw how people bowed down to the King. The
> quarryman got the lamp and summoned the genie. He told the genie, *"I'm not
> happy. If I had more power, then I would be happy."*
> So the genie granted him his wish and made him King.   *Cont'd over*

MASTER YOUR EMOTIONS

The quarryman felt the power surge through his veins and revelled in his might. Now he was happy. In his palace one day, he noticed the sun and realised how much more powerful the sun was than he. Although he had power of all people, the sun could give life to all things on the planet. The quarryman got the genie out of the lamp to tell him, *"I'm not happy. If I was the sun, then I would be happy."* And the genie made him the sun.

How happy he was to be able to give life to all things on the planet. Now he had the power he had always wanted. Until one day a black rain cloud covered the sun and began to rain. No matter how hard the sun tried, he could not break through the rain cloud. Wailing about his misfortune he summoned the genie, *"I'm not happy. Clouds are more powerful than I. If I were cloud then I would be happy."* The genie granted him his wish.

As cloud, he could block the sun when he wanted, he could give life through water from his rain, and he could travel where he pleased. He could transform anything. At last he was happy. However, one day cloud noticed that no matter what he did, rock was unmoving. He saw how rock stayed where it was, strong, unmovable, and unchangeable. Bitter disappointment welled up in him and he called out to the genie, *"I'm so unhappy. Rock has power much stronger than I. If I were rock, then I would be happy."* And so, the genie granted him his wish and made him rock.

How strong he felt as rock. Such power that no matter what sun, wind or cloud did, nothing could move him. He laughed and acknowledged that yes, now he was happy.

Until, one day a quarryman arrived.

> *"Happiness doesn't depend on any external conditions, it is governed by our mental attitude."*
>
> —DALE CARNEGIE, AUTHOR

Cliff Says...

It's a little known fact that... over 150 big surveys have been done in many countries since WWII to find out whether money increases happiness. The results are all the same, showing that although money brings satisfaction, the effect is minimal. When it comes to happiness, once people have risen above the destitute level, there is no difference between the rich and middle class.

Science says...

A sociological experiment with teachers in both rich and poor areas showed they both had the same levels of happiness. Further research showed that the teachers in the rich areas were happier at work and their happiness levels dropped off after work. The teachers in the poorer areas were happier when they left work, yet they considered themselves happy. It shows how poorly people assess their own lives and how they aren't always aware of the reasons for their happiness. Both groups were satisfied but only one group was happy at work.

> *"We act as though comfort and luxury are the chief requirements of life, when all we need to be happy is something to be enthusiastic about."*
>
> —CHARLES KINGSLEY, CLERGYMAN & NOVELIST

Happiness is a state of mind. It's simply an emotional state that feels good. You can make yourself feel good at any time if you choose. Remember:

Energy flows, where attention goes

If something you deem to be bad happens to you and you focus on the pain and not the lesson it contains, then you will remain depressed and down. However, if you look for the learning, the message in the pain, then you will start to feel better and get back on your success track quicker. That doesn't mean living in denial of any pain that may come into your life; it's about shifting your focus, choosing to put your attention on what will help you grow.

In some situations you may need time but ultimately, by creating a positive meaning and a positive outcome for everything that happens in your life, you can't help but feel happy. We dare you to try it!

Be unreasonably happy

A word about Eastern vs Western philosophy here. Sure, the East says give up total attachment to all material things and you will be happy. Now, if your ambition is to be a Buddhist monk then, yep, that's good advice. However, if you want to partake fully in life (and we're not bad-mouthing Buddhist monks here) then you'll be wanting to have nice things.

And why not? You deserve it. You're human and you're alive, that means you qualify for all the good things that life has to offer. We're not saying don't go for the jet ski and Parisian holiday – just realise that those things alone don't make you happy. YOU make you happy. Your mindset. The story you tell yourself every day. The meaning you give your life. YOU!

> *"Most folks are about as happy as they make up their minds to be."*
>
> —ABRAHAM LINCOLN, POLITICIAN

So although you may feel different things create happiness in your life, it really comes down to you giving yourself the permission to be happy, to be unreasonably happy.

Happiness variations

Here are four different variations of happiness you may experience:

1. **Pleasure** – positive physical sensations
   Eg: Feeling happy eating a good meal

2. **Excitement** – positive arousal
   Eg: Feeling happy about your new work project

3. **Relief** – end of pain
   Eg: Feeling happy when you've finished a tough physical workout

4. **Ego** – positive affirmation
   Eg: Feeling good when complimented or when you achieve something

These different types offer you different depths of happiness and they are not mutually exclusive. You may feel a combination of them at one time.

EXAMPLE: If you're hungry and eat something you may feel relief and pleasure happiness.

Imagine if your boss tells you not only is your job secure in the restructure, but you'll also be getting a promotion, then you may feel a combination of all four types of happiness. Of course, if you actually wanted to leave your work, then you will create a different meaning of this event and probably feel upset and disappointed at this news.

If you get most of your happiness from relief (and many people do), then you need to shift your focus onto the other three types and look for what you could enjoy, what you're excited about and what you enjoy doing well. When people tell you to follow your bliss and live your passion, what they're really saying is do what excites you!

The same mechanisms are at work in your brain no matter what gives you the sense of enjoyment. It may be chemical energy coming in the form of the smell of beautiful flowers or thermal and physical energy coming from a deep tissue massage. Ultimately, when the stimuli reach the brain, the happiness is the same.

> *"Remember that happiness is a way of travel, not a destination."*
>
> —ROY M. GOODMAN, POLITICIAN

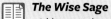

The Wise Sage

A king sought out the wisest sage in the land to come up with the secret of happiness. The sage invited the king to return in five days. Five days later the king visited the sage, who gave the king a rolled-up parchment. The king unrolled the parchment to reveal simply:

Parent dies

Child dies

The king flew into a rage. *"What is this?"* he demanded. *"How is this happiness?"*
The sage looked calmly at the king and asked him, *"Would you like it to be the other way round?"*

What do we want? HAPPINESS! When do we want it? NOW!

Want to be consistently (-ish) happy NOW? Not when you're making one million dollars a day, or when you have the six-pack or when the boat is parked behind the Maserati but NOW!

Step 1: Make your mind up to be happy regardless of where and when you are on your life path.

Step 2: Consistently think and do things that reinforce that belief.

Step 3: Enjoy the feelings and rewards that naturally result from those thoughts and actions.

It sounds simple, but usually the most profound things are.

And remember, you don't have to be happy all the time. There are times when you'll be upset, angry, frustrated, disappointed, confused and experiencing other negative emotions. It's part of life to take the downs with the ups. You're not a failure if you have bad days. It's only a problem if you stay down. Remember: get the message your emotions are telling you and move on.

> *"Now and then it's good to pause in our pursuit of happiness and just be happy."*
>
> —GUILLAUME APOLLINAIRE, POET

Other-centred happiness

We think it's prudent to remind you of the difference between being selfish and being positively self-centred. We don't want you to get the wrong idea and think that we're saying as long as you look after yourself you'll be happy. Most people (if not all) have peak experiences and a sense of fulfilment when they are helping others. We strongly recommend that you find your ways of being other-centred.

> **Gesundheit!**
> Watch the movie *Patch Adams* to see the benefits of other-centred happiness. What can you do to bring more fun and laughter into your life?

The happy trio
The latest in neuroscience research, according to science journalist Stefan Klein, shows that if you want to increase your level of happiness, you must have the following in your life. They are in order of impact on your happiness.

1. Good relationships with other people
The most important thing is for you to have family, friendship and love in your life. It doesn't have to be an intimate relationship but you are a social creature whose well-being can be determined by your relationships with others.

2. Exercise
Due to the mind/body connection, activity is a surefire way of getting a natural high, whether it's going for a walk, having sex or doing the gardening.

3. Variety
The same old same old can get you in the dumps. Variety stimulates the mind and body in a positive way.

Happiness killer
Believing there isn't any silver lining doesn't help. You may believe that if you think the worst and things aren't so bad then you'll be happy. Unfortunately it's not that simple. Pessimism is not a good motivator. Why would you bother doing something if it's not going to be very good?

REMEDY: Manage your perspective. Focus on what you have rather than what you don't have.

> **A Guy Walked into a Bar...**
> One of our workout participants was a stand-up comedian. Sometimes he'd take the stage to a small audience and couldn't help noticing the empty seats. When he trained himself to shift his focus from the empty seats to the full ones his performance greatly improved resulting in an increase of his happiness.

> **Cliff Says...**
> *It's a little known fact that...* people who win bronze medals at the Olympics are happier than those who win silver. Those who come third are happy to have placed whereas those who come second focus on what they've missed rather than what they've gained.

Remember, your level of happiness is a direct reflection of the level of your thoughts and behaviour. Only you can manage these, therefore only you are responsible for your happiness.

And if none of the above made any sense whatsoever or you thought it was New-Age hippy rantings, then just ponder on the following proverb:

> *"Be happy while you're living, for you're a long time dead."*
>
> —SCOTTISH PROVERB

REMEMBER:

1. Happiness is a mindset that YOU are ultimately responsible for.

2. There are different ways and depths of experiencing happiness so make sure you have a combination of these in your daily routine.

3. Having good relationships, exercise and variety are the three main ways of being happy.

Week 5 Day 4:   Optimism

> *"The notion of potential, without the notion of optimism, has very little meaning."*
>
> —MARTIN SELIGMAN, PSYCHOLOGIST

The jury is back in and the verdict is... the glass is half full.

Well, it should be if you want to achieve more at work and live a longer healthier life. Research shows that optimism is good for increasing motivation, it's more fun and promotes a better way of life than for the pessimist.

Optimism is when you have a positive viewpoint of the world. It is reflected in your thinking. When things don't go your way, you have very different thoughts compared with the pessimist. Psychologist Martin Seligman, one of the leading researchers in positive psychology, distinguishes optimists from pessimists in terms of how they define problems and setbacks:

OPTIMIST	PESSIMIST
Temporary	Permanent
Circumstantial	Personal
Isolated	Pervasive

i) Temporary vs Permanent

An optimist thinks that any setback or frustrations are temporary and not final, whereas a pessimist thinks the setback is permanent and therefore nothing they do really matters.

Optimists use words like "sometimes" and "recently" to describe a recent run of bad luck.

EXAMPLE: *"Recently things haven't gone my way with closing the sale."*

Whereas pessimists have a tendency to over-generalise with the words "always" and "never" when things don't go their way.

EXAMPLE: *"This always happens to me"* and *"I never get the computer to do what I want"*.

When a string of good luck occurs, it's the total opposite. The optimist thinks *"good things usually happen to me"* while the pessimist thinks good things are a rarity.

ii) Circumstantial vs Personal
When faced with challenges a pessimist will blame themself, while an optimist thinks that defeat is not their fault and can attribute it to circumstances, other people, or just plain bad luck.

Obviously, this could be interpreted as ditching responsibility for your own actions, which is not what we're recommending here. In fact, if you want to change your thoughts and behaviour into actions that lead you to your idea of success and fulfilment, then you will need to be responsible for what you do. What is being highlighted here is that pessimists will blame themselves for things outside of their control.

EXAMPLE: *"It always rains on my day off."*

An optimist doesn't necessarily consider themself faultless, but they are able to see challenges as future opportunities.

iii) Isolated vs Pervasive
An optimist limits a negative experience to that one experience, while a pessimist believes that the negativity spreads to all areas of their life.

EXAMPLE: Failure to reach a project deadline for the pessimist means that they think they are a failure in everything they do. This results in them losing focus in their relatioship at home, failing to see any humour in anything and often becoming depressed. The optimist can categorise the failure and say it was only for that project and not in everything they do.

The important thing to note here is that both the optimistic and pessimistic beliefs are just that – beliefs. And beliefs can be changed as you'll see next week. We're not saying that it's easy but it is simple. What you have to do is change the quality of your thoughts.

Next time when things go wrong (because they will, that's life) or when things go right for you (because they will, that's also life), notice your reaction in regards to how you interpret that event.

Ask yourself is this likely to carry on this way (permanent)? Are you to blame/credit for this (personal)? Is this reflective of your whole life or just a part of it (pervasiveness)?

Happily Seeking
Watch the movie *The Pursuit of Happyness* from the viewpoint of optimism and continuing in the face of disaster. How would you respond if you were in the main character's shoes?

Two Seeds

Two seeds were planted by a farmer in a field. As they lay there in the dirt the first seed wondered what existed around her. As time passed she became more and more intrigued as to what was happening both above her and below her. She said to the second seed, *"Let's go find out what's around us."*

However, the second seed didn't want to know. He said, *"It could be dangerous up there. And we don't know what's below us either. It may be scary."* The first seed wasn't to be put off though. She thrust her roots down and began to push up through the earth. As she burst through the earth she enjoyed the warmth of the sun and felt herself growing. Her roots were now giving her nourishment and energy. She was revelling in her new environment and continued to grow and become strong while the second seed stayed where he was, playing it safe. Until a bird came along and ate him up.

> *"No pessimist ever discovered the secrets of the stars, or sailed to an uncharted land, or opened a new heaven to the human spirit."*
>
> —HELEN KELLER, AUTHOR & ACTIVIST

Cliff Says...

It's a little known fact that... in the last three decades of the 20th Century, there were 46,000 psychological papers published in journals on depression and only 400 on joy. Hmm, perhaps a shift of focus is required?

Using optimism

Being an optimist doesn't mean being one of those annoying people who are "feeling up" all the time even when their partner leaves them, their dog dies and they get fired all on the same day. As you know already, "negative" emotions are healthy. It's not about losing touch with reality. There are things that are going to happen to you in your life that suck, that cause pain and may bring you to your knees. Being an optimist is how you deal with these things. It's focused around the quality of your inner voice, which you'll explore in detail next week.

Yes, there are times when it pays to be an optimist and times when it pays to be more cautious. Obviously if you're so optimistic that you have departed from reality then it would be prudent to be more careful. Any time when risks are high you should not blindly hope for the best and throw good analysis out the window.

EXAMPLE: If you're about to invest all your savings into a new business venture then you should be wary and careful. You should ask yourself, how well do I know this person from Nigeria who wants my bank account number so they can deposit $30,000,000 into it?

EXAMPLE: If you have a family member, friend or colleague who is upset, to start off by happily telling them to cheer up will not get you into their top 10 empathisers' list. Be empathetic by actively listening, which builds allowing you to steer them in a more positive direction.

There are times when even self-doubt can be beneficial.

EXAMPLE: The person who is unsure of how well they'll do in an exam, will use their self-doubt as a motivator to increase their study.

Beware, most people use the phrase *"get real"*, *"you're being unrealistic"* or something similar to those people who dream big unreasonable dreams. It is said these put-downs are usually out of fear as discussed in Emotional Barriers (Week 5 day 2). These people don't want you to succeed for fear of feeling inferior. So they project their doubts and insecurities on you, in an effort to keep you on their level. Or maybe they're just pessimists.

"Our deepest fear is not that we are inadequate. Our deepest fear is that we are powerful beyond measure. It is our Light, not our Darkness, that frightens us."

—MARIANNE WILLIAMSON, AUTHOR & SPIRITUAL ACTIVIST

Thunderbirds Are Go!

In a corporate training session, we overheard a group of senior managers discussing different ways of communicating to their team about the new company values roll-out. One of them said he loved the Thunderbirds and was going to put together a presentation based around that. Another manager said *"You can't do that. It sounds stupid"* causing the first manager to shut down his enthusiasm.

Which would you rather watch – a presentation coming from someone who is passionate about what they're doing or a standard PowerPoint/chalk 'n' talk presentation? Fortunately a well-timed voice in the ear of the manager meant that the Thunderbirds won the day.

Realism is often just positive pessimism

Don't get sucked into the 'be realistic' mentality. Too often it's used by people who are happy to settle for less in life. Research proves that if you have a positive mental response to adversity then you will enjoy a higher quality of life.

Your psychological state affects all areas of your life, from achieving in your career to boosting your immune system. So use optimistic thinking if you want to achieve a goal, whether it's health, wealth, or career orientated, or if you want to inspire others and have them want to have you in their lives.

And if you still aren't convinced that you should check the quality of your thinking, then ponder this:

> *"For myself I am an optimist – it does not seem to be much use being anything else."*
>
> —WINSTON CHURCHILL, POLITICIAN

REMEMBER:

1. Optimists enjoy a better quality of life in all areas from health through to wealth.

2. An optimist doesn't ignore setbacks; they just don't take them personally by holding on to them and letting them infiltrate and ruin all areas of their life.

3. Optimists have a high-quality inner voice that helps them see the glass as half full.

Week 5 Day 5:   Desire

> *"Whatever the mind of man can conceive and believe, it can achieve."*
>
> —NAPOLEON HILL, AUTHOR

On a basic level a desire is a want and not all desires are equal. Some of your desires will provide you with a sense of fulfilment and others will result in you feeling frustrated and disappointed. The desires that are deep within you and essential to your being are the ones that, once attained, help you build a life of meaning.

Wanting vs Liking

Wanting and liking aren't the same thing. Ask anyone who has sat on a bar stool all night. The first cold beer may have been wonderful. But by the seventeenth drink, liking the beer isn't really part of the equation.

> *"Desire is the essence of a man."*
>
> —BENEDICT SPINOZA, PHILOSOPHER

Although desire and enjoyment are closely linked, you can't be happily enjoying something while in a state of desire. And when you are happily satisfied, there's no desire.

Dopamine (Brain & Body Chemicals: Week 2 Day 4) is the substance that drives you; it's the molecule of pleasure. The sad thing is, pleasure doesn't last. Think of any time when you've strived for a goal. You felt good that you'd achieved it but as soon as you'd done it, it's like great, now what?

Remember:

Pleasure comes more from the expectation of the reward, not the reward itself.

📖 ***Ironman Glory***

  One of our workout participants who trained for months for the Ironman Triathlon highlighted how it's the journey not the goal. In a competition based on time, the last thing you'd do is purposefully slow down. However, in the last stage of the run she realised that it was all about to be over. All the months of hard training was about to reach its final peak and come to an end. On the way down the final hill she slowed right down to delay the ending and make the moment last longer.

Think of the excitement you may have had as a child waiting for Christmas Day or your birthday. Once the presents are open, the pleasure of the actual toys itself is short-lived. Many a parent has experienced the frustration of the child opening up the expensive present only to be more interested in the box and wrapping it came in than the present itself.

I'll have the lot, thanks!

As a human being you are designed to want it all. This doesn't mean it'll bring you happiness even if you could have it all. This doesn't mean that desires are bad. Not at all. Next week you'll explore your values, so you know what's important to you in all major areas of your life. This will allow you to align your desires with your values.

> *"You don't have to have it all. You just have to have what's important."*
>
> —WADE JACKSON, ACTOR & AUTHOR

Unless you're a monk, you don't have to totally surrender your desires. This can be just as harmful as obsessing about them. What's wise to surrender is your attachment to the way you fulfil your desires. It's beneficial for you to eliminate your unrealistic and self-limiting desires, but not desire itself. Besides, wanting and trying to give up desire is of course, a desire in itself.

Desires will change as you grow. Where people sometimes fall into a trap is that they keep holding on to an old desire that they've actually outgrown and don't really want.

 Give It Up
A JOLT Challenge workout participant shared with us a goal they've had for as long as they could remember. As a child he had always wanted to be competent at gymnastics – to have the ability to tumble and flip and do long handstands. Even into his twenties, it remained a longing. When asked to think of personal goals, this one always emerged. When, on the Challenge, he was asked to map out what it would take to achieve this goal, he realised that it wasn't really worth the effort and no longer desired it as much as he thought he had. He could quite happily let this goal go and file it as a goal he had once had.

Another trap is that many people make the mistake of focusing their attention on what they don't want.

Imagine a child walking into a candy store and being asked what they want. The child replies, *"Well, I don't want licorice!"*

What does the child get? Nothing! Because the child has focused on what they don't want rather than what they do want. In Gratitude (Week 4 Day 1) you looked at how whatever you think, you attract into your life.

It's hard to hit the target in life if you don't even know what the target is

This mindset is the reality for many people. When asked what they want to create in life, they respond with what they don't want. They don't want to work long hours, they don't want to feel stressed, and they don't want to fight with their partners. If real desire is missing in your life then it will be very challenging to create anything of value for you because basic motivation and commitment are lacking.

Your heartfelt desires

These are the desires that you truly feel in your heart. They're made up of your deepest values and your highest aspirations. They're your deepest motivators that drive your behaviour and they are within you, not outside of you. You'll know something is your heartfelt desire when you don't require any external motivation to go and live it. We will be looking at this concept in more detail in Driving Need (Week 7 Day 3).

> *"Desire is the starting point of all achievement, not a hope, not a wish, but a keen pulsating desire which transcends everything."*
>
> —NAPOLEON HILL, AUTHOR

You will know you are living your heartfelt desires when you feel that you have found your place in the world, when you wake up and are excited to be alive and get on with living that day. It's a passion that burns within you and is something that you commit to. Not the fleeting passion that is the same flame as inspiration. That sort of passion is a good kick start but it can be here today, gone tomorrow. The passion we're talking about is just there, you don't have to manufacture it. When you're confronted with the reality of day-to-day life, moments of fleeting passion and inspiration can fade. When you take away all the extrinsic motivators like the motivational CDs or self-help books you may find your temporary passion has gone with it, leaving you with nothing but best intentions.

Long-lasting passion may be something you've always wanted to do and still want to do. On the other hand, it may be something that you've discovered recently and just seems so right for you.

> **Cliff Says...**
> *It's a little known fact that...* Picasso was already enrolled in adult art school by the age of thirteen and Mozart had written his first symphony by the age of twelve. On the other hand, poet U.A. Fanthorpe published her first collection at 50 years old and Mary Wesley became one of Britain's most successful novelists at the age of 70 when she published her first novel for adults.

The Master Diver

Watch the movie *Men of Honor* to see what passion can help you achieve when you decide to act upon your heartfelt desire.

> *"There is only one thing more powerful than all the armies of the world, that is an idea whose time has come."*
>
> —VICTOR HUGO, POET & PLAYWRIGHT

To Egypt and Beyond

One of our workout participants was a lawyer who was passionate about ancient history. She didn't know why she liked history so much (a good clue that it's a long-term passion), she just did. She didn't really enjoy her work as a very well-paid lawyer as it didn't fulfil her. Nonetheless, she had to pay the mortgage.

After the JOLT Challenge she found ways she could incorporate her passion for history into her life. She wasn't prepared to stop being a lawyer and jump into studying ancient history full time. Instead she cut her work down to four days a week and took on some part-time study.

The next family holiday was to Egypt and she went round to travel and guide companies and found one that was impressed by her knowledge and interested in her helping out with tours during their busiest part of the tourist season. So she now studies ancient history and for four weeks of the year she works in Egypt guiding day tours.

For some people that wouldn't be enough, for others too much. For her it was taking steps outside her comfort zone but not too far that she couldn't manage it. What kept her going was her desire. She understood that life is not a dress rehearsal and if she were to be true to herself she would have to take action. She didn't have the end result in her head when she cut down her work and started studying either. It was her son's suggestion to go to Egypt.

Being clear on your desires doesn't make them just magically appear. It's just simply an understanding about what is important to you. You still need to take action.

And you'll slip up and make mistakes. Human beings are inconsistent. Remember the –ish word (S.U.C.C.E.E.D.: Week 1 Day 2). Be *consistent-ish!*

Imagine you have been saving for a house and have worked consistently towards this goal. Then one day a friend tempts you into a trip to Fiji and you blow a big portion of your savings. Does this mean you are a weak-willed hypocrite who is always doomed for failure? No. You are a human being who can be inconsistent like everybody else.

This inconsistency can ruin your plans so you need to reconsider what your heartfelt desires are. A heartfelt desire remains unchanged by the circumstances you find yourself in.

> 🍺 **Cliff Says...**
> *It's a little known fact that...* when Winston Churchill was asked by the King of England to form a government and get a woefully under-prepared nation ready to battle the might of the advancing Nazi army, he felt a *"profound sense of relief"*. Churchill, in his own words, said, *"I felt as if I were walking with Destiny."* Now that's a man who was clear on his heartfelt desires.

A heartfelt desire is a long-term desire. We're not talking about desiring the latest mobile phone or dress here. We're talking about desires that transcend short-term gain and take time to create. All careers, businesses, skills, talent, relationships take time. Not so much time that you can never see the outcome – that's just wishful thinking. But true desires can be achieved in the not-too-distant future.

> 📖 **Breathe in the Enlightenment**
> A young Zen monk had accompanied his master to the river where they were sitting on the riverbank. The young monk told his master how he had never achieved enlightenment despite many hours of meditating. He asked his master, *"What must I do to reach enlightenment?"*
> His master grabbed his head and held it under the water of the river. He held it strongly and after failing to break free, the young monk gathered all his strength and broke the master's grip. Spluttering water and gasping for air he breathlessly asked, *"Why did you do that?"*
> To which the master replied, *"When your desire for enlightenment is as strong as your desire for that breath, then you will be ready."*

Base your desires on your values and aspirations. Once you have identified these then you will be on the right road to creating the life you truly desire.

REMEMBER:

1. Pleasure comes from the expectation of the reward, not the reward itself.

2. Focus on what you want, rather than what you don't want.

3. Heartfelt desires are usually long-term desires that can be achieved in the not-too-distant future (eg: three to ten years).

Week 5 summary map:

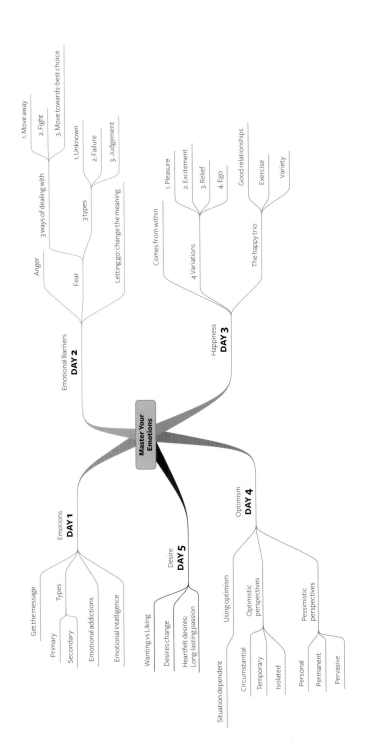

Master Your Emotions

Emotions
DAY 1
- Get the message
  - Primary
  - Types
  - Secondary
- Emotional addictions
- Emotional intelligence

Emotional Barriers
DAY 2
- Anger
  - 3 ways of dealing with
    1. Move away
    2. Fight
    3. Move towards: best choice
- Fear
  - 3 types
    1. Unknown
    2. Failure
    3. Judgement
- Letting go: change the meaning

Happiness
DAY 3
- Comes from within
- 4 Variations
  1. Pleasure
  2. Excitement
  3. Relief
  4. Ego
- The happy trio
  - Good relationships
  - Exercise
  - Variety

Optimism
DAY 4
- Situation dependent
- Using optimism
- Optimistic perspectives
  - Circumstantial
  - Temporary
  - Isolated
- Pessimistic perspectives
  - Personal
  - Permanent
  - Pervasive

Desire
DAY 5
- Wanting vs Liking
- Desires change
- Heartfelt desires: Long-lasting passion

Explore Your Behaviour

Purpose
To better understand the impact beliefs, values, and self-dialogue has on your day-to-day behaviour

Overview
Day 1: Beliefs
Day 2: Inner Voice
Day 3: Values
Day 4: Value Alignment
Day 5: Choice

Benefits
This week's experience in the Challenge guides you to:
- gain a deeper awareness and appreciation of yourself
- enhance your communication skills with yourself and others
- enjoy the freedom and power of making decisions based on your own values and beliefs
- understand the effects of conditioning
- reclaim your personal accountability
- shift yourself from a critical mental state to a positive one
- tap into your own intuition rather than thinking other people's thoughts
- take risks in a safe and nurturing environment
- acquire new perspectives on matters of importance to you
- have self-confidence readily available at all times
- express your values in different forms and gain further personal insight
- develop empathy and acceptance.

Week 6 Day 1:   Beliefs

"If you think you can do a thing or think you can't do a thing, you're right."

—HENRY FORD, BUSINESSMAN

Your beliefs are powerful things. They determine what values you hold and the decisions you make. Beliefs shape your experience and how you see the world. So what exactly are these almighty things we call beliefs? A belief is a cognition (mental process), focusing on how information is processed. It represents your level of confidence that something is true or right. This is reflected in statistics by probability theory.

For example, if the sun has risen every morning that you've been alive, then statistically speaking, it's probable that it will rise tomorrow morning.

Where do beliefs come from?

Your beliefs are the result of nature and nurture as they come from your genes as well as your own experiences. You also inherit beliefs that aren't even yours. They come from other people's experiences, from your parents, schools, church, media, peer groups and cultural traditions. Your beliefs are a result of conditioning and while they can help you succeed, they can also block you. When stumbling blocks occur in life it often comes down to the limiting beliefs you have about yourself.

> **Cliff Says...**
> *It's a little known fact that...* research tells us 50% of our belief system has been set by the age of two and 80% is set by the time you turn eight years old. And 85–90% of your beliefs are set by the time you're fifteen and will remain in place if unchallenged.

Challenging beliefs

Why is it often hard to change your limiting beliefs?

Because most beliefs operate at an unconscious level. The good news is most of your unconscious thoughts are able to be brought into your conscious mind purely by focusing your attention, exploring and thinking about your actions and behaviour. Another reason why it's challenging (but not impossible) to change beliefs that don't serve you is that most people think their beliefs are *true*. Beliefs often function as facts and truths, so when you believe something, you look for evidence that reinforces that belief rather than challenge it or accept contrary information.

> ### 📖 Because They Said So
> One of our workout participants said they were having particular trouble with one of the exercises. She said she couldn't do it because she had it from a good authority that she *"wasn't creative"*. When asked who told her that, she said it was the result of a personality profile exercise she did at work. Happy to destroy the negative influence of a misused personality profile, the trainer, with the help of the participant, pointed out many examples where indeed she was creative.

It was a universal belief that the world was flat, that the sun revolved around the earth and that people would never fly. The first Harry Potter manuscript was turned down by many publishing houses because they believed it was too long and slow for young readers.

Here are some examples of other beliefs in recent history:

"This 'telephone' has too many shortcomings to be seriously considered as a means of communication. The device is inherently of no value to us."

—WESTERN UNION INTERNAL MEMO, 1876

"Who the hell wants to hear actors talk?"

—H. M. WARNER, WARNER BROTHERS, 1927

"There is not the slightest indication that nuclear energy will ever be obtainable. It would mean that the atom would have to be shattered at will."

—ALBERT EINSTEIN, 1932

"We don't like their sound, and guitar music is on the way out."

—DECCA EXECUTIVE AFTER TURNING DOWN THE BEATLES, 1962

"With over 50 foreign cars already on sale here, the Japanese auto industry isn't likely to carve out a big slice of the US market."

—BUSINESS WEEK, 1968

"There is no reason anyone would want a computer in their home."

—KEN OLSON, PRESIDENT OF DIGITAL EQUIPMENT CORP., 1977

"640K ought to be enough for anybody."

—BILL GATES, 1981

> **Cliff Says...**
> *It's a little known fact that...* according to aerodynamic theory, the bumble-bee is unable to fly due to its size, weight and the shape of its body in relation to the total wing spread. Looks like no one told the bumblebee this.

Conditioning

By experimenting with dogs, Russian physiologist Ivan Pavlov showed how human behaviour becomes conditioned. Just as the dogs associated Pavlov's bell with food, you learn simply by associating one thing with another.

Remember:

Neurons that fire together, wire together

There are two types of conditioning – external and internal. External conditioning is when external events happen to you and they influence and shape your beliefs. Internal conditioning is what you do to yourself by keeping those conditioned patterns alive and well in your day-to-day life.

So what do you do if you've had some pretty tough experiences in life that resulted in some dreadful external conditioning? What if you grew up in an unloving and unsupportive household, or had a traumatic experience such as physical or sexual abuse, were exposed to violence, had failed relationships, or maybe went off the rails as a young or not so young person? Well, according to statistics, that would make for a fairly standard upbringing. The problem lies when you keep those external experiences alive with your current belief system.

Imagine you had an overbearing father who berated you, made you feel small and bullied you, and you took on the belief that all men are bullies. This would probably cause you problems in how you relate to men as an adult.

Imagine you have a bad experience at a particular task and remind yourself of it every time you come to that task. You're keeping it alive with a preconceived idea of your performance the next time you do it.

> *"Your present is your past of tomorrow."*
> —ALBERT ELLIS, PSYCHOLOGIST

Changing beliefs

The good news is, as with all your beliefs, you can change them. It's not always necessary to go back into the past and heal your inner child to do this. You can stay in the present, be aware of your limiting beliefs and work towards more beneficial beliefs. This concept of letting go of the past was covered in Emotional Barriers (Week 5 Day 2).

Easier said than done? Of course! You've had years of reinforcing those beliefs and keeping them alive daily. They are a part of you. However, by challenging them with constant thinking and reinforcement, along with new experiences, you can change your unwanted beliefs. And because your beliefs are interrelated, changing one belief can have an impact on others.

Just as the neurons that fire together wire together, old disused neural connections fall apart.

Shift happens!

Before you make any belief changes you need to check and make sure you want to change the belief. You're unlikely to change any beliefs you're happy with, so think about the consequences of your beliefs and if you find those consequences acceptable.

Examine your beliefs and the impact they have on your life. Identify your limiting beliefs and challenge them, because beliefs change when you alter your experiences accordingly.

There are three main ways of dealing with limiting beliefs:
1. **Autosuggestion**
2. **Positive experience**
3. **New decision**

1. Autosuggestion

This is all about the way you talk to yourself. You'll be going through this in a lot more detail tomorrow in Inner Voice (Week 6 Day 2). It's a lot more than just good old "positive thinking".

Émile Coué, a psychologist and pharmacist who pioneered autosuggestion (self-hypnosis) in the early 1900s said, when it comes to giving suggestions to yourself (and others) there are three laws that are always in action:

i. *Law of concentrated attention*
   Whatever you focus on tends to happen and be expressed mentally and physically. You already know this as energy flows where attention goes.
ii. *Law of dominant affect*
   States that the suggestion linked to the strongest emotion will dominate.
iii. *Law of reversed effort*
   Whatever you try *not* to do, will end up happening.

Imagine you're standing in a room and are asked to walk across a 3 m long plank that is 150 mm wide. You would probably do that with little concern. Now imagine that the plank is 15 storeys above the ground in between two buildings. The idea of falling would be at the forefront of your mind, and the law of concentrated attention means this will probably happen. The dominant emotion would be fear and would reinforce the law of concentrated attention. The law of reversed effort in action is that the more you try not to fall increases the likelihood of you falling.

Now imagine your child or a young loved one is at the end of the plank 15 storeys above the ground and the building they're in is on fire. All of a sudden the fear of falling isn't the dominant emotion. It's still there but the love for your child will overcome that fear and you'll have the motivation to save them.

You can also use this crossing-the-plank scenario as a way to decide your values (Week 6 Day 3). You probably wouldn't cross it for a million dollars when it's 15 storeys up but you would to save a loved one. What and who else would you cross it for?

To start changing any limiting beliefs, use your imagination to switch out your stuck thought patterns. It doesn't even matter whether the new belief is "true" or not. Start imagining new beliefs rather than defaulting to old patterned thinking that may not serve you.

How does this work?
As we looked at in Visualisation (Week 4 Day 3), the brain doesn't know the difference between a real experience and one that's been imagined. That's because they fire the same electrical patterns between the neurons in the brain.

Think of a task you believe you're not good at before you read on. Got one? Now imagine that you are very proficient at this task. What did you have to do to get good at this task? How do you move, speak, think, feel, and behave now that you're good at this task? The answers to these questions hold the key to becoming good at this task.

So using your imagination, along with practice and new experiences, you can disrupt the hold that limiting beliefs have on you.

> *"When the will and imagination are antagonistic or in conflict, it is the imagination that wins without exception. When the will and imagination are in agreement, one doesn't merely add to the other, but one is multiplied by the other."*
>
> —ÉMILE COUÉ, PSYCHOLOGIST & PHARMACIST

2. Positive experience
Positive experience is about building up enough evidence to show that your beliefs are now out of date. If you do something that contradicts your beliefs then you will alter your beliefs to match your behaviour. Psychologists call this cognitive dissonance.

> **Cliff Says...**
> *It's a little known fact that...* social psychologist Leon Festinger first proposed the cognitive dissonance theory in 1957, when he infiltrated and monitored a cult group that believed a great flood would wipe out non-believers and purify the earth. He wanted to know how they would reconcile their beliefs when the prophecy didn't occur as they said it would. They lessened the dissonance by creating a new prophecy – their actions had spared the world.

Imagine you believe that you aren't and never will be a good public speaker. However, if you suspend this belief long enough to do the appropriate training, your skill level will increase over time. People notice your improvement and slowly (because we're always the last ones to) so do you. You will now have to alter your belief.

So start building up positive experiences that gradually take you from a limiting belief to an empowering one. Look for people who will encourage you to take on this new belief.

3. New decision

This is a different take on the traditional ways of changing your limiting beliefs. The new decision is to decide it doesn't really matter if you have some limiting beliefs about yourself when it comes to achieving the life you desire.

You're still going to have desire and things you want to achieve. Know the steps you need to take to reach this goal and take them. What you think about yourself as you progress on this journey may change or even become totally irrelevant to you. Think of a continuum with self-hatred at one end and self-love at the other. You will fit somewhere on this continuum in the different areas of your life. Making this new decision accepts this and you can remain non-judgemental of yourself.

> **Cliff Says...**
> *It's a little known fact that...* there's a large body of research that shows people with low self-esteem still achieve well in the classroom, the workplace and in getting along with others.

Make the decision that you can live with these limiting beliefs and still reach your desired level of fulfilment.

As with everything in this Challenge, you need to find which way or combination of ways works best for you and then do it!

> **On Death Row**
> Watch the movie *Dead Man Walking* and see what impact different beliefs have on people in this film.

Shoulda, woulda, coulda

Absolute thinking is when you hold unrealistic ideals about yourself and live your life to incredibly rigorous standards. While we have nothing against having high standards, and in fact encourage you to raise your standards – just be careful not to raise them to a point where there can be no compromise or slip-ups without you feeling worthless as a result.

Absolute thinking leads to pain

Look for, when you say to yourself: I should have done that, I would have done this or I could have done that if I had more... (insert your reason here).

Are you holding yourself to rigid rules? When you jump to conclusions, blow things out of proportion, over-generalise and try and be perfect, chances are you have a case of what psychologist Albert Ellis calls *'musterbation'*.

You believe you *must* not fail, you *must* be the best, you *must* do things right, you *must* be the best parent, you *must* never be late, you *must*, you *must*, you *must*!

By holding yourself accountable to rigid rules, you're setting too big an expectation for you to meet. Of course, if realistically you could have performed better and you were resting on your laurels, then learn the lesson and do what's required next time. Remember in S.U.C.C.E.E.D. (Week 1 Day 2) we talked about how *must* can also be a positive motivator.

Lower your expectations and raise your standards

This may sound like a contradiction but let's put it into context. Expectations deal with other people, whereas standards are yours and yours alone.

Imagine there's a certain task at work that you do very well and you're proud of the job you do. One day you have to delegate this task to someone else, and they do the job differently, but not as good as the way you would have liked it done. You're upset with them and tell yourself you'll never get anyone to do it for you again.

The problem is your expectation for that person was too high. You expected them to reach your standard. No one has your exact life experience and view of the world so no one can do things the way you do. Don't confuse lowering your expectations with lowering your standards. You can still set them the high target to reach; you just need to clarify expectations in advance and put the way they do things into perspective.

Imagine you're new to a role and want to do a good job. However, because you don't know the ins and outs of the role things don't go smoothly. This is another opportunity to lower your expectations. Of course you're not going to get it right first time. This doesn't mean you don't try for the high performance standard though. Personal growth lies down the path of constant self-improvement.

Lower your expectations = saves yourself pain
Raising your standards = increases your potential

REMEMBER:

1. You're constantly reinforcing your beliefs by conditioning yourself with your thoughts.

2. Beliefs are feelings and can be changed with imagination, new experiences and a new decision.

3. You can maintain high standards without absolute thinking.

Week 6 Day 2:   Inner Voice

> *"If you had a friend who talked to you like you sometimes talk to yourself, would you continue to hang around with that person?"*
>
> —ROB BREMER, PGA COACH

You talk to yourself. Don't worry, you're not alone there, everybody does. We all have that inner voice. And if you're not sure if you do have an inner voice and you just asked yourself in your head, *"Do I talk to myself?"* then that's the voice we're talking about!

The question is – HOW do you talk to yourself? Is it an empowering voice or a critical one the majority of the time? Do you regularly tell yourself that you are talented, loveable and worthy of success? Do you criticise and talk yourself down? Do you replay the same old dialogue day in or day out? Are you even aware of the constant chatter that goes on in your head?

🎥 Danger's My Middle Name

In the comedy movie *Austin Powers*, Mike Myers' character comes out from being cryogenically frozen and has lost the ability to keep his inner voice internal.

"My God, Vanessa's got a fabulous body. I bet she shags like a minx. How do I let them know because of the unfreezing process, I have no inner monologue? I hope I didn't just say that all out loud just now."

Quite a scary predicament if you can't stop voicing your thoughts!

🍺 Cliff Says...

It's a little known fact that... research tells us on average 77% of everything we think comprises negative, counterproductive or banal banter, and doesn't serve us.

In his book *As a Man Thinketh*, James Allen likens the mind to a garden. It may be cultivated or allowed to run wild. Regardless of whether it's cultivated or neglected, it will bring results. You must regularly weed out unresourceful thoughts and sow empowering thoughts into your mind.

> *"All that a man achieves and all that he fails to achieve is the direct result of his own thoughts."*
>
> JAMES ALLEN, AUTHOR

163

When you make a mistake or fail at something, do you say to yourself *"Boy, do I suck!"* and beat yourself up? Or do you say, *"Boy, did I learn something there!"*? This positive reframing isn't about being detached from reality and seeing the world through rose-coloured lenses, but actually empowering yourself through positive self-talk.

A different kind of system

The good news is that you not only have a physiological immune system that protects you but also what Harvard psychology professor Daniel Gilbert calls your *psychological immune system*. The role of your psychological immune system is to protect you from unhappiness and you do this by talking to yourself.

Imagine you sit an exam and fail it. Your first action is to look to see who else failed in order to make yourself feel better. That's your psychological immune system in action. Your inner voice rationalises bad experiences that can't be changed. People who have been maimed, divorced, fired from their jobs or lose a winning lottery ticket will sincerely tell you it's the best thing that's ever happened to them.

> **Cliff Says...**
> *It's a little known fact that...* actor Christopher Reeves who was paralysed in 1995 talked positively of his experience, saying, *"I didn't appreciate others nearly as much as I do now."*

Your psychological immune system usually kicks in on major events that can't be changed. For example, becoming paralysed, going to jail, your partner leaving you, being fired or a sick parent dying. You can consciously activate it for the small things that don't go your way by reframing (Choice: Week 6 Day 5) and selecting better words when you talk to yourself.

Words

Words are incredibly powerful. When you choose them well you can create trust, close a deal, make someone fall in love with you, inspire people and achieve personal greatness. Of course words can also be used to inflict harm, undo good work and cause pain to others and yourself.

The words you choose affect the way that you feel and your attitude, on a daily basis.

EXAMPLE: Which of the following responses would you normally choose when someone asks how you're doing?

    a. I'm good
    b. Okay, I guess
    c. Can't complain
    d. Fine thanks
    e. Not bad
    f. Surviving

Now imagine how you'd feel if you chose one of the following responses to the same question.

- a. Excellent
- b. Fantastic
- c. I'm superb
- d. Rock 'n' roll baby
- e. Outstanding
- f. I am king of the world

You would feel different right? You may fear that you'd become one of those annoying, overly positive people who seem "up" all of the time or that you'd feel fake doing this. However, by using S.U.C.C.E.E.D. to gradually incorporate this behaviour, you *will* feel better. For example, if your usual response is *"good"*, take the step up to *"great"*. After this becomes a habit, step up to *"fantastic"*. You'll find others will treat you differently too. Emotions are contagious and no one likes being around a sad sack. If you are positive then you'll attract positive people around you. Like attracts like, birds of a feather, etc. etc.

> *"The greatest discovery of my generation is that a human being can alter his life by altering his mind."*
>
> —WILLIAM JAMES, PSYCHOLOGIST & PHILOSOPHER

You may remember as a child running home crying to your mother after being picked on and her telling you to say next time *"sticks and stones may break my bones but names will never hurt me"*.

While you can choose to be upset by others, what often goes unnoticed is the bullying that goes on internally. Be aware of the quality of the words of your inner voice and choose high-quality words.

Self-image

> *"What you think of yourself is much more important than what others think of you."*
>
> —SENECA THE YOUNGER, PHILOSOPHER & DRAMATIST

Pretty much everything you say and do reflects your sense of worth on some level. Your self-image is found in the words you use to describe yourself and you can have many different self-images.

Some examples:

I'm a great athlete	I'm a smoker	I'm a terrible cook
I'm a brilliant driver	I can't take rejection	I'm clever/stupid about this
I'm a good parent	I'm hard to love	I'm not attractive

The way you talk to yourself helps define your self-image. This in turn guides you throughout your journey in life. You say and do things according to all the definitions you have of yourself. The *"I've always been shy"* self-image will prevent someone from starting up a conversation and feeling comfortable within themselves around other people. On the other hand, a person with the *"I am outgoing"* self-image will make new friends and acquaintances easily and enjoy social situations.

Warning: I think I can, I think I can, I think I can

We are talking about your identity here, not just positive thinking. The term "positive thinking" has been abused over the years with people using it unrealistically and even dangerously. No amount of positive thinking is going to help you if you jump out of a plane without a parachute. It's very challenging for mantras, daily incantations and positive affirmations to help you if you hold on to a whole lot of negative beliefs around your self-image. Think of your self-image as the vehicle that helps get you to where you want to go. If you're sitting on the wrong bus then no amount of positive self-talk will get you to your desired destination. However, if you can detach from the negative beliefs or, better yet, question your negative beliefs and ask yourself what's the value in thinking this way, you'll find reframing (Choice: Week 6 Day 5) a valuable tool.

The person who thinks they're a failure and always will be, will create a self-fulfilling prophecy. There's no value in that, so take on an inner voice that serves you. Don't identify yourself with your failures. You are not your failures any more than you are your successes. You are more than your behaviour, your character, your fears and your dreams alone.

Remember: the whole is greater than the sum of its parts

> **Cliff Says...**
> *It's a little known fact that...* a study done in the US showed that 96% of four-year-olds had high self-esteem and a strong self-image. By the time they reached eighteen years old, less than 5% had a good self-image. Interestingly enough, parents on average, tell off or speak negatively to their children 90% of the time. Hmm, could there be a link?

Improving your inner voice

> *"If you don't like something, change it; if you can't change it, change the way you think about it."*
> —MARY ENGELBREIT, ARTIST

You may know of people who complain about the same old thing all the time (we're not saying it's you...). If they're not going to change the thing they don't like or change the way they think about it, then at the very least tell them to shut up about it!

You can use your inner voice to change habits, build up self-esteem, improve your attitude, motivate yourself and gain a new perspective on any unpleasant or undesired situation.

If your inner voice uses the right words in a very specific way, you can literally adopt the self-image and positive habits that you want. Train your inner voice to use words and action statements that command you to be the kind of person you need to be in order to do what you want to do.

Be your own coach if required, offering yourself words of encouragement and support. Take on a sergeant major inner voice if you know you need to get out of bed and go for that run rather than coaxing yourself into five more minutes of sleep. Use your inner voice to cultivate winning habits.

Maxwell Maltz was a cosmetic surgeon who noticed that many of his patients still remained unhappy even after successful treatment. This led him to create Psycho-Cybernetics, a philosophy that believed having a healthy and accurate self-image is the cornerstone of all positive change in life. If your self-image is inaccurate or unhealthy then you will continue to repeat past mistakes.

> *"Our self-image and our habits tend to go together. Change one, and you automatically change the other."*
>
> —MAXWELL MALTZ, COSMETIC SURGEON

You have to ensure if you do have a low self-image, that you're not using it as an excuse to keep treasured habits and receive any secondary gain (Emotional Barriers Week 5 Day 2).

Affirmations

> *"The happiness of your life depends upon the quality of your thoughts."*
>
> —MARCUS ANTONIUS, ANCIENT ROMAN POLITICIAN

An affirmation is an expression that confirms a belief. You can use affirmations to help strengthen the image of your desired state. Affirmations work by repetition. By positively reinforcing a suggestion over and over, you program your unconscious mind with this image that it then takes on to be true.

This is simply how clinical hypnotherapy works. You are in a relaxed state with the conscious mind (critical voice) kept at bay while the hypnotherapist provides you with suggestions that speak directly to your more suggestible and ever-working unconscious mind.

Émile Coué, the psychologist and pharmacist who named the three laws of suggestion (Beliefs: Week 6 Day 1), noticed that patients who used positive autosuggestion with their remedies were a lot more successful than those using just remedies alone.

His most famous affirmation that he got patients to recite was *"every day and in every way, I'm getting better and better"*. Notice that affirmations work best in the present tense. It's not *"I'm going to"* or *"I will be"* but *"I am"* and *"I have"*. This is because you're painting a picture in your unconscious mind of how you want to be and in time the unconscious mind will accept this self-declaration. How long this takes depends on the desired outcome and your committment to it.

> *"Autosuggestion is an instrument that we possess at birth, and in this moment, or rather in this force, resides a marvellous and incalculable power."*
> —ÉMILE COUÉ, PSYCHOLOGIST & PHARMACIST

P.P.P.S – guidelines for positive affirmations
1. **P**resent tense
    eg: *"I have an excellent memory"* not *"I want an excellent memory"*.
2. **P**ositively framed
    eg: *"I am a non-smoker"* not *"I don't smoke any more"*.
3. **P**ractical
    eg: *"I have healthy eating habits"* not *"I never eat chocolate"*.
4. **S**pecific
    eg: *"I am able to relax easily"* not *"I can relax at certain times"*.

You can see top-performance athletes talking to themselves using affirmations and autosuggestions all the time before an event. You can use it too. And not just when things are tough but also when things are going well. This way it's easier for your mind to accept the repeated expressions allowing for quicker results. Success depends on your commitment and the emotion you invest in repeating your affirmations.

Cliff Says...
It's a little known fact that... the most often used and well-known affirmation is the word *"Amen"*, which can be translated simply as *"so be it"* or *"and so it is"*, affirming the truth of whatever was written or said immediately prior.

Critical voice vs Play state
Your critical voice often wages war on your peace of mind and stops you from achieving the play state (The Growth Cycle: Week 1 Day 1). In life's major events, the psychological immune system kicks in to protect you, but in the day-to-day happenings of life, your critical voice can dominate your mind. This means your natural ability is stifled as your critical voice judges you and shuts down the learning opportunity. As you'll experience in Peak Performance (Week 7 Day 2), your best performance occurs in times of relaxed alertness. The first step is to practise becoming aware of your critical voice. Then work on switching it to a positive one.

> **Cliff Says...**
> *It's a little known fact that...* Shell Oil in Rotterdam, Holland, employed a team of psychologists to establish what made some people creative and others uncreative. The result? Simply that creative people thought they were creative and uncreative people believed they were uncreative. The irony is people who say they're uncreative are often very creative when it comes to coming up with reasons why they aren't creative.

The quality of your inner voice is something far too important not to pay attention to. It really plays a major part in whether you'll reach your desired level of success or not. So be smart, talk positively to yourself.

REMEMBER:

1. Words are powerful so choose carefully the words you use to talk to yourself.

2. How you see yourself guides how you act, think and feel every moment of your life.

3. Work towards silencing your critical voice so you can be in a positive state.

Week 6 Day 3: Values

> "We can tell our values by looking at our cheque book stubs."
>
> —GLORIA STEINEM, JOURNALIST & FEMINIST ICON

The word "value" originally comes from the French verb *valoir*, meaning "to be/have worth". Values are deeply held views of what you find worthy. They are abstract concepts that are important to you and express what you *value*. You have a hierarchy of values, ones that are more important to you than others. Your values are the result of your beliefs. They are the reason behind the decisions you make, thus they drive your behaviour.

EXAMPLE: If you strongly believe that people should treat others how they'd like to be treated themselves, then kindness and respect would be included in your higher values. Although beliefs and values are closely related, there is a slight difference in that the beliefs are the *why* you believe something whereas your values are the *what* you believe in.

This area is so important we've divided it up into two parts: values and value alignment. What values are, and then how you live life in harmony with them.

One life, different values

You only have one life but it is divided up according to how you spend your time. You probably talk about your work life and your family life, etc. but the reality is, it's one life. You can't be going through an acrimonious divorce and function fine at work. Likewise, you can't be all warm and fuzzy when you walk through the door at home after just having a big argument with your boss.

Nonetheless, you will have a different set of values in the different areas of your life; your personal life, your relationships, your career and even the company you work for has its own values too. Why is this? Because your values are relational. This means that you will behave in accordance with your values depending on the circumstances. What may be important to you on a personal level may be different to what's important to you in a relationship or in your career. Your values will shift accordingly.

Imagine a colleague bumps into you right before they're about to make a presentation to a very important client. You think that he isn't a very good presenter and is a bit under-prepared. He asks you how you think he'll go. If you value honesty over kindness you may tell him you think he stinks and will do a terrible job. But chances are, you will let your kindness and support values come to the fore in this situation and say he'll do fine. Afterwards you may suggest presentation coaching so that the issue doesn't go ignored.

Men who are asked by the wife or girlfriend *"Does my butt look big in this?"* know this

EXPLORE YOUR BEHAVIOUR

6

very well. They may be very honest people but the circumstances dictate to raise love (and perhaps peace and tranquillity) over honesty.

Everyone has values in these different areas but for most people they often sit at an unconscious level. Many of your values are set early on in childhood. Values will change as you grow and have new experiences but your core values are likely to stay with you throughout your life. Everything you do is determined by your beliefs and values.

Value types

There are three types of values – espoused, governing and desired.

    i. Espoused values are those people say they value.
    ii. Governing values are those that people actually have that govern their behaviour.
    iii. Desired values are those that people want to have.

A gap between espoused and governing values is best described as someone who doesn't "walk the talk". A gap between governing and desired values is an opportunity for you to grow.

People can believe that their actions are congruent with their values, but others may perceive discrepancies and, therefore, hypocrisy. Being clear on what a particular value means to you, helps you live them.

Values are ideals that you spend your whole life living. However, they are on a continuum that is affected by your circumstances. Your values are constant even if you are not acting on them constantly. You don't have to be 100% honest or kind all the time to have these values.

Although challenging, you can change your values. What you have to do is change the priority of them. You can change a value by changing the definition or your understanding of a particular value.

Your values affect you every moment of your life. Remember the RAS, the reticular activating system (Neurons: Week 2 Day 3) – it's the part of the brain responsible for paying attention and filtering the information that comes in through your sensory perceptions. The filters are influenced by your values and emotions, by what you consider to be important at the time. Your values influence where you put your attention. Therefore your values help determine how you make sense of the world you live in. Your brain is a self-organising system that seeks meaning. When you know what your governing values are, then you can be more effective in everything you do and experience a sense of peace that comes with congruence in your beliefs and actions.

What values aren't

In clarifying your values it's good to know what values aren't. Values aren't emotions, morals, attitudes, principles or needs.

- Emotions lead to your feelings.

- Morals are judgements based on what you feel is right or wrong.
- Attitudes are how you view, judge and react to specific people or events.
- Principles are agreed-upon truths.
- Needs are what you require for survival and growth.

Values are preferred ways of meeting your needs; they are preferred ways of acting on your beliefs and attitudes, in order to meet your needs.

Competence vs Moral values

There are two categories of values: competence (focusing on abilities) and moral (focusing on character). Milton Rokeach, social psychologist and leading authority on values, called these two categories the two great drives: the drive for greatness and the drive for goodness.

Material possessions are the result of a competence value (getting what you want reflects on your ability), while honesty would be a moral value (seeing yourself as truthful reflects on your character). Values are based on beliefs about what's true and false, good and bad, and they have affective and behavioural consequences.

You need to be aware that money isn't a value. Although right now you're probably saying to yourself, *"but I DO value money"*, you have to remember: values are abstract, you can't hold them in your hand. However, like the quote at the start of this section says, what you do with money, how it makes you feel and what it means to you are values.

EXAMPLE: Money may symbolise freedom, security, achievement or something else to you. Therefore money is just a way of expressing a value.

Imagine you've just won a million-dollar lottery prize. What would you do with your winnings? Invest some of it? Buy a new house? Give some to your family? Donate some or all of it to charity? Go on a holiday? Buy a new wardrobe?

Whatever you do first shows what you value. If you invest, then security and/or freedom is important to you. If your first thought is to give money to family or donate to charity, then belonging/community and/or generosity are most important to you. It doesn't mean that your other values aren't important, they may be very important to you, but they're not as important.

A good way to get at your core values is to ask, *"What would you die/kill for?"* Acts of heroism, often dormant, reveal these underlying values. Think back to the 15-storey high 'crossing the plank' story in Beliefs (Week 6 Day 1). What and who would you cross the plank for?

Anyone Got a Light?

Watch the movie *The Insider* from a values perspective. What values in particular stand out in the main characters?

Now let's look at how values greatly impact **The Big** $\boxed{3}$

i) Personal (Health)   ii) Career (Wealth)   iii) Relationships

i) Personal values

> *"Just because you feel good, doesn't make it right."*
> —SKUNK ANANSIE, MUSIC BAND

These are the values that guide you on a day-to-day basis. What you need to keep in mind is that values are not emotions. Just as Skunk Anansie sang in the song *Hedonism*, you may feel good doing something but that doesn't mean it's good for you. As was discussed in Emotions (Week 5 Day 1), when you feel guilty it is because you've violated one of your personal values. When you feel angry, someone has violated one of your values. As you'll discover next week, you also have needs and at times you will violate your own values in order to meet these needs.

> 🍺 **Cliff Says...**
> *It's a little known fact that...* employers who help their staff determine their personal values raise engagement levels that result in a 20% increase of discretionary effort and reduce the probability of leaving the company by 87%.

An important point to realise is, that if you're in a committed relationship, your significant other may not automatically rank as your number one value. There's nothing wrong with this. You will have certain beliefs and views that would still exist even if you weren't in this current relationship. The fact that you have other values ranking higher (which may be aligned to your partner's) may be the very reason they fell in love with you and enjoy being with you.

ii) Career values

> *"Nothing is really work unless you would rather be doing something else."*
> —J. M. BARRIE, NOVELIST & DRAMATIST

These are the values you hold when it comes to work. You spend almost half of your waking life at work each week so it's well worth you knowing what you value when it comes to your working career. If your current working situation is in conflict with your career values (or your personal values) then chances are you are unhappy in your role.

Imagine you're in a position where you can't make decisions that have any real impact. If contribution is high on your career values this will result in you feeling frustrated and powerless.

Imagine you're working in a position largely on your own and are unhappy about it. You discover that collaboration is one of your highest-ranking values so you know no matter what work you do, you need to be in a team.

When You Gotta Go, You Gotta Go

We were asked to present to a senior executive team of four about the importance of value alignment in organisations. They had called us in because of the low morale and high staff turnover. After our presentation on value alignment, two of the four senior executives did up their CVs that night, and one handed in their notice of resignation shortly after.

These two senior executives realised the cause of the disharmony was due to the values the managing director was living, and they realised that his values weren't about to align to the company's any time soon.

How effective is someone who isn't really into their work? Not very. It's better for the individual to move on and find something that best suits them, and likewise for the organisation to have someone better suited for that position. That way both parties win.

Conversely, clarifying values has resulted in participants realising how happy they are in their job. They didn't realise the extent of how their work actually fulfilled them. It made them appreciate what they had a whole lot more.

iii) Relationship values

"The greatest relationships are those in which the desire for each other greatly outweighs the need for each other."

—DALAI LAMA, SPIRITUAL TEACHER

There are certain values that will rise to the fore in your close and intimate relationships, which may not be as important to you on a personal or career level.

EXAMPLE: Communication may not be such a strong personal or career value, but it may be very high on your list for relationships.

I See Dead People

In the movie *The Sixth Sense,* Bruce Willis stars as a child psychologist dedicated to his work. His wife at the start of the movie comments on how his work always came first with him. By the end of the movie, he corrects her and tells her that she was always first.

Clarifying your relationship values can benefit you whether you're in a committed relationship, a casual relationship or even if you're single. Once you know what's important to you in a relationship you can seek someone who holds the same values. If you're in a casual relationship looking to take things to the next stage, then this is one way to check your compatibility. If you're in a committed relationship then clarifying yours and your partner's values may bring understanding to any hot spots in the relationship and help you grow together, knowing what's important to you both.

EXAMPLE: One of you may find out that support is highly important to you, more than you realised. You can then discuss ways that your partner can give you that support whether it's for your work, sport, hobbies or just around the house.

Such accommodations are necessary to make a relationship work.

REMEMBER:

1. Values are positive abstract concepts that you prefer and hold in a hierarchy.

2. Values are the results of your beliefs.

3. Values drive your behaviour whether you're aware of it or not.

Week 6 Day 4:
Value Alignment

> *"Things that matter most must never be at the mercy of things that matter least."*
>
> —JOHANN WOLFGANG VON GOETHE, POLYMATH

Your values, although abstract nouns, become real through your actions and behaviour. Therefore they need to be verbs (*doing* words) in order for you to be living in alignment with your values. Look at your day-to-day behaviour to see if you are living your high-ranking values.

Imagine you discover intimacy is one of your high-ranking relationship values. However, a look at your behaviour shows that when you get home you're tired and don't open up to your partner to share your thoughts and feelings with them. Instead you go through the motions of a relationship without scheduling in quality time alone together.

Imagine you recognise that control is one of your high-ranking values. However, at work you are often stressed by fighting fires with problems that just keep popping up. You are reactionary and only deal with things when they urgently need your attention.

These examples clearly show a misalignment between your values and behaviour.

> *"Open your arms to change, but don't let go of your values."*
>
> —DALAI LAMA, SPIRITUAL TEACHER

Decisions, decisions

Values are the criteria for all your decision making and how you set your priorities. So now, decision making can be made easy once you are aware of your high-ranking values. Any time you face a tough decision, you can simply come back to your value set. Once you know what's important to you, you'll know where to devote the majority of your time and energy that's fulfilling and meaningful for you.

The Glass Jar

A time management expert stood in front of a group of high-powered overachievers and said, *"I have a simple question for you."*

She pulled out a big glass jar and put it on the table. She then brought out six big rocks and put them into the jar until it was filled to the top.

"The question is, is this jar full?" asked the expert.

Everyone nodded and replied, *"Yes."*

"Are you sure?" she asked, as she picked up a bucket of gravel and poured it in.

6

176

She shook the jar causing pieces of gravel to shift in between the big rocks. *"Is the jar full now?"* she asked.

The group was less sure now but still replied, *"Yes, it's full now."*

"Really?" she replied. And she took a bucket of sand and started tipping the sand in. The sand went into all the spaces left between the rocks and the gravel. Once more she asked the question, *"Is this jar full?"* However, one or two people in the group were now onto her.

"No," they said.

"Well spotted," said the time management expert as she picked up a pitcher of water and began to pour it in until the jar was filled to the brim. The question came again, *"Is this jar full?"*

"It is now," said those who had said no moments earlier.

"Ah, but wait, there's more," joked the expert as she picked up some fine dry salt and carefully dissolved it in the water at the top of the jar. *"Now,"* she said, *"this jar is full."* She looked at the group and asked, *"What's the point of this demonstration?"*

One of the overachievers raised a hand and said, *"The point is, no matter how full your life or your schedule is, if you think smart, you can always fit some more in."*

"That's one interpretation," the expert replied smiling, *"but not the point I'm trying to make. This demonstration can also teach us that whatever you do in life, get the big rocks in first or you'll never get them in at all."*

What are the big rocks in your life? What do you value? How much are the pebbles like the little tasks that fill your time? What might the sand and water represent? Your big rocks may be family, personal growth, kindness, health, education, community, whatever you deem important in your life. Remember to put these big rocks in first or you'll never get them in at all.

> *"I don't believe people are looking for the meaning of life as much as they are looking for the experience of being alive."*
> —JOSEPH CAMPBELL, MYTHOLOGY SCHOLAR

What Is your Kwan?

Watch *Jerry Maguire* from a value alignment and decision-making viewpoint. In which ways do Tom Cruise's character's values affect his decisions throughout the movie?

Balance

Trying to live a balanced life on a daily basis is a recipe for frustration, disappointment and even madness. To live a balanced life you must think long term. There will be times when your personal life is more important to you than your career and times when your career takes precedence over your relationships and family time. Accept this and understand that as long as you tend to all areas of your life over time, you are leading a balanced life.

The 80:20 rule

The 80:20 rule states that 20% of effort creates 80% of the results. This split shouldn't be taken literally as it refers to the minority often controlling the majority. Companies have found that 80% of their revenue comes from 20% of their clients. This rule means that 20% of what you do creates 80% of your achievements. It also applies to things like you spending 80% of your time with 20% of your friends, 80% of the music you listen to makes up only 20% of the CD collection, 80% of the clothes you wear makes up only 20% of your wardrobe.

> **Cliff Says...**
> It's a little known fact that... the 80:20 rule, also known as the Pareto Principle, was named after the Italian economist Vilfredo Pareto who observed in 1906 that 80% of the wealth in Italy was owned by 20% of the population. He carried out surveys on other countries and found a similar distribution of wealth applied.

"The greatest journey you can undertake in life is to cover the distance between you and your full potential."

—MICHAEL HENDERSON, AUTHOR

What may come as a shock or perhaps no surprise to you at all is – what you spend your money on a day-to-day basis is not necessarily on things that actually represent your values.

Imagine how much money, space and energy you could save by knowing which 20% to focus on.

Knowing your value set will allow you to know how to best spend your time to create more results for you. It will lessen the time and physical and mental energy you waste on things you deem not as important.

Remember that your values are relational, they will shift according to the context. When it comes to values you need to think hierarchically. You have to make sacrifices in order to achieve things in life and it helps to know that you're making the right sacrifices.

EXAMPLE: You decide you want to be in excellent physical condition. So you start by waking up early every morning and going for a run. You give up going out late at night and socialising with friends so you can achieve this. You eventually enter half marathons and do well and decide to train for a marathon. This takes an even bigger commitment of your time.

This could make you feel one of two ways. The reward for completing the marathon is tremendous. You're in great shape, your self-esteem is boosted, and you are proud of your achievements. If you feel this way the chances are you value health/vitality and achievement over community and belonging. You don't mind sacrificing time with friends and family because although they may be important, they're not as important to you.

However, if you made this sacrifice but felt unhappy about the lack of social contact and thought it was too big a price to pay, then the chances are you value friendship and belonging more than your individual success. Only you can tell what's right for you.

What are you doing in life that's living your values? What activities are you doing, what decisions are you making that's not living your values?

> *"Values are like fingerprints. Nobody's are the same, but you leave 'em all over everything you do."*
> —ELVIS PRESLEY, THE KING

Aligning to the organisation

It's important to note that although organisations have values, they don't hold them – only the people working for them do.

In Ken Hultman's book *Balancing Individual and Organisational Values*, he lists six main research-based reasons why it's good for you and the company you work for to have aligned values:

1. Profits are higher when values are aligned.
2. Values for trust and camaraderie increase shareholder value.
3. Companies with an enduring core ideology outperform the stock market.
4. Firms that consider the employees, customers and stockholders outperform those who don't.
5. Organisations' change efforts fail when culture is ignored.
6. Value-based leadership increases job satisfaction and overall bottom-line performance.

In order for you to get the most satisfaction out of your job, align what you do with the company's values.

REMEMBER:

1. Align your big decisions in accordance with your high-ranking values.

2. Life satisfaction comes from living in alignment with your values.

3. It's good to know which 20% of what you do gives you 80% of your results.

Week 6 Day 5:   Choice

> *"There's nothing good or bad but thinking makes it so."*
> —WILLIAM SHAKESPEARE, THE BARD

There are many things in life that are out of your control – your gender, the country and time in history you were born in, the weather and the latest football results. However, there are a lot of areas in your life where you do have control. Probably more than you realise. You have the power of choice. As a human being, you are a constant choice maker.

One of the biggest choices you can make in life is to answer the big question:
What is the meaning of life?

Of course the big answer is:
Life has no meaning except the meaning you give it.

What does that mean? Let's put it another way.
   Viktor Frankl, author of *Man's Search for Meaning*, was a Jewish psychiatrist who survived the horror of Auschwitz and wrote the following:

> *"Between stimulus and response there is a space.*
> *In that space lies our freedom and power to choose*
> *our response. In those choices lie our growth and*
> *happiness."*

As Shakespeare wrote in Hamlet, there are no positive or negative experiences unless you deem it so. All there is in life are events. Losing your keys, missing a deadline, your pet dying, your partner being upset with you, winning the lottery, your car breaking down, getting a promotion, going to Fiji for a relaxing holiday, waking up in the morning – all these events are just stimuli.

Your choice

You choose what they mean to you. You *choose* your moods and attitude by how you interpret the events in your life. So yes, you are in *total* control over how you feel every moment of your life. That's a big responsibility and definitely worth thinking about next time you get upset, angry or are feeling frustrated and stressed. It's not other people making you upset but rather you choosing that particular reaction.

Three Pots

A young woman visited her mother complaining about the stresses she faced at work and the hardships of her relationship with her husband. She was tired of the constant battle she seemed to be waging with life.

Her mother put three pots on the stove each filled with water. Once they boiled she put a carrot into the first one, an egg into the second and some tea leaves into the third pot. She let them boil away for about 20 minutes and then put each one into three separate bowls. She asked her daughter, *"What do you see?"*

Her daughter replied a bit exasperated, *"A carrot, an egg and a bowl of tea."*

Her mother made her feel the carrot, and the daughter felt the limp vegetable. The mother handed her the egg and asked the daughter to peel off the shell to reveal the hardboiled egg. Finally, the mother asked the daughter to sip the tea. The daughter enjoyed the rich smell and taste of the freshly brewed tea. Confused she looked at her mother and asked her, *"But what does this mean?"*

Her mother explained, *"My dear, each of these things faced the same adversity – boiling water. Each had a different reaction. The carrot went in hard and strong. But after being subjected to the boiling water, it became soft and weak. The egg had been fragile. The thin shell had protected the liquid interior, but after sitting through the boiling water, it became hardened. The tea was different again. After the tea was in the boiling water, it changed the water's colour and taste."*

She continued, *"Which are you, my love? When adversity knocks on your door, how do you respond? Do you appear strong but then wilt? Do you appear soft and fluid but then harden your heart on the inside? Or does the very thing that comes to bring you pain get transformed as you release the latent power within you? Are you like the carrot, the egg or the tea?"*

> *"No one can make you feel inferior without your consent."*
>
> —ELEANOR ROOSEVELT, AUTHOR & POLITICAL LEADER

Life is Beautiful

Watch *Life is Beautiful* and note the choices Roberto Benigni makes as the father throughout the movie. How does his interpretation of events affect other people?

If you don't like the outcome of a particular situation then change the meaning!

Be proactive by choosing to look for the positive in events. This means you are staying in control of your life rather than constantly being in a reactive state to all the things that happen to you.

Your "response-ability" is your responsibility.

"We are not creatures of circumstance; we are creators of circumstance."

—BENJAMIN DISRAELI, POLITICIAN

Defence mechanisms

You need to watch out for such defence mechanisms as:

- Denial — telling yourself that there is no problem
- Rationalisation — making excuses to carry on undesired behaviour
- Displacement — snapping at your spouse when you're really angry at your boss
- Projection — attributing your undesired thoughts or behaviour onto others
- Blame-shifting — blaming others for your own deeds or situation
- Minimising — making out something isn't as bad as it really is

If you say that *"I've always been this way"* or *"it's in my nature"* or *"it's just who I am"* then understand you are abdicating your responsibility to make positive changes in your life.

Sure, there is a genetic influence that scientists say makes up roughly 50% of your mental processes, but that still leaves plenty of opportunity for you to develop the life you desire.

Stephen Covey, author of *The 7 habits of Highly Effective People,* inspired by Viktor Frankl's words, wrote in *The 8th Habit:*

"Fundamentally, we are a product of choice, not nature (genes) or nurture (upbringing, environment). Certainly genes and culture often influence very powerfully, but they do not determine."

Bottom line, you are always self-determining because you always have a choice.

Often the space between stimulus and response is so small that we don't realise we choose all our actions. Imagine your phone rings and you answer it. Did you choose to answer it? You sure did. Your behaviour has been conditioned to answer a ringing phone but you still had a choice.

"The strongest principle of growth lies in human choice."

—GEORGE ELIOT, NOVELIST

Find the choice

Listen to your language where you may be putting the power, meaning and happiness of your life into other people's hands. You may be exhibiting a victim mentality by blaming other people and circumstances for your current position in certain areas of your life. Even things you consider obligations are choices.

EXAMPLE: I would rather do something different with my life but I can't because my family depends on me.

There is a choice being made here. It's easier/better to stay in the current situation rather than change. Have you discussed it with your family? What assumptions are being made? Which is the higher priority for you?

Take the power back by truly understanding that you ALWAYS have a choice

This doesn't mean you won't make bad choices or mistakes in life. You as a human being have the right to make mistakes. Making mistakes is how you learn. It's from your bad choices that you gain experience. You sure didn't pop up onto your two little legs at around 10 months old and just start walking around. You spent some time falling on your butt and you didn't give up then. You processed the information, stored the lessons and went at it again. This falling on our butt happens metaphorically to all of us throughout life. Sometimes you're walking tall, other times you're hitting the ground and kissing the carpet.

> **Cliff Says...**
> *It's a little known fact that...* a baby falls over on average 240 times and still gets up. It shows that you ain't no quitter!

"What matters most is how we respond to what we experience in life."

—STEPHEN COVEY, AUTHOR

Emotional Barriers (Week 5 Day 2) looked at the different fears that often immobilise you and appear to take away your choices. The fear of failure, the unknown and judgement need to be overcome in order for you to proceed in your desired direction.

Reframe

"Nothing can stop the man with the right mental attitude from achieving his goal; nothing on earth can help the man with the wrong mental attitude."

—THOMAS JEFFERSON, POLITICIAN

In psychology the word "frames" is used to describe the process of making sense of complex information. Frames help you make sense of the world around you and communicate that world to others. Reframing is simply taking a fresh perspective on the exact same stimulus.

EXAMPLE: It took Thomas Edison over seven hundred attempts until he found the right material for the light bulb filament. One could reasonably argue that he failed many times. Edison himself didn't see it as a failure but rather *"I've just found seven hundred ways of not making a light bulb"*.

Friedrich Nietzsche the philosopher once said, *"There are no facts, only interpretations"*, so you can use reframing to help you look at a troubling situation from a new angle, making it easier for you to find a better way to handle it. For reframing to work effectively, the alternative views have to be something that you can genuinely believe in. That's why it works better if you train your brain to look for the positive yourself, rather than relying on others pointing it out.

> *"If one does not begin with the right attitude, there is little hope for a right ending."*
> —CHINESE PROVERB

Challenge expectations

Choice gives you freedom. However, what may be blocking you from your deserved state is that you are living up to other people's expectations that you've conjured up yourself due to your belief system. Understand that even if you choose not to decide, you have still made a choice.

You must start looking at the reasons behind your *can'ts*. Discover what expectations, assumptions and beliefs are at play that are stopping you from achieving what you want.

If you're a part of a group within or outside of work, then usually there are certain behavioural norms that the group has silently agreed to follow. You may feel pressure at times to abide by this agreed-upon code of conduct. Even then, you still have a choice. You can choose to conform, choose to act differently or choose to leave that particular group.

> *"One cannot make a slave of a free person, for a free person is free even in a prison."*
> —PLATO, PHILOSOPHER

If you choose to make a change you may find that others follow suit as they also wanted a change. Management expert Jerry Harvey called this the Abilene paradox. It's when a group of people collectively decide on a way of doing things which goes against the way any of them as individuals would want things to be done. It's one of the perils of compromise.

📖 *Is That The Bell?*

A JOLT Challenge participant would work late most nights well beyond what he wanted to and what he was paid for. He and the rest of the staff did this as the manager worked late and no one wanted to be seen to be slacking off and leaving first. The standard had been set and the participant was unhappy because his family time was suffering.

After doing his Values Set, the participant understood that he now had a bigger desire to spend more time at home and felt comfortable leaving earlier than normal. He realised he was choosing to stay late and complain about all the extra work he "had" to put in. He still put in extra time but would be the first to leave. He was happy to put up with any negative comments about leaving early, as he would explain the reason for leaving. Sure enough, it didn't take long till he wasn't the only person who started leaving at a much more reasonable time.

The more you accept that you can choose your words and behaviour, the more good things will come to you.

There are no have to's but only choose to's

"The meaning of life is whatever you ascribe it to be. Being alive is the meaning."
—JOSEPH CAMPBELL, MYTHOLOGY SCHOLAR

🍺 *Cliff Says...*

It's a little known fact that... Walt Disney challenged expectations from day one when he refused to sell out his idea of the original Mickey Mouse character "Steamboat Willie" to studios, as was the norm, and instead preferred to release Mickey Mouse independently.

So life isn't about discovering yourself and what the meaning of life may be.

Life is about YOU choosing the meaning you want for your life. That's real power. That's real control of your destiny. That's real happiness. That's something that no one or no circumstance can ever take away from you.

Or not. It's your choice.

REMEMBER:

1. You always have a choice in what you feel, think and do.

2. Look for the learnings from things that go wrong for you.

3. Examine the barriers and assumptions that are limiting you and challenge them.

Week 6 summary map:

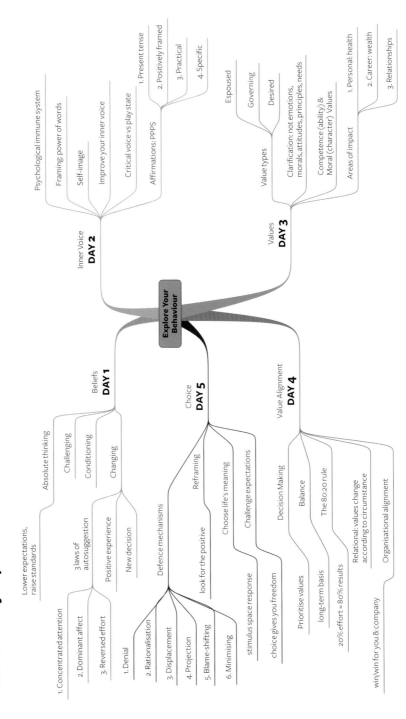

Explore Your Behaviour

Inner Voice — DAY 2
- Psychological immune system
- Framing: power of words
- Self-image
- Improve your inner voice
- Critical voice vs play state
- Affirmations: PPPS
  - 1. Present tense
  - 2. Positively framed
  - 3. Practical
  - 4. Specific

Values — DAY 3
- Value types
  - Espoused
  - Governing
  - Desired
- Clarification: not emotions, morals, attitudes, principles, needs
- Competence (ability) & Moral (character) Values
- Areas of impact
  - 1. Personal: health
  - 2. Career: wealth
  - 3. Relationships

Beliefs — DAY 1
- Lower expectations, raise standards
- Absolute thinking
  - 1. Concentrated attention
- Challenging
- Conditioning
  - 3 laws of autosuggestion
    - 2. Dominant affect
    - 3. Reversed effort
- Changing
  - Positive experience
  - New decision

Choice — DAY 5
- Defence mechanisms
  - 1. Denial
  - 2. Rationalisation
  - 3. Displacement
  - 4. Projection
  - 5. Blame-shifting
  - 6. Minimising
- Reframing
  - look for the positive
  - Choose life's meaning
  - Challenge expectations
- stimulus space response
- choice gives you freedom

Value Alignment — DAY 4
- Decision Making
  - Balance
  - The 80:20 rule
    - Prioritise values
    - long-term basis
    - 20% effort = 80% results
- Relational: values change according to circumstance
- Organisational alignment
  - win/win for you & company

Align Your Needs

Purpose

To be able to consistently perform at your best, understand your needs and link them to your purpose in life.

Overview

Day 1: Stress Alignment
Day 2: Peak Performance
Day 3: Driving Need
Day 4: Self & Belonging
Day 5: Structure & Change

Benefits

This week's experience in the Challenge guides you to:

- achieve a peak performance state regularly
- handle stress more effectively
- feel that you're on purpose in life
- experience transformation and positive change
- enjoy freedom of expression and gain clarity on things that are important to you
- develop awareness of your patterns and values related to friendship
- respond to adversity in a positive manner
- understand the roles that *self* and belonging play in your life
- spontaneity and mental flexibility while dealing with structure and change.

ALIGN YOUR NEEDS

⑦

187

Week 7 Day 1:
Stress Alignment

"It's not stress that kills us, it is our reaction to it."

—HANS SELYE, ENDOCRINOLOGIST

Stress is a word that has been adopted to cover a wide range of mental and physical components. There are many misunderstandings of what stress actually is. For example, in a 2006 study in the United Kingdom, 68% of people defined stress as "having a really bad day". Hans Selye, an endocrinologist (your endocrine system deals with your metabolism, growth and development) coined the term "stress" and originally defined it as "the rate of wear and tear on the body". A stressor causing a stress response describes any mental, emotional or physical strain that tests an individual. Excessive heat or cold are physical stressors, pain is a mental stressor, while a demanding job or interpersonal problems are emotional ones. Stress is now commonly used to mean something negative as in *"I'm under a lot of stress right now"*. However, there is good stress and bad stress.

The good and the bad

Stress is required for you to grow. Just like a muscle grows bigger and stronger when put under stress, so do you. Good stress is called eustress (euphoric stress) and it's a stimulation that enhances your performance. It's stress you feel you can handle and it is only sustained for short periods of time.

"What man actually needs is not a tensionless state but rather the striving and struggling for a worthwhile goal, a freely chosen task."

—VIKTOR FRANKL, AUTHOR & PSYCHIATRIST

If the stress lasts longer than you feel you can handle it or you feel over-stimulated, then you have left the eustress stage and entered the bad stress stage, called distress. Not having a sense of control is a major factor in causing distress. We all have different stress thresholds so the stage where you leave eustress and enter distress is going to be different for each person.

Imagine doing a parachute jump. This event may cause you distress if you're doing it for the very first time. You're nervous, sweating, your heart is beating faster as adrenaline pumps through your system, you feel physically sick and are probably thinking of what might go wrong. Fast-forward to your 20th jump, the same event may cause eustress. You've got the same adrenaline pump but you're excited, thinking of the best positive outcome, and can't wait to leap out of that plane.

The event is the same but the experience of it is different. Think back to Choice (Week 6 Day 5).

There is always going to be stress, so whether stress is negative or positive is purely in your interpretation of the event, which means that you're ultimately responsible for there being any stress in your life.

Sympathetic vs Parasympathetic response

"Tension is who you think you should be.
Relaxation is who you are."

—CHINESE PROVERB

Your sympathetic response (Emotional Brain: Week 2 Day 2), better known as your fight or flight response, is one that helps you in time of need. It gives you the emergency dose of adrenaline for a particular time and activity. Although there are times when you need adrenaline, if it stays on it will lead you to burnout.

> **Cliff Says...**
> *It's a little known fact that...* American physiologist Walter B. Cannon coined the fight or flight term in 1915. He also coined the term "homeostasis", meaning the stable condition or balanced state of a living organism.

With today's hectic pace, your sympathetic response can be constantly activated by the small but consistent triggers that come with a busy life. Therefore stress is often now a chronic (long-term) problem rather than the acute (short burst) experience it used to be.

> **"I'm the bad guy?"**
> In the movie *Falling Down* Michael Douglas plays a character who has lost his job, been recently divorced and is stuck in a traffic jam with a broken air conditioner on the hottest day of the year. The stress makes him snap and he wreaks vigilante justice, which leads to his own demise.

The **3** stages of distress

Hans Selye described three stages of stress:

Stage One – Alarm   Stage Two – Resistance   Stage Three – Exhaustion

Stage One: You experience a stimulus that triggers a biochemical reaction with adrenaline and cortisol being pumped into your system.

Stage Two: You either freeze in fright, stay and fight or flee in flight.

Stage Three: You can't stay too long at stage two without becoming exhausted. Distress takes its toll on the body.

Stress can be experienced in many ways and result in mental, emotional, physical, behavioural problems if left, so you need to be aware of what triggers your distress.

You need to allow the body to rest and recover. This is your parasympathetic response, when your serotonin levels are restored. There are plenty of ways to help alleviate distress and return to a more productive balanced state.

Some ways include:

- any relaxation technique (self-hypnosis, progressive muscle relaxation, autogenic training, meditation, breathing exercises)
- doing physical exercise (eg: favourite sports/exercise, yoga, jogging, walking)
- getting quality sleep
- getting a massage
- writing down a strategy to deal with the issue
- being surrounded by nature
- change of scene (eg: go shopping, take a short break)
- talking to a friend
- adjusting your diet accordingly (eg: drink water)
- laughing
- having a bath
- playing with a pet
- enjoying positive self-talk.

> *"Take rest; a field that has rested gives a bountiful crop."*
>
> —OVID, POET

You don't have to do these things only when you feel stressed. As they say, prevention is better than cure, so if you make these activities a part of your regular routine you will handle stress better and avoid burnout. You will feel healthier and live better.

Two different takes on stress

So while Hans Selye pioneered the response-based perspective on stress, there are two other stress theories. There is the stimulus-based perspective which pays more attention to the characteristics of the stressors. When someone says, *"I have a stressful job"*, they're referring more to a demanding situation, than their response to that situation. The emphasis is on reducing the number of stressors, rather than increasing activities such as those listed above that stimulate the parasympathetic response.

EXAMPLE: If driving to work in rush hour puts you under stress, rather than listening to calming music, you can instead change the stimulus and catch a train instead.

The other perspective is the Transactional model, that looks at stress as an interaction between people and their environment. This model was developed by psychologist Richard Lazarus who maintained that the most important factor is how you appraise situations that arise in your environment, ie: what beliefs you hold about the situations you confront.

Any particular situation can be appraised as either a challenge or a threat. If you appraise a situation as threatening, then you will have the appropriate emotional and behavioural response, such as anxiety and looking for ways to cope. Likewise, if you appraise the situation as challenging then you'll trigger enthusiasm and positive motivation. Appraising situations accurately is very important, so that challenges aren't misperceived as threats. This reinforces the power of words (Inner Voice: Week 6 Day 2). Avoid statements like *"this is difficult"* and use instead *"this is challenging"*, *"this is an opportunity"* or *"this is exciting"*.

> **Shoes For Africa**
> Two shoe salesmen were sent to a remote part of Africa to explore the opportunity of selling shoes there. The first salesman looked at his target market and couldn't believe what he saw. He reported back to head office, *"This is a waste of time. They don't even wear shoes here."*
> The second salesman reported back, *"Send me all the shoes you've got. This is an untapped market."*

You can't live without stress

You can't avoid stress and nor should you want to. It's what helps you grow and develop.
The trick is to align the stressors in your life so you spend the majority of your life

in eustress rather than distress and use the tools to get you from feelings of distress back into balance.

> *"Grant me the courage to change the things I can change, the serenity to accept the things I can't change, and the wisdom to know the difference."*
>
> —REINHOLD NIEBUHR, THEOLOGIAN

Remedy for the Mind

You've already learnt reframing (Choice: Week 6 Day 5) as one method of removing stress by regaining control of your negative thoughts and replacing them with positive ones.

Remedy for the Body

As you discovered in Breathing (Week 3 Day 3), focusing on your breathing is a simple way of alleviating stress as it loads your blood with oxygen. Shallow breathing doesn't oxygenate your blood very efficiently. Consequently, toxins pile up in the cells and make you feel sluggish and down. If your organs don't receive enough oxygen to remove toxins then this eventually leads to organ malfunction. Breathing is the best tool you have to profoundly affect your body and mind.

REMEMBER:

1. There is good stress and bad stress, be aware of the difference.

2. Prevention is better than cure so put little relaxing activities into your schedule.

3. There's no avoiding stress but there's plenty you can do to make it work for you.

Week 7 Day 2:
Peak Performance

"True enjoyment comes from activity of the mind and exercise of the body; the two are ever united."

—ALEXANDER VON HUMBOLDT, EXPLORER

Anybody can learn to reach the level of peak performance but most people reach it through chance. There are four areas you need to consider in order to consistently achieve peak performance in whatever challenge or task you attempt:

Mind, Body, Emotions, Spirit

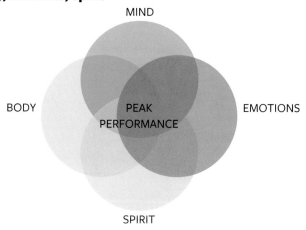

MIND = This is your understanding of the challenge. It takes into account your knowledge and ability to focus and concentrate on the task at hand.

BODY = This is your skill level. It takes into account your competencies and technical ability.

EMOTIONS = This is your desire for the challenge. It takes into account your emotions and attitude.

SPIRIT = This is the belief that the challenge serves you on all levels and that it's the right thing for you to do.

You cannot achieve peak performance if one of these areas is missing.

EXAMPLE 1: If MIND is missing, then you have skills, desire and belief but no understanding of the task.

EXAMPLE 2: If BODY is missing, then you have the understanding, desire and belief but lack the necessary skills to do the task.

EXAMPLE 3: If EMOTIONS is missing, then you have the understanding, skills and belief but no desire to undergo the task.

EXAMPLE 4: If SPIRIT is missing then you have the understanding, skills and desire, but lack the belief that it's in your best interests to do the task.

Misaligned action equals poor results for you. It is your responsibility to get yourself into alignment so you can gain maximum benefit from the challenges ahead of you.

Flow

Have you ever had a time when you have been totally engaged in a project at work and your partner calls and you tell them you'll be leaving work in 10 minutes, only to look at the clock a little while later and see that an hour has passed?

Psychologist Mihaly Csikszentmihalyi, who has spent 40 years studying peak performance states, coined the term *flow* to describe this state. Flow fits into the Play stage of the Growth Cycle (Week 1 Day 1). In sport it is also known as being in the zone. You've probably experienced this state when absorbed in a good book, movie or in an engaging activity. Everything seems easy, fluid, and your perception of time can slow right down. However, time has continued normally so when you come out of the zone you may notice hours have passed like minutes. Hence the saying, *"Time flies when you're having fun."*

FLOW DIAGRAM

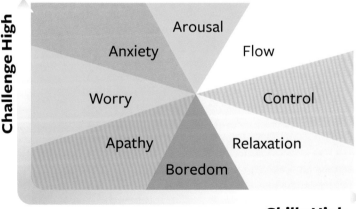

Adapted and used with permission from Csikszentmihalyi 1997

As Csikszentmihalyi's graph shows, you are in flow when the challenge of an activity is met by your relevant skill set. This results in you being fully engaged in the process rather than the outcome of the activity.

EXAMPLE: Rather than stressing about a looming deadline and having the thoughts of whether you're going to make it on time or not affecting your work, you are fully engaged in the doing of the work and will meet the deadline as a result of this.

Too much challenge and not enough skills results in worry causing distress. Too much skill level and not enough challenge results in boredom.

Remember, as we discussed in Neurons (Week 2 Day 3), neuropsychological research shows the brain responds to excess challenge and not enough challenge in a similar way.

The human brain responds poorly to boredom. If your brain is under-challenged then it loses its ability to focus and allows your critical voice to kick into action. People who engage in negative behaviour such as gossiping, backstabbing others or being a pain in the proverbial, are often bored. The Growth Cycle (Week 1 Day 1) gives you ways of getting back into the cycle.

Getting into flow

"The most powerful weapon on earth is the human soul on fire."

—FERDINAND FOCH, SOLDIER & WRITER

It would be near impossible to be in flow all the time because of the nature of life. You can't force yourself into flow either. However, you can set up your environment so you achieve flow more consistently rather than haphazardly.

The **8** characteristics of flow as defined by Csikszentmihalyi are:

1. Clear goals
You need to know where the goalposts are for you to be absorbed in any activity. As you discovered in Desire (Week 5 Day 5), the real pleasure lies in the journey towards the goal, not the achievement itself. The pleasure is in the eating of a nice meal, not actually finishing it. Don't worry about the end result, put your focus on the process. So remember:

Get off outcome and get on purpose!

2. Immediate feedback
The feedback doesn't have to be from other people, it can be from yourself or even the actual task itself. You will know how things are going. If you're a boxer you'll know things aren't going well when you're getting hit in the head. If you're having a terrible round of golf then that's your feedback.

ALIGN YOUR NEEDS

7

195

3. Challenge matched by skill

You've got to feel that you can do the task. It's not entirely comfortable, there is a stretch component, but it's not too far out of your reach.

4. Deep concentration

You become fully engaged in the activity and experience a focusing of attention. This is when people say they become one with the activity rather than watching and judging themselves or becoming easily distracted.

5. Being in the moment

You are totally present, with the past and future having no place in your focused conscious mind. People are often unable to recall exactly what they did or what was going on around them because of such focus. Others have the capacity to be fully present in what they're doing and yet be able to observe themselves in the action.

6. Control

You feel you have control of your own performance. You don't have to have total control. You may be at the mercy of the environment but within that you are able to make things happen positively for you.

7. Time distortion

Time is distorted. It can quicken or slow depending on what the task is. You're no longer on clock time.

8. Ego-less

You lose your sense of *self* when you are in flow.

> **Cliff Says...**
> *It's a little known fact... that* people enter the flow state more at work than anywhere else. People have a distorted view of work due to the cultural perception that work is bad. However, the majority of people say that they would work even if they didn't have to.

> *"I don't think anybody yet has invented a pastime that's as much fun, or keeps you as young, as a good job."*
>
> —FREDERICK HUDSON ECKER, BUSINESSMAN

There is a difference in leisure activities. Some are active like sports and hobbies whereas some are passive like watching TV and sunbathing. It's the active leisure activities that allow people peak experiences. This explains why many people after two or three weeks of blissing out on a beach on holiday are ready to head back to work. You desire peak performance states and you get them more at work than anywhere else.

The task that gets you into flow is worth doing for its own sake. It's intrinsically motivating (ie: you don't require external rewards). Just because you may be paid for your work doesn't mean you can't take pleasure in it.

> ### 📹 Show Me The Money
> In the movie *Jerry McGuire*, Tom Cruise plays a sports agent to Cuba Gooding Jnr's American football character. He is more interested in playing for money and fame rather than the game itself. When Tom Cruise tells him he's a head player and not a heart player, he starts playing for the love of the game again and the money takes care of itself.

You can achieve peak performance in any activity. Even people who are in jobs that are monotonous by nature such as production lines and data entry, or where there's perceived to be not much challenge, can achieve peak performance.

How? By looking at what you can learn on the job. By holding yourself to a higher standard and finding ways you can improve what you're doing even if no one else knows or recognises it.

In W. Timothy Gallwey's book *The Inner Game of Work*, he writes about training a telecommunication company's call centre operators who were bored and had nothing new to learn after six weeks of training. By simply training them to listen to the voice of the customer, they were able to understand more about the customer, if they were stressed or in a hurry. By being more aware of the customer's voice they were able to vary their own voice, increasing warmth and understanding accordingly. Customer satisfaction increased as a result, with job satisfaction increasing 30% and boredom and stress decreasing on average 40%. The key was that even those who couldn't enjoy the work, enjoyed *themselves* at work.

We're not denying that sometimes people take a job purely for pragmatic reasons and engage in more meaningful pursuits outside of work. Philosopher John Stuart Mill had a boring day job, which left him with energy at night to devote to his scholarly writing. He wrote an article about this entitled *"In praise of dull work"*. However, if you're going to spend 40 hours or so doing a job, you'll find it more fulfilling to find ways of entering the 'Play' state of the Growth Cycle (Week 1 Day 1).

Focus

> *"Concentrate all your thoughts upon the work at hand. The sun's rays do not burn until brought to a focus."*
>
> —ALEXANDER GRAHAM BELL, INVENTOR

When you were a child did you ever get a magnifying glass and burn holes in pieces of paper? Or maybe you were the kid who tried it on ants. Either way, how could the sun's rays accumulate such intense heat? The answer is focus. Focused energy is a powerful force that can accomplish things that the very same energy unfocused cannot.

Experienced actors know this. While some may be nervous before going on stage, others take that nervous energy and channel it into the feeling of excitement of going on stage. It's the same energy but just with a different focus.

When you combine the demands of life along with not knowing your purpose, it's very easy to spread your energy far and wide and accomplish little. You may be busy but it's not busy in a good way, it's busy with busyness. Successful people do the opposite. They focus their energy, time and talent on exactly what they want to achieve. They live their purpose and in that way follow their bliss. This doesn't mean you have to become a workaholic obsessed with achieving a perfect life. All you do is to refuse to let your attention become distracted from achieving your desires. It's not a matter of never losing focus but rather shortening the times in which you lose focus. Focus is something you can practise.

> *"Concentration is the secret of strength."*
> —RALPH WALDO EMERSON, AUTHOR & PHILOSOPHER

Setting your intention (Week 4 Day 2) is an excellent way to train your mind to focus. When you are focused, your mind tunes in to things that are relevant to your goal. You stop blocking the information that may be useful to you and you begin to notice all sorts of things around you that you didn't notice before. You are attuned to coincidences such as meeting people who introduce you to a person who can help you. Or while sitting in the doctor's waiting room you pick up a magazine and come across an article on the exact thing you needed to know for your project.

Play your strengths

So while choosing a positive meaning for your life and your daily activities is a path to happiness, it is not the only one. Playing your strengths is also another path. You don't want to confuse skill and knowledge with your talents and your strengths. Too often people aren't happy because they are doing their competencies rather than playing their strengths. By strengths, we don't mean just something you're good at, but something you're good at AND enjoy doing.

EXAMPLE: If you are good at accounting but it doesn't set you on fire then it's a competency, not a strength. If you live for accounting and are good at it then it's a strength.

Marcus Buckingham and Curt Coffman in their book *First, Break All the Rules*, show the results of a 25-year Gallup Organization study of over a million employees. The study found that the following 10 management practices were associated with productivity, profitability, employee retention, and customer satisfaction:

1. Clarify performance expectations
2. Provide necessary materials and equipment
3. Provide opportunities for employees to do what they do best
4. Give employees recognition for good work at least once a week
5. Care about employees as persons
6. Encourage employee development
7. Consider employees' opinions
8. Make employees feel their job is important
9. Talk to employees about progress
10. Provide opportunities for employees to learn and grow

 Cliff Says...
It's a little known fact that... only 20% of employees feel that their strengths are engaged at work every day.

One way to improve your happiness is to stop thinking thoughts and doing things that make you *un*happy.

Imagine you're having a shower and happiness is the lovely, relaxing hot water. One way of getting more hot water is to turn up the hot water tap, ie: think and do the things that make you happy. However, another (and circumstantially often more so) effective way is to turn down the cold water tap, ie: stop the unhappy thoughts and actions.

As Bob Dylan said – you're a success if you get up in the morning and go to bed at night and in between do what you want to do.

Which activities make you happy? What aspects do you enjoy the most about your job? When are you at your best? The answers to these questions are your strengths.

Which activities make you unhappy? What aspects do you enjoy least about your job? These are pouring cold water on your happiness. Turn them down a bit. Alongside your To Do List create a Stop Doing List.

Of course, if there was no cold water at all then it may be too hot so there will always be aspects of work that we need to do rather than want to do. These are opportunities to have appreciation for the things that help you feel fulfilled and happy. The question is what can you stop thinking and doing that will increase your fulfilment, and what can you start doing?

REMEMBER:

1. Peak performance is a result of your mind, body, emotions and spirit being fully engaged.

2. Flow can happen in any activity if you set it up right.

3. Understand the difference between skills and strengths and focus on your strengths.

Week 7 Day 3:   Driving Need

> *"I am the master of my fate; I am the captain of my soul."*
>
> —WILLIAM ERNEST HENLEY, POET

There is an urban myth that a philosopher posted the following message on his answering machine: *"This device is programmed to ask two simple questions: Who are you and what do you want? Most people go throughout their entire lives without answering either question."*

So far in this Challenge you have made big inroads with the first question and now you will have the opportunity to delve into the second and come up with some answers.

One could rightly argue that adults have very few actual needs outside of the basic human physiological needs such as oxygen, water, food and sleep. The argument goes that the rest of our so-called needs are actually things that we *want*, eg: love, power, freedom, etc, therefore these are values rather than needs. However, in order for you to create a *fulfilling* life you do have certain needs that must be met. We call these the Driving Polarity Needs. These will remain constant regardless of your values.

> *"Life is the coexistence of all opposite values. Joy and sorrow, pleasure and pain, up and down, hot and cold, here and there, light and darkness, birth and death. All experience is by contrast, and one would be meaningless without the other."*
>
> —DEEPAK CHOPRA, DOCTOR & AUTHOR

These are so-called because they are made up of one driving need that underlines two polar opposite needs.

POLARITY ONE
Self & Belonging

Driving Need:
The need for Purpose

POLARITY TWO
Structure & Change

The polar opposite needs follow the Yin-Yang theory. These Polarity Needs do not have any absolutes and therefore they exist within each other. This may seem contradictory, but they create balance and you cannot achieve harmony by having one without also having the other.

The Driving Polarity Needs have been adapted from Maslow's Hierarchy of Needs, probably the best-known work on human needs, developed by psychologist Abraham Maslow in 1943. Maslow believed that people needed to meet physiological, safety, social and self-esteem needs before working on self-actualisation (living your purpose). However, many psychologists today recognise that once the basic physiological needs are met (ie: you have food, water and shelter), then there is a coexistence of needs rather than a hierarchy.

Driving need: The need for purpose

> "To forget one's purpose is the commonest form of stupidity."
>
> —FRIEDRICH NIETZSCHE, PHILOSOPHER

The need for purpose is called the driving need because it is the driving force that underpins all that you do. It's also known as your dharma, your self-actualisation, your duty, your role in life, your highest goal, your heartfelt desire, your vocation, your mission, your essence, your calling in life, it's the very thing that you can't not do. It's all the same thing. If you're not moving towards your purpose, you're slowly dying.

> "Your vision will become clear only when you look into your heart. Who looks outside, dreams. Who looks within, awakens."
>
> —CARL JUNG, PSYCHIATRIST

Your driving need goes beyond success and failure and achieving goals by going into the realm of fulfilment and living a life of meaning. No matter what you do, how you do it, when you do it, there is a why, an *intention* beneath all of your behaviour. As a human being you have a need for purpose. The purpose defines who you are and that what you do has meaning.

 Build It and He Will Come
Watch the movie *Field of Dreams* from the perspective of the main character's driving need.

According to many eminent philosophers, scientists and theologians, your major purpose in life is to create. Therefore a significant part of your purpose is the need for creativity. People need to create. We're not just talking about artistic expression, but the need to create relationships, the need to create a family, or the need to create time so you can do your taxes.

The result of creativity is growth

This can be physical, mental, emotional, and/or spiritual growth.

So what is your purpose? As we've said, it's not something you have to discover, although you may – but it's something you can definitely create!
Remember:

Life has no meaning except the meaning you give it.

> *"Life isn't about finding yourself. Life is about creating yourself."*
> —GEORGE BERNARD SHAW, PLAYWRIGHT

The Cathedral
A man was walking past a building site where he saw three people working.
He asked the first person, *"What are you doing?"* The man, stopping to wipe the sweat from his brow, replied, *"I'm laying bricks."*
He asked the next builder, *"What are you doing?"* The man, standing up, replied, *"I'm building a wall."*
He asked the third person, *"What are you doing?"* The man, who had been humming as he worked, looked around him and smiled. *"I'm building a cathedral."*

Creating your driving need

You have the power to choose your purpose in life and strive to be the best you can. You don't have to climb Everest, start a billion-dollar company or be the world's number one 10-metre springboard diving champion. It's the journey more than the destination that satisfies you and brings you pleasure. Life is just a series of moments that are combined into one experience that you come to regard as your life.

You are totally unique and therefore will have a talent that is specific to you. You might already be doing it or maybe not. A good way of finding out is to answer these questions.

1. Do you wake up, leap out of bed brimming with energy and full of enthusiasm for the day's activities?
2. Do you enjoy your work so much that you would be willing to be paid less than you are at the moment?
3. Is the constant flow of ideas that drive you to do more and be more, beyond your ability to keep up with them?
4. Do you feel that other people value who you are and what you are doing?
5. Are you genuinely content with your role in society and the success of your daily interactions with others?

6. Do you have an inner peace brought about by knowing that you're on purpose?

If you have failed to answer yes to these questions then it is likely you are not working towards your ultimate destiny. Therefore you need to spend a little time to find out what that is.

Destiny comes from Destination – what path are you on?

> *"Is life not one hundred times too short for us to bore ourselves?"*
>
> —FRIEDRICH NIETZSCHE, PHILOSOPHER

Nietzsche is right. Life is too short to be other than rewarding and enjoyable. No one else is going to make it this way for you, so you have to step up. A job or occupation that does not provide fulfilment is simply a prison without bars. This doesn't necessarily mean that you have to throw in your current job, but rather look at what you're doing and find ways to achieve fulfilment within it. There may be people you need to influence or things you need to do differently in order to achieve this. If you want clues about your purpose, look back at the Growth Cycle (Week 1 Day 1) and identify the areas and times you are in the Play state.

> **Money Schmoney**
> Mother Teresa didn't receive much financial compensation for working in the slums of Calcutta. Once a visitor said to her, *"I wouldn't do your work for all the money in the world."*
> To which Mother Teresa replied, *"Neither would I."*

Fulfilment means that financial reward is an end product and not the motivating factor. If your work is fulfilling, you live in an environment that supports your physical and mental health, and you have loving relationships, you are meeting your driving need.

> *"There is no such thing as chance; and what seems to us merest accident springs from the deepest source of destiny."*
>
> —JOHANN FRIEDRICH VON SCHILLER, HISTORIAN & PHILOSOPHER

Know your path

Being consciously aware of your driving need provides you with an image that you can use to affirm that what you're doing has a long-term purpose. Knowing you're on the right path enables you to constructively face challenges and obstacles, as you realise they are simply an opportunity to draw on your resources to end up a richer and wiser person.

Finding your purpose in life doesn't mean you have to meditate on a rock under a waterfall undergoing deep personal introspection. It is more often than not simply changing the question from *"what should I do with my life?"* to *"what do I enjoy doing?"*.

If you really enjoy something, go for it!

It doesn't have to be your official purpose in life but what if it was? As long as it was ecologically good for you, what if you spent your life doing what you enjoy doing? People who choose to do this are called many things including eccentric, obsessed or geniuses. But they are living *their* dreams. Remember from Overcoming External Barriers (Week 1 Day 4):

Be positively self-centred!

> **I Believe I Can Fly**
> Watch the inspirational movie *October Sky* to see how following your dream can change your life.

Make the change from doing what you think you are supposed to do to what you are meant to do. You owe it to everyone to follow your dreams, live your purpose and find your bliss.

> **Man on the Moon**
> In the early days of the space race, John Kennedy visited Cape Canaveral to meet with NASA scientists and all the people who were working to put a man on the moon. As he was leaving he came across an old African-American man wearing blue overalls and mopping the floor. President Kennedy asked him what he did there at Cape Canaveral.
> The old man, straightening up, looked the President in the eye and said with pride, *"Sir, I'm doing the same as everybody else here. I'm working to put a man on the moon."*

> *"Keep away from people who try to belittle your ambition. Small people always do that, but the really great make you feel that you, too, can become great."*
> —MARK TWAIN, AUTHOR

Be wary of the critic. Many people will shoot down your dreams because they are justifying their life choices. They may be embarrassed to admit what they want out of life because they believe they can't accomplish it or they are not worthy of such a life.

Whenever anyone tells you that you "should/ought /must" do something, they are merely reflecting their values in life and often projecting their fears on you.

> **Cliff Says...**
> *It's a little known fact that...* the term Tall Poppy Syndrome originates from two sources, the philosopher Aristotle, and Livy, a Roman historian. A 7th Century BC tyrant was advised to cut off the tallest ears of corn, meaning that he must get rid of the eminent people who may threaten him. In Livy's *History of Rome*, a tyrant gave a message to his son to put to death all the society's prominent people by going into his garden and sweeping a stick across it resulting in the heads of the tallest poppies being cut off. This was the signal for his son to do the same.

Notice that tyrants created the Tall Poppy Syndrome. You need to rise above that.

Driving need defined

> *"What lies behind us and what lies ahead of us are tiny matters compared to what lives within us."*
> —OLIVER WENDELL HOLMES SNR, PHYSICIAN & POET

You'll get to your driving need when you answer the questions *"what drives me to live out this purpose?"* or *"what gives me the strength to endure the tough times?"*.

The key to knowing your driving need is recognising the source of your inner power and that you are able to use your unique talents, strategies, strengths to achieve your desired level of fulfilment.

> *"He who has a why to live for can bear almost any how."*
> —FRIEDRICH NIETZSCHE, PHILOSOPHER

You are the only person who knows what truly makes your heart beat faster, gets your juices pumping, keeps your mind engaged and draws you in like a magnet. You need to put yourself in the driver's seat and take control of your search.

REMEMBER:

1. Life is too short not to live a life of purpose.

2. You can overcome any challenges when you are on purpose.

3. Tapping into what drives you results in knowing your purpose.

Week 7 Day 4:   Self & Belonging

The first of the Polarity Needs is your need for both self and belonging.

The need for Self

Self is all about your identity, knowing who you are and feeling a sense of importance, that you have a place in this universe. You need a sense of self-worth, a feeling that you are significant and competent in what you do. You have a need to be loved, to feel accepted for who *you* are, and that you are unique and are living a life of meaning.

> *"I think therefore I am."*
>
> —RENÉ DESCARTES, SCIENTIST & PHILOSOPHER

> **Cliff Says...**
> *It's a little known fact that...* patients in a rest home who were given the option of choosing their own meals, visits and when they could do certain activities, experienced an increase in health and happiness compared with those who weren't.

Human beings are thought to be the only creatures on the planet with a sense of self. Why? You can consciously reflect about yourself and then even think about your thinking! This ability to reflect is crucial because if you don't know who you are, how do you know what to believe in, what to desire, how to make sound judgements and decisions?

This need for self, of knowing who you are, is very strong and can lead to both inner and outer conflict as you seek to satisfy this need.

We all have different ways of fulfilling our need for self. Some people do it amassing a fortune, others do it by travelling, others by raising a family that they're proud of, by doing good deeds, working hard, being a good friend, having a relationship with God, being a solid member of a community, playing sports, getting an education, being an artist – there's no limit to how you may satisfy this need. There is nothing wrong with satisfying this need and feeling special.

Inner conflict

> *"You can't learn how to fulfil your needs by reviewing examples of how you weren't able to do that in the past."*
>
> —WILLIAM GLASSER, PSYCHOLOGIST

However, inner conflict can arise as you go about answering the question that philosophers have tried to answer since man first walked upright out of the cave – who am I? Do you identify yourself by how you fulfil this need? This means: do you identify yourself by your occupation, your possessions, your achievements, your reputation, your role in the family, your gender, your sexual orientation, your education, your values, your emotions, your bad habits, your friends, what other people tell you, or something else? Do you believe and conform to stereotypes in your head?

Of course, there's no one right way of answering this age-old question, but the beauty is that you can distil the inner conflict by choosing to create your own identity now rather than trying to discover it.

This way, your past limitations fall away as you focus your attention on who you are now or even who you would like to become. Think back to your Driving Need (Week 7 Day 3) to help create your identity.

Don't confuse the different roles you play in life with your identity. There are many roles you could identify yourself as: partner, parent, sibling, friend, professional, employee, colleague, coach, manager, volunteer and mentor to name a few. You may be confused as to which one best defines you as you are all of these people. There's nothing wrong with having different roles. Some will be more important to you than others. Like your values, roles are relational – they will change in relation to the situation you are in. And like your values, it's good to know which roles are your priority. None of those roles you play actually define who you are in their own right as you're a sum of them and more.

Outer conflict

Outer conflict is conflict with other people. You may be fulfilling your need for self in a non-conforming way and conflict is caused by pressure from others to conform.

> *"The protruding nail gets hammered down."*
> —JAPANESE PROVERB

You have the right to be positively self-centred (Overcoming External Barriers: Week 1 Day 4) and live your life. If you have inner peace and accept yourself unconditionally then the conflict lies with the other person – it's not yours!

If you don't accept yourself and seek approval and worthiness from others then this inner conflict will manifest in outer conflict. You will need to feed your ego and this results in undesirable behaviour towards others.

Imagine a boss who through their own insecurities has a need to micromanage their staff and put others down. They will claim credit for other people's ideas as a way of boosting their image in the eyes of others. This controlling nature will spill into their relationship with their staff, and talented employees won't hang around long in this environment.

Ego

> *"Ego is simply an idea of who you are that you carry around with you."*
> —WAYNE DYER, AUTHOR

The need for self when taken too far can run into some obvious problems; namely, an out-of-control ego. This may result from the desire to be approved of, the desire to win, the desire to be right or simply to be recognised as someone different from everybody else. When you satiate this need for self in excess, it can lead to isolating yourself from others, resulting in loneliness.

Unconditional self-acceptance

Psychologist Albert Ellis offers a way to avoid an extreme desire for approval, and that is to practise unconditional self-acceptance. This means that you accept yourself for who you are right now. You accept the fact that you have a place in this universe and a given right to be happy. Who gives you that right? You do! Self-acceptance has nothing to do with self-confidence or self-respect – it's all about accepting that you are alive and therefore deserve happiness. Self-acceptance is a prerequisite to accepting others. It's a very liberating choice to make. To paraphrase the philosopher Descartes, all you have to do to accept yourself is think '*I exist therefore I am worthy*'.

> *"Self-importance is man's greatest enemy."*
> —CARLOS CASTANEDA, AUTHOR

The desire to win or be right, or simply to be recognised as being different, can lead you to judge the way other people fulfil their need for self. Judging one person's way of fulfilling their need for self as good or bad is about as accurate and useful as judging one type of car being better than another. One is neither right nor wrong; it's purely a vehicle for that person to travel to where they want to go. Ego checking can be gained by detaching from having to win or be right all the time.

Another way to keep your ego in check is to remember that ultimately you are connected and not separate from everyone else. It may appear that you are different but when you get past the surface level, science shows we are made up of the same matter and that we're all just bundles of energy and information. Regardless of your religious or spiritual beliefs or whether you don't have any, we are all connected.

This leads to the polar opposite need, the need for belonging.

The need for belonging

You can fulfil the need of belonging through groups, friends, family or intimate relationships. Your need for people to love and to be loved is very strong. As a human being, you need to gather in groups and have a sense of community. It is even better when you are involved with like-minded people in your group. Your need for belonging, as highlighted in Happiness (Week 5 Day 3), is the number one contributing factor to your well-being.

> *"If you take the friendship out of life, you take the sun out of the world."*
>
> —CICERO, STATESMAN & PHILOSOPHER

We are social beings and your need for belonging is part of your genetic make-up. Your ancestors quickly learnt that those who were part of a community had a better rate of survival than those who went it alone. This makes it a very powerful need.

Imagine a person who so desperately wants to belong to a particular group that they don't even eat, and eventually develop anorexia. That sense of belonging is so strong that it overrides their in-built desire to eat.

Choose your peers

It's pretty much a given that you can't choose your family but you most certainly can choose your friends and peers. Now that you know your values and what's important to you, check to see that it's aligned with who you spend the majority of your time with.

> *"When the character of a man is not clear to you, look at his friends."*
>
> —JAPANESE PROVERB

Saving Norman
Watch *City Slickers* from the viewpoint of having purpose in your life, your peer group and gaining a clearer sense of identity.

Your peer group is a reflection of you. Are the people you're surrounding yourself with the people who are going to support you and help get you to where you want to go? Are they people you aspire to be? You need people around you who are going to stretch you and who live, or are trying to live, at the same level you wish to.

This goes for not only all relationships but any goal you have. If you desire to improve yourself in a sport or activity then you need to play against someone at a higher level than yourself.

EXAMPLE: You wish to get better at badminton. You won't get better playing someone at or below your level. You can only achieve this if you start training with someone who is better at it than you. Although it may be frustrating to be beaten all the time at first, you will rapidly improve. You don't want to play with someone who just thrashes you either. They need to be supportive and want you to get better.

There is enough research to show that an unhappy relationship, whether it's an intimate, social or work one, causes suffering. So choose your friends and peer group carefully.

When you take this need for belonging too far you begin to lose your sense of identity. Cults know this and that's why part of their recruitment process is to separate you from your normal environment for sustained periods of time while they indoctrinate new beliefs and a new sense of identity. They understand that what a person thinks of themselves is directly influenced by interactions with others in social situations.

The balance of self and belonging

> Excess self creates loneliness. Excess belonging creates a lack of identity.
> Hence we need a balance of both for harmony.

Give up the idea that there's a perfect balance between these two needs. As you'll see with the Structure & Change Polarity Needs (Week 7 Day 5), there is no perfect balance zone.

What Is Your Deepest Fear?

Watch *Coach Carter* from the viewpoint of the balance between self and belonging. How do the basketball players balance individuality and team work? What values are most prized? How do the players achieve fulfilment?

Your need for self can be fulfilled in many ways. It drives people to climb mountains, read books, jump out of aeroplanes, commit fraud, make pottery, have extra-marital affairs, volunteer for charity, control others, raise pets and a whole host of other ways of feeling special. Remember, disempowering and excessive ways eventually lead to the feeling of being alone, which ultimately results in depression and ill health.

Empowering and balanced ways lead to a life of fulfilment. Your need for belonging causes you to seek satisfying relationships with partners, family and friends all your life and is at the core of your happiness.

REMEMBER:

1. You need a sense of self and a sense of belonging in your life.

2. Ensure you have empowering ways of fulfilling your need for self.

3. Choose your peers wisely as they are a reflection of you.

Week 7 Day 5:
Structure & Change

*"Everything is dual; everything has poles; every-
thing has its pair of opposites; like and unlike are the
same; opposites are identical in nature, but different
in degree; extremes meet; all truths are but half-
truths; all paradoxes may be reconciled."*

—THE KYBALION

The second of the Polarity Needs is your need for both structure and change.

The need for structure

Structure is all about order, certainty, comfort and safety. You need to have structure in your life. From waking up in the morning to going to work, to having dinner at night and going to sleep – it's all about structure. There is comfort in knowing that the person who was your mother today is still going to be your mother tomorrow.

Having structure in your life allows stability in an ever increasingly changing world. You more than crave structure – you need it. Communication, language, logic all require structure. Your brain is designed for structure. It takes in something new and novel and categorises it so that it can easily recognise it again later. This in-built evolutionary process has aided human survival for generations and it aids your survival on a daily basis. Centuries ago when your ancestors were wearing only a fur loincloth, they quickly learnt which berries not to eat. Those who didn't learn quickly don't have any offspring around today.

Evolution is slow and this hasn't changed much today. A modern-day example is that you know to look both ways before crossing the street. This keeps you safe. Unsafe is that feeling you quickly get when you first try and cross the street in a country where people drive on the other side of the road. You've wanted to feel safe ever since you were a little one in nappies and structure gives you that feeling.

Structure provides security and in the case of earning money, most people want job security. It's tied into meeting your basic physiological needs, knowing that you can put food on the table and a roof over your head. That's why there's an increase of fear when an organisation announces a restructure. Of course, the best way of assuring your job security is to ensure that you are employable to other organisations and not just the one you're currently at. That way the security rests with you and not your boss, industry or the economy.

Having structure frees you from the need to reinvent everything, so you can focus on what's really important. In your work environment it allows you to get things done, and brings you satisfaction as a result. Having structure in your relationship with your significant other allows you to grow more intimate with that person. Structure is a need, and when it is met it brings you pleasure. To a point.

What happens when there's too much structure in your life? Think back to the Growth Cycle (Week 1 Day 1). Your behaviour becomes automated. There's no challenge, no excitement because you know *exactly* what's going to happen. You get bored!

Relationships suffer from this. It's not that a person doesn't love their partner any more, it's just that they're bored. As a result, they invest their time elsewhere, either in their work, hobbies or other interests. They may invest their time in unresourceful ventures, like drinking excessive alcohol or having an affair, anything to relieve the boredom of too much structure.

> **What Day Is It?**
> The movie *Shirley Valentine* is a story about a woman who breaks free from her very structured existence. Her lifestyle is structured to the point where Thursday means it's steak for dinner – *Every* Thursday.

Like Shirley Valentine, it takes courage and determination for you to break free from excessive structure and it may upset those around you who like and are used to such structure.

Now, we're not suggesting that you run off to Greece and have an affair (well, you could run off to Greece, that would be fun) but rather, be aware of areas in your life where you are embedded too heavily into structure. Ponder on which areas of your life you are bored with or don't feel very excited about.

People crave structure and often wrongly think it gives them more control. However, too much structure also means there's less flexibility. This can be costly in many areas. Highly structured military powers know this when they're up against a fast-moving enemy. Big business can't respond to a constantly changing environment as quickly as smaller, more agile businesses. Being flexible can actually give you more control of your life than just structure alone. If you are a highly structured individual, then chances are you often get very frustrated and let down as things don't fit neatly into your structured world.

The remedy for this of course is the polar opposite need, the need for change.

The need for change

The need for change is all about detachment, uncertainty, variety and the unknown. You need change in your life otherwise your life just becomes a repeat of the same events over and over again. Day-to-day changes in your life are a gradual process. Depending on the desired change, it can take time to see and appreciate your development.

> *"Variety's the very spice of life, that gives it all its flavour."*
>
> —WILLIAM COWPER, POET

Not Again!
Watch Bill Murray's character in the movie *Groundhog Day*. How does he use the experience of having the same day over and over again to slowly develop into a much better person?

Variety gives you pleasure. Changing your pleasures more frequently helps you to stop taking events in your life for granted. At the beginning of the New Year many people stay up to see the first sunrise and marvel at its magnificence. But rarely do people wake up on 6 June to marvel at the sunrise. Why not? It's the same sun! The same beauty. Because if we did that every day, the novelty and meaning we attach to the event dissipates.

Now this need may not always come naturally for you at first. The good news is the brain is attracted to novelty. If your brain comes across something it hasn't experienced before, it works hard to assimilate it and understand it. The bad news is, depending on the level of skill and knowledge required, your brain does quickly assimilate things and then it's not new to you any more. Knowing this, you must actively look for ways of doing things differently and having new experiences. Even if you're doing the same old, same old, you need to ask *"what else can I learn from this experience?"*, as was discussed in Peak Performance (Week 7 Day 2). It is with this creative outlook and action in dealing with change that your growth as a person is stimulated.

You need to embrace change. This doesn't mean if you're bored in your relationship you go and change your partner. It doesn't necessarily mean you go and change your job. Knowing what to change and what not to is very important and only you know the areas in your life that can do with change. It means that you look to bring variety into the areas you need it most. It may be your daily routine, your work or certain relationships in your life.

> *"Things do not change, we change."*
> —HENRY DAVID THOREAU, AUTHOR & PHILOSOPHER

Of course, like with structure, you can have too much change in your life. All the uncertainty can bring chaos to the point where you don't know whether you're coming or going. This constant change creates chaos, which results in stress. As you discovered in Stress Alignment (Week 7 Day 1), you begin to break down physically and mentally under stress. When you're under stress, you then start looking for structure in your life, things that you can count on.

People who go live in a totally foreign country understand this. At first everything is exciting and new. But after a while they often start to crave the familiar – food they're used to, people who speak their language, things and events they're comfortable with.

Often it takes a big event in your life to bring change. A heart attack may make you take more care of your health. Burnout may inspire you to go on vacation or change jobs. The death of a close friend may force you to take stock of your life. The good news is – you don't have to wait for these events to happen before you make a change. Impose the change on yourself if only for the reason that you can!

 Ultimate Reality TV

Watch *The Truman Show* to see Jim Carrey's character Truman Burbank go through the conflict of wanting structure in his life but also adventure. Pay particular attention to how a person can be controlled by those around them to live a life that isn't theirs.

The balance of structure and change

> *"When the way comes to an end, then change – having changed, you pass through."*
>
> —I CHING

Excess structure creates boredom. Excess change creates stress.
Hence you need a balance of both for harmony in your life.

There's no constant balance, as things are always in flux and different people have different preferences or comfort zones. Some people aren't happy going to work the same way two days in a row and must always go somewhere new for vacation. Other people like to have two sugars in their coffee every morning and go to the same holiday spot every year. And then there are those in the middle of these two extremes. They're the kind of person who when hiring a DVD for the night could watch either an old favourite or a new release they haven't seen before.

There's no right or wrong with any of this, where balance is for you on this continuum comes down to personal preferences. However, the key to a fulfilling life is to make an informed decision. Ensure that you've tried other options and that you're not stuck in a set routine for routine's sake. And likewise, avoid constant change for change's sake. It'll just drive you and everyone around you nuts.

These two needs may seem contradictory but they are actually complementary. They go together like night and day, and like this cycle, you need both for completeness.

And so life is about enjoying this constant flux between these two needs. As long as you realise they're not exclusive and that you can't have one without the other, then you will win this game of life and be happy.

REMEMBER:

1. You need both structure and change in your life.

2. Structure gives you security while excessive structure results in boredom.

3. Change keeps you stimulated and engaged, too much change results in stress.

Week 7 summary map:

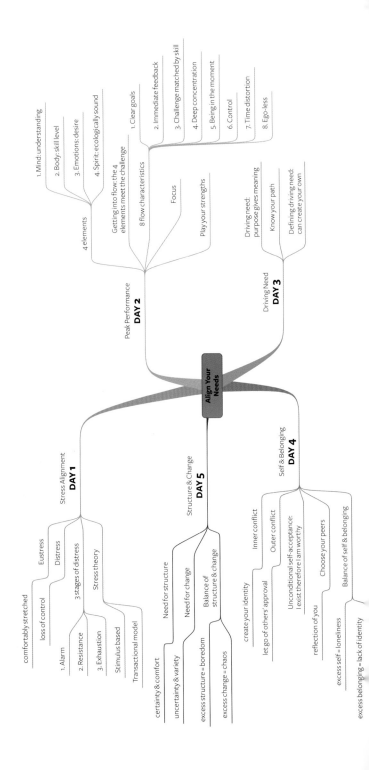

Align Your Needs

Stress Alignment — DAY 1
- comfortably stretched
  - Eustress
  - Distress
- loss of control
- 3 stages of distress
  - 1. Alarm
  - 2. Resistance
  - 3. Exhaustion
- Stress theory
  - Stimulus based
  - Transactional model

Structure & Change — DAY 5
- Need for structure
  - certainty & comfort
- Need for change
  - uncertainty & variety
- Balance of structure & change
  - excess structure = boredom
  - excess change = chaos

Peak Performance — DAY 2
- 4 elements
  - 1. Mind: understanding
  - 2. Body: skill level
  - 3. Emotions: desire
  - 4. Spirit: ecologically sound
- Getting into flow: the 4 elements meet the challenge
- 8 flow characteristics
  - 1. Clear goals
  - 2. Immediate feedback
  - 3. Challenge matched by skill
  - 4. Deep concentration
  - 5. Being in the moment
  - 6. Control
  - 7. Time distortion
  - 8. Ego-less
- Focus
- Play your strengths

Driving Need — DAY 3
- Driving need: purpose gives meaning
- Know your path
- Defining driving need: can create your own

Self & Belonging — DAY 4
- create your identity
  - Inner conflict
  - Outer conflict
- let go of others' approval
- Unconditional self-acceptance: I exist therefore I am worthy
- Choose your peers
  - reflection of you
- Balance of self & belonging
  - excess self = loneliness
  - excess belonging = lack of identity

Unleash Your Creative Mindset

Purpose

To understand how to use creative thinking to generate effective solutions.

Overview

Day 1: Detachment
Day 2: Being in the Moment
Day 3: Attunement
Day 4: Pattern Disruption
Day 5: Problem Solving

Benefits

This week's experience in the Challenge guides you to:

- flex your imagination and increase your ability to generate ideas
- break old patterns that no longer serve you
- detach from your own perspective by gaining insight and understanding of others
- learn the importance of detaching ego from your ideas
- tap into your intuition and trust your instincts
- improve your spontaneity and lateral thinking skills
- activate your innate physical genius and fine-tune your peripheral vision
- develop a deeper awareness of yourself and your surroundings
- centre yourself by being totally present
- embrace ambiguity and see how it can positively impact your life
- build on ideas and be able to give up control
- create a supportive environment to nurture creativity
- develop empathetic listening skills.

Week 8 Day 1:   Detachment

> *"The first problem for all of us men and women is not to learn, but to unlearn."*
>
> —GLORIA STEINEM, JOURNALIST AND FEMINIST ICON

Detachment is being able to let go of any attachment or fixation to process and structure, people, and environment. To be able to detach from the material and non-material. It means you are free from any addictions, preconceptions, expectations, judgements, opinions, memories and your critical inner voice. You are not held hostage to the past or future and are free from any emotional clutter.

Human beings are very suggestible, just ask any stage hypnotist! Unfortunately most people are very poor at knowing to what extent they are suggestible. The majority think they are a lot less suggestible than they really are. What you think are your thoughts and beliefs, are often in fact alien beliefs, that is thoughts and beliefs that you've inherited from other people (Beliefs: Week 6 Day 1).

Know when to let go

Social psychologist Erich Fromm wrote in his book *Beyond the Chains of Illusion*:

"Often one believes he has thought through something, that his idea is the result of his own thinking activity; the fact is that he has transferred his brain to the idols of public opinion... he believes that they express his thoughts whilst in reality he accepts their thoughts as his own... he is their slave because he has deposited his brain with them."

Detachment releases you from these set thoughts and beliefs. You are no longer trapped in a rigid mindset but able to move freely in thought and action to discover your true self.

> *"Freedom discovers the man the moment he loses concern over what impression he's making or about to make."*
>
> —BRUCE LEE, MARTIAL ARTIST & FILM STAR

Dualistic vs Synergistic thinking

Dualistic thinking is black and white thinking. It's the "either/or" mentality, one plus one equals two. You're either happy or sad, creative or uncreative, guilty or innocent. It's a too simplistic way of looking at things for the complex world we live in. A better view is a synergistic one. This is a "both/and" mentality where one plus one equals three. As you bring two parts together you create a greater whole. This synergistic way of thinking and being is evident in nature. Perhaps the ultimate example of synergy is procreation – a child results from a man and woman.

Creativity is full of paradoxes. It simultaneously involves analysis and intuition, structure and chaos, judgement and non-judgement, and thinking and non-thinking. You've probably heard the sayings, *"if it ain't broke, don't fix it"* and *"if it ain't broke, break it"*. Which one is right? They both are – depending on the circumstances. Detachment helps you detach from dualistic thinking and look from a synergistic viewpoint. Life becomes a whole lot more exciting and less complicated when you think "this *and* that" rather than "this *or* that".

When you achieve genuine detachment you basically get the hell out of your own way and achieve flow (Peak Performance: Week 7 Day 2). You will experience your true self, that pure state, on a continued basis, rather than as a one-off isolated event. It's a powerful way to live and has a major impact on your creativity and goals.

It is this state of mind that is often being credited as the source of entrepreneurial success. Entrepreneurs have learnt that detachment results in achieving great things.

EXAMPLE: Steve Jobs, the founder of Apple Computers and the IPod says:
"When we started, we didn't know what we were going to do, we didn't know what products we were going to make. All we knew was that the first commercial radiation machine was about to come to the market."

Detachment allows you that time to stop and organise your thoughts and allow neurons to connect with other neurons resulting in new ideas and strategies. With these new ideas it also pays to be detached from your ego. Your brain works incredibly quickly and can come up with many creative solutions if you just let it. You don't want to be suffering from analysis paralysis. Avoid having your self-worth tied up in your creativity. When it comes to allowing creativity to flow – lower your expectations!

"Creativity requires the courage to let go of certainties."

—ERICH FROMM, PSYCHOLOGIST

Characteristics

There are certain characteristics that go with being detached.

Embracing the unknown – Detach from what exists

It takes a lot of courage sometimes to venture into the unknown. Fear is the main deterrent for many people, as covered back in Emotional Barriers (Week 5 Day 2). People get duped into thinking that there's no risk in the known, but this is an illusion. There is comfort in the known but the security it provides can prevent your personal evolution.

Just Keep Swimming
Watch the movie *Finding Nemo* to see how the father, Marlin, experiences the fear of the unknown and what he does to overcome this.

By detaching and embracing the unknown you will allow yourself to discover newness. Of course, be practical about things too. Know at least you will have some skills to deal with what may appear.

Sailing Away
Christopher Columbus was the first person to sail the Atlantic crossing because he detached from what everyone else did. Everyone else sailed parallel to the shore whereas Columbus sailed perpendicular from the coast, leaving the safety of the shore behind him and discovered new lands.

Fluidity – Detach from rigidity

"Surrender is the most important thing you can do to bring about positive change."

—ECKHART TOLLE, SPIRITUAL TEACHER & AUTHOR

Be able to move your mind freely from one thought, element and/or industry to another. Staying rigid keeps you on the same path, whereas fluidity allows you to flow from one area to perhaps a totally unrelated area, creating a synergistic relationship between two or more areas.

Ambiguity – Detach from the obvious

Things are not always as they appear. Interpreting an experience as ambiguous, should prompt you for other interpretations. Let random elements influence your imagination and look at things from multiple perspectives. Look for what else things could mean. Don't try and have *the* right answer but look for several probabilities and then several possibilities.

Recreation / Fun – Detach from routine

Make time to relax and take away the stress of needing a good idea. You need quiet time to allow all the thoughts, concepts and ideas generated to incubate. You also need time to create new neural connections in your brain resulting in new thoughts and ideas.

> 📑 **The Peaceful Meeting**
> Emperor Hirohito of Japan was in Thailand with an itinerary jam-packed with meetings and appearances, scheduled right down to the last minute. One particular visit had the emperor and his travel party meeting with some monks from a small Buddhist temple. They were to chat for ten and a half minutes before moving on. However, the monks didn't show and the emperor was left standing alone silently in the temple. The emperor's aide who was responsible for his schedule flew into a panic and tried in vain to find the monks.
> After ten and a half minutes exactly, the emperor gave signal that it was time to carry on with his schedule. As he exited the temple, he summoned his aide and said in a quiet voice, *"Thank you. I enjoyed that appointment very much. Please schedule me another one tomorrow."*

When it comes to creative thinking, the importance of both physical and mental time out is repeated in the stories of thousands of successful people whether they be entrepreneurs, artists or sports people. In order for you to maximise your creativity, make time to have regular down time, and get away from the stress of everyday life. How you do this is up to you. It may be going for a massage, having a long soak in the bath, playing sports, watching a movie, listening to music or just getting a change of scenery.

Charles Thompson in his book *What a Great Idea 2.0* states that the most common places people have ideas are (drum roll please):

7. Exercising
6. During leisure reading
5. During boring meetings
4. Falling asleep / waking up
3. On the toilet
2. Commuting to work
1. Showering / taking a bath

> *"If your mind is empty, it is always ready for anything: it is open to everything. In the beginner's mind there are many possibilities, in the expert's mind there are few."*
>
> —SHUNRYU SUZUKI, ZEN PRIEST

Overflowing Ego

A respected university professor went to visit a famous Zen master to ask many questions about Zen. The master welcomed him into his monastery and sat down to listen to the professor and answer his questions. The professor talked for some time about his interpretation of Zen. The Zen master served some tea. He filled the professor's cup to the brim and continued to pour till it overflowed. The professor noticed that tea was spilling onto the table and couldn't refrain himself any longer.

"Stop, it's overfull," he said. *"No more will go in."*

"Precisely," said the Zen master, putting down his teapot and looking at the professor.

"Just like this cup, you are so full of your own ideas, views and opinions that there is no room for any new understanding."

Detaching from a situation also means ending the worries of past mistakes and future anxieties. You will find a great inner peace when you realise that no matter what happens to you in life, you will be all right. Your critical inner voice will become silent and you will live in the moment trusting yourself. You will achieve the freedom to be truly creative and perform at your best throughout your life.

> *"He who would be serene and pure needs but one thing, detachment."*
>
> —MEISTER ECKHART, PHILOSOPHER

Like most of the best advice, achieving a sense of peace is both simple and very difficult. All you've got to do is shut down the critical voice and live more in the present. How can you do this? By focusing your attention on the task at hand and giving up contradictory thoughts and actions.

EXAMPLE: When you eat, focus your attention on the smell and taste of the food. Don't read the paper while eating or do other activities.

EXAMPLE: When at a meeting, detach from *your* agenda and truly listen to what others have to say.

> *"When you eat, you eat; when you sleep, you sleep; when you work, you work."*
>
> —CHINESE PROVERB

As your life is composed of lots of moments strung together, living a full life means living fully in each moment. And don't worry if you find it difficult at first, it takes practice. And sure, you'll forget to do it. But when you remember to detach and be more present, do it at that moment. Know that failures are something to learn from and to use as a spring board for new opportunities. Once the decision to proceed is made then there is no need to think about success or failure. You can detach from judgement and concentrate to do your best in each moment.

REMEMBER:

1. Detachment is being able to let go of any attachment or fixation to a process or outcome.

2. You need down time in order to be at your creative best.

3. Knowing you can cope with anything in your life gives you ultimate freedom.

Week 8 Day 2:
Being in the Moment

"Life can only be found in the present moment. The past is gone, the future is not here yet, and if we do not go back to ourselves in the present moment, we cannot be in touch with life."

—THICH NHAT HANH, BUDDHIST MONK

Being in the moment is having the ability to be present without preconceived ideas and judgements. It's also known as being present and living in the now. Eckhart Tolle, spiritual teacher and author of *The Power of Now*, suggests that simply being present is enlightenment. We say, although being present may be simple, it's not easy!

If you've ever experienced the state of flow, then you've experienced being in the moment. The biggest barrier to being in the moment is the constant chatter that takes place in your mind (Inner Voice: Week 6 Day 2). This makes it very challenging and you may feel it's a state that only monks can achieve. However, you can do it. Like anything worthwhile, it just takes practice.

Being in the moment is a state of being that can help you with any challenges you have in life, whether it's to solve a problem or come up with new strategies and ways of doing things. The solution to any problem already exists – you just have to discover it. This is true creativity. Being present allows you to do this. You can seek guidance by tapping into your intuition where silent knowledge lies.

Your unconscious mind servant

Your unconscious mind is there to serve you. It constantly observes all that is going on and sends you messages. Being in the moment allows you to be more attentive to your thoughts and these messages. You can then begin to consciously observe them without judgement as they happen. You are now both the thinker of the thought and the observer of it. It's when you become conscious of these observations of your thoughts that you are being in the moment. This act is one of a higher level of consciousness as you no longer identify yourself with any problem or painful situation and therefore are more open to solutions.

Imagine you've missed the ferry that will get you to an important meeting on time.

Your critical voice pipes up as soon as you've missed it and starts you down the path of 'stinking thinking': you'll be late now, this always happens to you, you're an idiot, you shouldn't have cleared your email first, etc. Being in the moment means you start noticing these thoughts without judging them or yourself for thinking them. You simply notice that those thoughts aren't you. You are now free to choose other thoughts rather than automatically default to the old 'stinking thinking' voice in your head.

Imagine an ocean setting, the sun is shining, the water is calm and there's a slight breeze with only one or two white fluffy clouds in the sky. Suddenly a storm breaks out with dark clouds taking over the entire scene. The wind picks up intensity and disturbs the water making it unsettled. The sun, which never stops shining, is still behind the dark clouds trying to break through. The wind eventually moves the dark clouds on, leaving the sun shining with the white clouds and some time after the water settles again.

It's as if your unconscious mind is the sun. It is always there serving your best interests. Bad events like missing the ferry is the storm that brings the dark negative thoughts that overpower everything else. Your emotions, like the water, become disturbed and unsettled, causing distress. However, your unconscious mind is always sending you messages. Sometimes it takes you a long time, sometimes a short time to observe the message but when you do, like the wind, it always brings change. The negative thoughts pass, being replaced by more positive ones, and the negative emotion, although still felt, dissipates till you come into balance.

Being in the moment is a more powerful state to act as a guide for life's challenges rather than using your memory. As discussed in Neurons (Week 2 Day 3), information you store in your memory is filtered by the way you see the world, resulting in memories becoming distorted. Being in the moment allows you to notice emotions as soon as they happen without being changed by other thoughts and memories.

EXAMPLE: In the past you've dealt with missing the ferry by just waiting for the next one. If you go with what your memory tells you, you'll do this, as this is what you know. This time, however, you notice a pamphlet on water taxis and make enquiries. You find out they're not as expensive as you had imagined and make the booking that will get you to your meeting on time.

"I do not want to foresee the future. I am concerned with taking care of the present."

—MAHATMA GANDHI, SPIRITUAL LEADER

> **The Strawberry**
> A monk running for his life was being pursued by a tiger. He came to a cliff and started to climb down. Just as he grabbed hold of a branch that was growing from the cliff face, the cliff face under him gave way. Hanging on for dear life he looked down and saw another tiger at the bottom of the cliff. With a tiger behind him, and a tiger in front of him he clung even tighter to the branch.
> After a while, he noticed a strawberry vine growing alongside the branch and at the end of the vine was a giant strawberry. The monk plucked the strawberry and popped it into his mouth. As he enjoyed the succulent flavour of the strawberry, he didn't even notice the tigers tire of waiting for him to fall, and leave.

The past is gone and the future hasn't happened yet so all the solutions to life's problems exist in the moment that is now. Now is the best time for you to do what's right for you, to make the start on the things you've procrastinated on in the past. You know this. You don't need us to tell you, but here's a little handy saying you can remember to keep you on track:

There are only two moments in life: NOW and TOO LATE!

> **Cliff Says...**
> *It's a little known fact that...* an aeroplane pilot can fly up to 95% of the time off course.

The take-off point and landing destination are as planned, but the journey is constantly being evaluated to make sure the best course is taken. This is exactly the same as a successful person achieving their goals. Being in the moment allows you to make the necessary adjustments to the continually changing circumstances until your desired destination is reached.

Intuition

> *"The only really valuable thing is intuition."*
> —ALBERT EINSTEIN, PHYSICIST

One of the major benefits of being in the moment is that it allows you to tap into your intuition. Intuition is *"knowledge from within"*; direct knowledge that hasn't been analysed or reasoned. It begins with self-awareness and then integrates with awareness of your surrounding environment combining to make sense of a situation. When you combine intuition with reason and logic, it creates a fertile new ground for perception and thinking.

Characteristics

In order to be in the moment and tap into your intuition you need to be living certain characteristics.

Being open

You need to have an openness both mentally and physically to go wherever the creative journey may take you. Your mind and body are two parts of one system and you cannot change one without having an effect on the other, therefore both must be open. Open yourself up to new experiences, be open to what people are and aren't saying to you, look for what is new, what you could learn, and what you could attempt.

Paying attention / Being observant

Intuition and creativity require an attentive state. If you pay attention and observe without being fixated, then you can discover good ideas rather than trying to invent them, by being in your head, shut off to everything around you. Start looking at stimuli in your environment with fresh eyes. Everything is an opportunity, you just need to look at things in a different way.

Remember:

Stimulus   Space   Response

You choose your response to every situation. So start asking the kinds of questions that serve you: How can this help me? What are the benefits in this? Look for the positive and the learnings and you shall find them.

Spontaneity

Being spontaneous is being free from the past and not worrying about the future. Be present and you will be amazed at what creative forces come to you.

Relaxed alertness

Like a top performance athlete, you need to be relaxed and alert. That way, you're not in your head looking to prejudge situations or people and instead, are alert to discover everything around you. Relaxed alertness allows you to be present, whereas a stressful state has a narrowing impact on the mind and body and your reaction time is considerably less.

"Intuition is the function that explores the unknown, senses possibilities and implications which may not be readily apparent."

CARL JUNG, PSYCHIATRIST

Trust your inner voice when it is working positively for you. Go with your instincts and refrain from logic alone ruling you. Your mind and body have years of different experiences, so tap into this knowledge.

> **Cliff Says...**
> *It's a little known fact that...* research on intuitive decision making in business, found executives of the companies that more than doubled profits had a far higher intuitive ability based on predictive testing. The research also found dynamic people who got more done in a day had a far higher intuitive score.

> *"Creative people have much more confidence in their imaginative leaps, their intuition."*
> —LAUREL CUTLER, ADVERTISING EXECUTIVE

Okay, so you may be thinking, it's all well and good to say "be more intuitive". But how do you go about it?

Here's how (and remember, like anything it takes practice):

HOW TO ACCESS YOUR INTUITION	HOW NOT TO ACCESS YOUR INTUITION
Be still and centred	Be in turmoil and stressed
Be open and receptive	Be closed off mentally and physically
Be in a quiet space	Be in a noisy place
Believe you will receive guidance	Believe your inner voice knows nothing
Receive emotional and sensory info	Receive words only
Pick up subtle cues	Expect a neon sign accompanied solution
Practise!	Expect right answers first time, every time

How will I know if I'm being intuitive?

The language of intuition is emotional and sensory, so when you receive inner guidance there are certain feelings that accompany it, such as a deep sense of calmness, clarity and detachment. If you believe your intuition is telling you something and it makes you excited or agitated then chances are it's wishful thinking or you've projected your personal needs onto the situation.

> *"Intuition is a constantly evolving, fluid state of awareness that's always adapting to meet our present needs."*
> —J. DONALD WALTERS, AUTHOR & SPIRITUAL TEACHER

More Than Just An Itch

One of our workout participants told us that practising the intuition tool benefited him in making an incredibly hard decision. He had been in a relationship for seven years but didn't feel fulfilled. Although he still had feelings of love for his partner, he felt they had drifted apart and were no longer compatible. He'd tried to break up before but they had got back together for the wrong reasons.

On prasticing the intuition exercise he eventually used it for seeking inner guidance on what to do with his relationship. He told us:

"I just knew. I didn't know how I knew, but I just knew. The funny thing was I didn't feel relieved, excited, or even upset. I was calm. I knew it was the right thing to do and that everything would be all right."

This feeling of not knowing how you know is understandable. Intuition is non-rational, non-linear and non-data based.

How does it work?

Your brain is always taking in information and figuring out what works for you and what doesn't. This learning takes place in the more primitive parts of your brain such as the brain stem (Brain Map: Week 2 Day 1) and emotional brain (Week 2 Day 2). Therefore many of life's learnings aren't represented by words and logical thought but rather by feelings.

Cliff Says...

It's a little known fact that... the emotional brain activates circuitry from the limbic system that runs along the gastrointestinal tract resulting in literally, a gut feeling.

There are four main ways of receiving intuitive signals:

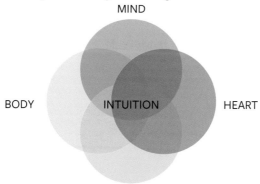

MIND (mental)	Eg: Eureka or Aha effect, pieces of a problem fitting together
BODY (physical)	Eg: Gut feelings, hairs rising on neck, tension headache, tingling sensations
HEART (emotional)	Eg: Immediate like or dislike, sudden change of mood without logical provocation
SPIRIT (spiritual)	Eg: Satori (enlightenment), awareness of a connection beyond the material world

Intuition is an extension of your five senses. Some people have a more dominant sense when it comes to intuition. Get to know yours. For Einstein, he felt a tingling sensation in his finger. For you, it may be a gut feeling or a vision, or something that just sounds right to you.

> **Cliff Says...**
> *It's a little known fact that...* intuition is neither feminine nor masculine. It's equally present in both genders although often in different areas. Generally speaking, women tend to be more intuitive in their understanding of people while men tend to be more intuitive in their work.

Asking intuitive questions

> *"Intuition will tell the thinking mind where to look next."*
>
> —JONAS SALK, PHYSICIAN & RESEARCHER

There are two key points when it comes to asking yourself the right kind of intuitive question:

1. Be specific.
Right question: Is company X a good company to work for?
Rather than: Will I be happy working for company X?

2. Ask simple rather than compounding questions.
Right question: Shall I take the new job offer?
Rather than: Shall I take the new job offer and look for a promotion within the year?

A question properly phrased is half answered as it shows you have an understanding of what you are asking and can reveal much of the answer. Poorly phrased questions are ambiguous and can be interpreted in more ways than one. So be careful what you ask for, as you may just get it.

In ancient Greece a powerful ruler was going to invade an enemy kingdom so he consulted the Oracle at Delphi whether a great battle would be won. The Oracle responded that indeed a great battle would be won.

The Oracle was correct; the battle was won. Unfortunately for the king, it was his rival who was victorious.

Now, if the king knew what you now know about asking the right kind of intuitive questions, he may have asked the Oracle something along the lines of *"will I be victorious in the great battle?"*.

> *"I have so much to do today that I must meditate twice as long."*
>
> —MAHATMA GANDHI, SPIRITUAL LEADER

Some people have said that with today's busy pace of life, they don't have time to slow down and listen to their intuition. It's more of a case they don't have time *not* to. What are your choices? You can choose moments to slow down and tap into your wealth of knowledge and make the best choice for you. *Or* you can rush rush rush and then spend a whole lot of time making up for mistakes that could have been avoided.

On some level, you know this makes sense. If you're not sure this is true, what does your gut tell you?

REMEMBER:

1. Being in the moment is a way of being that opens doors of opportunity for you.

2. You have access to a wealth of knowledge; silent, direct knowledge that you can tap into anytime.

3. Intuition takes a little bit of dedicated practice to access, but it's there for you.

Week 8 Day 3:   Attunement

"When you seek to understand through attunement,
you bring unconscious knowledge to the conscious."
—STEVE HILL, MIND WARRIORS CO-FOUNDER

Attunement is bringing yourself into harmony with your surrounding environment, tuning into yourself and experiencing a feeling of being at one with another person or group of people. This helps you understand what exists, to recognise patterns, and gain a systemic overview of your world. This overview is essential when exploring possibilities for change as it tells you what is there, what gaps, associations and replication there may be, and gives you relevant information for whatever it is you wish to achieve.

Attunement involves more than just your visual sense

> **Check mate!**
> On 11 May 1997, IBM's Deep Blue computer beat Chess grandmaster Gary Kasparov. The Deep Blue team had analysed many of Kasparov's matches and programmed the computer accordingly. The Deep Blue team knew that by tuning into Kasparov and recognising his patterns they would have a greater chance of defeating him.

Attunement is a natural tendency which involves at least two separate things moving, operating and working at exactly the same rate together.

EXAMPLE: World Ice Dancing Champions Jayne Torvill and Christopher Dean took attunement to new heights with their gold medal winning skate at the 1984 Winter Olympics. They earned unanimous 6.0s for presentation, the world's first ever perfect score.

UNLEASH YOUR CREATIVE MINDSET

Entrainment

When attunement happens in nature it's called entrainment. This is the process where systems come into alignment, often spontaneously. This was first recorded in 1665 when Dutch physicist Christiaan Huygens noticed that the two pendulum clocks on his wall always swung so that each pendulum was precisely opposite each other. Even if he intervened and disturbed the rhythm, the pendulums always synchronised the same way.

EXAMPLE: The human heart consists of over 10,000 pacemaker cells. These cells trigger the rest of the heart to beat properly. If these cells don't have the same rhythm as each other, the heart stops. By sending electrical currents to each other, your pacemaker cells communicate to keep your cardiovascular system functioning.

> **Cliff Says...**
> It's a little known fact that... geese fly 70% more efficiently by entraining to the leader's flight tempo.

Attunement is something that you can make a *conscious* effort to do. When you are attuned, you are aware of everything around you all the time, rather than just acting out of habit. Successful people are able to tune in and understand other people's perspectives. This doesn't mean they necessarily sacrifice their own views, but they are more able to truly listen and understand other viewpoints.

> **The Horse Whisperer**
> The movie *The Horse Whisperer* features Robert Redford as a horse trainer with a talent for understanding horses. He is able to tune in and be empathetic to the horse's needs, motives and desires, and achieves win/win results.

Characteristics

It is easier to achieve attunement when you follow these characteristics:

Pattern awareness / association

The brain is a self-organising system that creates patterns through association. Patterns are made up of how you interpret people and events around you and the meaning you associate with those people/events. Pattern awareness within yourself is a major part of attunement. Being aware of your habitual thoughts, patterns in your behaviours, emotional states and your environment is the first step to creating significant change. You need to know where you are and how things work before you look at where you want to be and how you're going to get there.

Rapport

Rapport is the ability to attune to others. The best way to achieve this is to genuinely give your attention to people. This allows you to tune into other people's perceptions and see from their point of view. When in rapport, you can combine your imagination and life experience with another person's to create a third mind, which dramatically increases your opportunity of finding a creative solution.

Complementarity

Think *"what goes with that?"* rather than copying what exists. This can be challenging because from a young age you learn by copying. You learnt to walk and talk by copying others. Look for a complementary idea/action. Beethoven asked what instruments go with a piece of music or Monet asked what colours go with each other. You will create a richer life for yourself by thinking in complementary terms.

Being supportive

Ideas need to be nurtured in a supportive environment. Rather than *"No, because"*, a *"Yes, and"* attitude is required. Creativity blooms with a positive outlook and withers in negativity. For ideas to be built upon each other you need to be positive and always looking for the positive. A high trust element is crucial for those working in the creative realm.

Types of pattern formation

Your brain is a self-organising system that actively seeks patterns to make sense of the world around you. It perceives patterns in different ways:

1. **Filling in** incomplete patterns
2. **Finding** a desired pattern often embedded in distracting surroundings
3. **Categorising** information into appropriate divisions
4. **Sequencing** the next part of the pattern

Imagine you are researching a project. You may look at what information you have and notice any gaps that require you to source the missing parts (filling in). You notice certain trends from that information (finding). You sort the information in appropriate ways so that the information is of use to you (categorising). From the information you can now identify what the past stages have been and where the future stages lie (sequencing).

> *"The capacity for delight is the gift of paying attention."*
>
> —JULIA CAMERON, AUTHOR & POET

> ### 📖 The Three Secrets of Life
>
> A businessman had heard that on a faraway mountain lived a Zen master who knew the three secrets of life. He had also heard that anyone could obtain these secrets and as a result one would know everything they needed to live a happy and fulfilling life. The businessman felt he had no purpose in life and spent many hours pondering what these secrets might be. What words could possibly answer all of life's problems and guarantee a constant feeling of well-being? Determined to find the answer he quit his job and began his search of this Zen master.
>
> Some time later he arrived at the right temple at the top of the right mountain. There, sitting in the centre, was the Zen master he had heard about.
>
> The man approached the master and bowing low said, *"Master, I have travelled a long distance and sacrificed much to find out the three secrets that will lead me to live a happy and fulfilling life. Please share those secrets with me."*
>
> The master bowed in return and said, *"Yes, I will tell you. The first secret is to pay attention. The second secret is to pay attention. And the final secret is to pay attention."*

How is that story for you? Did you feel cheated by the ending? Don't fret, if you want to know the secret of life, we'll tell you. You ready? Here it is:

The secret of life is that there is no secret!

Think about what the Zen master said. What does it mean to pay attention? What are you paying attention to? Are you attuned to your feelings, your thinking styles, your senses, your dreams, other people's perspectives, resources available to you, the strategies you use, the surrounding environment? So tune into what exists and remember...

Energy flows where attention goes.

"The answer to any problem pre-exists. We need to ask the right questions to reveal the answer."
—JONAS SALK, PHYSICIAN & RESEARCHER

Attuning yourself to your world will result in a new way of life in which you slow down. You will find yourself becoming more productive, efficient and energetic and able to focus on the task at hand without distraction.

Inner vs Outer awareness

The art of attunement requires that you do two things, both focus your attention and extend your attention. How can you do this seemingly contradictary action simultaneously? Here, we look to the arts for guidance. A good actor is totally in the moment, focused on what she's doing and yet also aware of everything around her, her next

UNLEASH YOUR CREATIVE MINDSET

235

movements, the end of the stage, her fellow actors, and the audience. In traditional martial arts, they practise Zanshin. It is having the awareness and control of one's surroundings while being completely focused. You can achieve this by being relaxed and defocusing your eyes slightly so you perceive more of what's going on around you, rather than becoming trapped in tunnel vision. It results in the relaxed alertness state described in Being in the Moment (Week 8 Day 2).

> **100% Each Way**
> A student once asked his Tai Chi master, *"What percentage of awareness should be given to the inner and what percentage to the outer?"* The master replied, *"Yes, 100% inner, 100% outer."*

> *"Leaders must be occupied with both their exterior and interior worlds. One cannot become preoccupied with one at the expense of the other."*
> —ED SELLNER, AUTHOR & TEACHER

Before anything new can be created or any problem solved it's important to take the time to attune yourself to the many possible areas that may be affected by your venture. When you have an intention to make a change, learn a new skill or take on a challenge, attunement will give you a better understanding of what may be involved.

When looking to achieve a goal you need to develop your attunement skills, as it's very challenging to reach your goal if you don't know from where you're starting.

There are three areas of exploration to consider:

1. **You**	– Identify the different parts of you – thoughts, emotions, behaviours, beliefs, values, capabilities
2. **Environment**	– Identify people, resources and sensory stimuli
3. **Strategies**	– Identify the strategies, processes and tools

1. You

This is taking into account your thoughts, emotions, behaviours, beliefs, values, knowledge, desires, needs, and capabilities. This is what you've been doing so far on this Challenge.

2. Environment

Your environment is made up of people, resources and sensory stimuli. Attunement is about identifying people who can help you achieve your desired level of success. It may be people you come into direct contact with, such as family members, friends, mentors, acquaintances, work colleagues, or indirect contact through books or the internet.

Are there people you could seek advice from or model yourself on? Modelling (Week 4 Day 5) yourself on successful people requires attunement into their behaviours and strategies.

As was discussed in Self & Belonging (Week 7 Day 4), be aware of who you spend the majority of your time with as your peer group is a reflection of you. Are these the people who are going to support you and help get you to where you want to go? You need people around you who are going to stretch you and who live or are trying to live at the same level you wish to.

 Educate yourself!

In the movie *Educating Rita*, Julie Walters plays a hairdresser who wants to better herself by studying literature. She is encouraged by her professor who is played by Michael Caine. She recognises she wants more for herself than her husband does, who just wants her pregnant and to stay at home. In order to fulfil her needs she has to part ways with her husband. It's upsetting for her at the time but in the long run they are both better off and he later finds his ideal partner.

Look around you. What's in your environment that can help you achieve your goals? What's missing? What environments do you need to be involved in to help you succeed? Is your environment conducive to creativity (Overcoming External Barriers: Week 1 Day 4)? How can you use sensory stimuli to aid you in your journey?

"Originality is simply a pair of fresh eyes."
—THOMAS WENTWORTH HIGGINSON, SOLDIER & AUTHOR

3. Strategies

Strategies include all the structures, processes, systems, and tools you have available to you that may help you achieve your desired outcomes. Successful people follow patterns of success. Unsuccessful people have the wrong strategies. What are your current strategies? What are you doing now that is taking you to your aim of living a fulfilled life? What aren't you doing that will take you to where you want to be?

Remember, probably at some level:

You know what to do, you just aren't doing what you know!

"When searching for a needle in a haystack, other people quit when they find the needle. I look for what other needles might be in the haystack."
—ALBERT EINSTEIN, PHYSICIST

Attunement is taking stock of where you are, what you're doing and how you're doing it. It is to look at your life with fresh eyes rather than just living by rote. Rather than simply being satisfied with what you're currently doing, look for patterns, gaps and other strategies that may serve you.

REMEMBER:

1. Attunement is a natural process that's enhanced with conscious effort.

2. Being relaxed and paying attention helps you to attune to your patterns.

3. Become aware of your whole world; You, your Environment and your Strategies (YES).

Week 8 Day 4: Pattern Disruption

"The definition of insanity is doing the same thing over and over and expecting a different result."

—BENJAMIN FRANKLIN, POLYMATH

Pattern disruption is simply that – disrupting your normal thought, emotional, behavioural and environmental patterns. First you need to know the patterns (Attunement: Week 8 Day 3) before you can disrupt them. The creative person uses tools and techniques to disrupt their normal patterns of behaviour and thinking in order to perceive new ways of doing things.

> **Cliff Says...**
> *It's a little known fact that...* your brain has approximately 60,000 thoughts a day.
> The scary thing is 95% of those thoughts you had today, you will have tomorrow. Multiply this by 7 days for the week, then by 52 weeks for the year and finally by your age and you have got some serious brainwashing! The question is – are you washing yourself with positive stuff?

PATTERN DISRUPTION

You already know that the brain is a pattern-making machine (Neurons: Week 2 Day 3) and that your mind is very good at recognising sequences, cycles, shapes, processes, similarities and probabilities. As you discovered in Week 2, patterns aren't necessarily bad, but a common problem is that because of the way your brain functions you become locked into one particular approach, method or strategy without acknowledging that other approaches may be more appropriate.

BREAK FREE! MAKE NEW CONNECTIONS

Rebel Rebel

An experiment was carried out where five monkeys were put into a cage with a hole at the top. Above this hole was a bunch of bananas that the monkeys could grab, except there was a sensor at the top of the cage. The cage was hooked up to a high-powered hose that would go off whenever one of the monkeys put their hand through the hole going for the bananas. The monkeys quickly learnt not to go for the bananas.

The scientists then disconnected the hose and sensor and replaced one of the monkeys in the cage with another monkey. This new monkey saw the bananas and went for them. The other monkeys beat the new monkey down until he stopped going for the bananas.

The scientists then replaced another original monkey with a second new monkey. This monkey also went for the bananas. The other monkeys, including the one who had never experienced the high-powered hose, beat this monkey too.

The scientists continued to replace the old monkeys with new ones until there were five monkeys who had never experienced the water blasts yet were conditioned not to go for the bananas.

Then the scientists added another monkey to the cage. This monkey was big and strong. When this monkey saw the bananas he went straight for them. The five other monkeys did what they'd always done, they went to beat down this monkey. However, this monkey rebelled. He fought back. He had a thick skin and could take their beatings and was still strong enough to power through to grab the bananas. He started to eat the bananas while the other monkeys looked on. Slowly but surely the other monkeys also started to eat the bananas.

Your challenge in life is to be the rebel monkey. Be strong and go for what you want. It may mean going against the norm. It may mean you take a "beating" from some people, but just like the monkeys, they don't know any better. They are not you, so remain positively self-centred and do what you need to do.

> *"If you don't like change, you're going to like irrelevance even less."*
> —ERIC SHINSEKI, RETIRED SOLDIER AND POLITICIAN

Caged monkey effect

You often go through this process:

1. You make rules based upon reasons that make sense.
2. You follow the rules.
3. Time passes and things change.
4. The original reasons for these rules are no longer in place, yet you continue to follow them.

> **Cliff Says...**
> It's a little known fact that... in the 1870s the keys of the typewriters of the day would stick together if the typists typed too fast. The solution to this challenge was to slow the typists down by rearranging the letters on the keyboard so that the most frequently used ones were now in positions that needed the typist's weakest fingers to depress them. The arrangement known as *qwerty* (because it's the first six letters of the standard keyboard) still exists today, even though keys interfering with each other and jamming no longer pose a challenge.

Resistance and judgement may come from within, so courage is required to be yourself.

> *"All truth passes through three stages. First, it is ridiculed. Second, it is violently opposed. Third, it is accepted as being self-evident."*
>
> —ARTHUR SCHOPENHAUER, PHILOSOPHER

Unfortunately, there is often a fourth stage to Schopenhauer's stages. It's when those not accepting the new truth are ridiculed. Hence, truth comes full circle.

Creative thinking involves not only generating new ideas, but escaping from obsolete ones as well. That's why it's important to periodically tune in to your ideas and beliefs to see if they are habit-bound and still contributing to the effectiveness of your thinking. Ask yourself, *"Why did this idea/belief/concept/project come to exist?"* Then check, *"Do these reasons still exist?"*

> *"We can easily forgive a child who is afraid of the dark; the real tragedy is when men are afraid of the light."*
>
> —PLATO, PHILOSOPHER

Disruption through pattern seeking

On a rudimentary level you discover everything by recognising common features. Perception itself is an active pattern-seeking process. Your brain has a highly developed ability to instinctively find meaning in the world around you, and will always try to close an incomplete picture by finding a desired pattern in its surrounding.

Think of the Rorschach inkblot test used by psychotherapists to discover the unconscious interests of their patients, by analysing how they interpret visual patterns.

Develop your natural pattern-seeking and analytical abilities and you will find more creative solutions to any challenges in your life. If you consider yourself a details person who chunks things down, then practise chunking up (Chunking: Week 4 Day 4) to see the bigger picture and view it in a different light.

Creative thinking is a process of identifying relationships and reorganising them until a new idea is perceived. Many popular creativity tools are based on this process such as random words, analogies, alternative viewpoints and combining concepts.

> *"A wonderful harmony arises from joining together the seemingly unconnected."*
> —HERACLITUS, PHILOSOPHER

The pattern that you perceive in a problem is strongly influenced by the way you attempt to solve the problem. The stereotyped thinker works with the first pattern that he sees, almost invariably a conventional one. The creative thinker re-centres his perception of the same problem by disrupting the original pattern and regrouping it into a variety of patterns.

Imagine your problem is that you have trouble making time to exercise daily. Your conventional method of attacking the problem is to try and fit it into your daily schedule but work is too busy and there just don't seem to be enough hours in the day. By asking, *"How can I exercise without exercising?"*, you come up with the idea of exercising at work. By simply replacing your chair with a Swiss ball you now spend hours engaging your abdominal, back and leg muscles keeping a proper posture, while sitting at your desk.

> **Cliff Says...**
> *It's a little known fact that...* the philosopher Aristotle believed that the individual who had the capacity to perceive resemblances between two separate areas of existence and link them together was a person of special gifts.

> *"Creativity involves breaking out of established patterns in order to look at things in a different way."*
> —EDWARD DE BONO, AUTHOR

> **Reflective Thinking**
> There were complaints about how long the lifts took in some high-rise buildings. The standard way of solving this problem would be to look at how the lifts could be sped up. However, a more creative and far cheaper solution was found.
> They simply put mirrors on the walls of the lifts. This gave people something to do in the lift, rather than stand there in silence. Brilliant!

Patterns can have a low impact or a high impact on your life. Remember: Not all patterns are bad, as you will have good patterns that bring you success. However, chances are, you have patterns that are unhelpful. As you've explored in Week 6, these thought and behavioural patterns are a result of your values and beliefs.

High- vs Low-impact patterns

The following are examples of potential high- and low-impact thought and behavioural patterns.

A. Low-impact thought patterns:
1. You think a little bit of chocolate won't harm you.
2. You think, given their performance, the All Blacks will win the tournament.
3. You think talkback radio is boring.

B. High-impact thought patterns:
1. You think you are uncreative because you are not good at art.
2. You think money is the root of all evil.
3. You think people are generally kind and generous.

C. Low-impact behavioural patterns:
1. You drive the same way to work every day.
2. You sleep on the same side of the bed every night.
3. You put your sock on your left foot first.

D. High-impact behavioural patterns:
1. You smoke a cigarette after dinner.
2. You become inconsolable when you think of someone close to you who has died.
3. You get defensive when your partner criticises you.

As is the microcosm, so is the macrocosm

Challenging your low-impact patterns is a good place to start positive change in your life.

Challenging the status quo is something you must actively do. By challenging the status quo and disrupting your thought and behavioural patterns you may start to develop new beliefs, which results in new thoughts and behaviours that serve you in your personal quest.

REMEMBER:

1. Generate new ideas and disrupt patterns that no longer serve you.

2. Expect to come up against resistance from various quarters, including within, as you make changes in your life.

3. Your brain is a patterning device, so you need to consciously challenge the status quo.

Week 8 Day 5: Problem Solving

> *"We cannot solve our problems with the same level of thinking that created them."*
>
> —ALBERT EINSTEIN, PHYSICIST

Imagination is your most valuable tool when it comes to solving the problems and challenges in your life, whether it's at home or work. It doesn't matter what the problem/challenge may be, you need to bring a fresh perspective to it. However, in order to get the most from the opportunity provided by a challenge, it is worth learning the problem-solving process. This process breaks down problems into stages, each stage having a different set of mental skills and tools.

> **Cliff Says...**
> *It's a little known fact that...* the Chinese symbol for crisis is composed of the symbols for danger and opportunity. Problems contain both negative and positive aspects. Consider your problems as opportunities and you are likely to seek the best solutions.
>
> 危
> 機

Two types of problem solving

There are two types of problem solving, proactive (prevention) and reactive (fire-fighting).

> *"The intellect solves the problem, the genius prevents them."*
>
> —ALBERT EINSTEIN, PHYSICIST

Proactive problem solving is when you identify opportunities for improvements or potential problems before they actually exist. This is when you *want* to think.

EXAMPLE: Things might be going well at work but you ask yourself, *"How might I speed up this particular process?"*

Reactive problem solving is when the problem already exists and is causing you strife. This is when you *have* to think.

EXAMPLE: You've got low morale within your team and need to create a solution to lift staff engagement.

Watch the movie *Apollo 13* for a good example of a fire-fighting problem. What mindset did the crew have and what actions did they take to solve the problem?

Cliff Says...

It's a little known fact that... the actual quote made by the Apollo 13 Command Module pilot was: *"Okay, Houston, we've had a problem here"* with Commander Lovell then adding, "Houston, we've had a problem." In the movie, however, using the present tense made it more exciting.

Process overview

The following process is relevant for both types of problem solving. It is divided into three distinct stages:

Stage 1
PROBLEM FINDING
1. Identify & define the problem
know what it is you're trying to solve
2. Knowledge acquisition
gather the facts on your problem

Stage 2
SOLUTION EXPLORATION
1. Idea generation
create as many solutions as possible
2. Evaluating & decision making
sort out which solutions are the best ones

Stage 3
SOLUTION IMPLEMENTATION
1. Planning & ecology check
planning your action steps, checking that it'll work and is an overall positive change
2. Implementation & review
taking action and monitoring progress

Your end-result solution will invariably lead you to more challenges, hence the ongoing nature of this process.

Stage 1: Problem finding

> *"A problem well stated is a problem half solved."*
> —JOHN DEWEY, PHILOSOPHER & PSYCHOLOGIST

Identify & define the problem

The first part of this stage is to identify and define the problem. Usually when it comes to looking at problems, people look at them in isolation, skimming over the big picture. Assumptions are often made or relied upon, which result in you putting all your creative energy into solving the wrong problem.

Imagine your problem is that you've been hit with a large unexpected dental bill and now don't have enough money to make ends meet for the month. Your first thoughts may be focused around where you can cut down on your spending. This carries with it the inherent assumption that your income is limited, so you don't really consider options of how to increase it instead. Or if you do, it isn't given much thought.

> **Farmer's Gift**
> A farmer in the United States had neighbours whose dogs were killing his sheep. Traditionally farmers dealt with this problem with lawsuits, barbed wire fences or shotguns. This farmer asked himself a different question. He framed his question, not *"How can I stop my neighbour's dogs from killing my sheep?"* but rather, *"How can I get these people to help me protect my sheep?"*
> His solution? He gave his neighbour's children lambs as pets. The neighbours then voluntarily tied their dogs up. In the process, the families became friends.

> *"Sometimes it is only a change in viewpoint that is needed to convert a seemingly tiresome duty into an interesting opportunity."*
> —ALBERTA FLANDERS, SINGER

Problem statement

When you start exploring your problem you need to identify and select a starting point. This is your problem statement. Looking at the bigger picture gives you many possible opportunities, although your problem/challenge/opportunity may initially seem rather broad and general.

Taking the example of not having enough money, you now might look at both increasing income and decreasing expenditure. It's wise to summarise the key points, and to synthesise and integrate ideas to gain focus on the different areas that make up your problem.

You might come up with ideas such as:

INCREASING $$	DECREASING $$
Ask for a raise	Ask for a rent reduction
Ask for an advance	Ask for a rent extension
Sell your surplus belongings on Trade Me	Reduce any surplus outgoings
Temporary second job	Find out which creditors will wait
Temporary overdraft	Car pool
Borrow from a family member	Refinance mortgage
Take on a foreign student	Bargain hunt

"A prudent question is one half of wisdom."
—FRANCIS BACON, PHILOSOPHER & STATESMAN

Ultimately, problem solving begins with a question. The way a problem is stated has a powerful impact upon your ability to stimulate solutions. So you need to check that you've come up with an effective problem statement that will focus your attention on your current reality and the gaps between that and your desired future.

Ensure your problem statement:
- has an invitational opener at the start. This invites you (and others) to open up your mind to think of possible solutions. Eg: *"How might I..."* or *"In what ways could we...?"*
- identifies the owner. Is it your problem, the team's problem, someone else's problem?

Effective problem statement: *"How can I make ends meet this month?"*
This opens you to the bigger picture and to explore all different areas.

Limited problem statement: *"How can I reduce my expenses?"*
This statement creates a narrow focus for your attention and shuts down your brain to all the options of increasing your income.

> **Cliff Says...**
> *It's a little known fact that...* Leonardo da Vinci believed that, to gain knowledge about the form of a problem, you begin by learning how to restructure it in many different ways. He felt that the first way he looked at a problem was too biased. Often, when the problem itself is reconstructed it becomes a new one.

Knowledge acquisition

> *"Get the facts, or the facts will get you. And when you get them, get them right, or they will get you wrong."*
>
> —THOMAS FULLER, CHURCHMAN & HISTORIAN

The second part of the problem finding stage is to get all the necessary facts. There are a variety of tools at your disposal that you've already covered so far in this challenge:

- The YES Chart (Attunement: Week 8 Day 3) can help you consider all the relevant information.
- Chunking (Week 4 Day 4). Both chunking up and down can give you a new perspective.
- Pattern Disruption (Week 8 Day 4). Look for assumptions in your fact-finding and challenge them.

Now that you've defined your problem and have all the necessary data, you're ready to move into Stage 2.

Stage 2: Solution exploration

> *"The best way to have a good idea is to have lots of ideas."*
>
> —LINUS PAULING, BIOCHEMIST

Idea generation

Idea generation is simply a numbers game and it's about quantity not quality. You don't want to have just practical ideas so you must suspend logic, reason and judgement. Don't worry, logic, reason and judgement will come into the picture but its place in the process is later on – not here!

> *"If at first the idea is not absurd, then there is no hope for it."*
>
> —ALBERT EINSTEIN, PHYSICIST

Think of your idea as a newborn baby. It needs lots of care, nurturing and a supportive environment to survive. The whole purpose of the idea-generation stage is to move away from the known, to broaden your horizons and explore new perspectives.

Divergent thinking

In order to be creative, you need to be mentally flexible, adaptive and prepared to rearrange your thinking style.

The main form of thinking used throughout this part of the process is divergent (lateral) thinking. This type of thinking starts from your problem statement and moves outward into a variety of perspectives. It allows you to come up with a number of responses and produce several different ideas. You must have different ways of generating possible solutions, otherwise you run the risk of falling into the single-mindedness trap.

> *"He that is good with the hammer tends to think everything is a nail."*
>
> —ABRAHAM MASLOW, PSYCHOLOGIST

It is at this stage of the process that you must embrace each of the characteristics of the four principles of creativity:

1. **Detachment**
2. **Being in the moment**
3. **Attunement**
4. **Pattern disruption**

This way you'll be able to generate many options by combining old ideas to create new ones, adding details, looking at the opposites, taking on new perspectives and more. When it comes to generating ideas, remember:

Quantity not quality!

A common pitfall at this stage of the process is trying to have good ideas or ideas that are practical and that could work. Don't fall into this trap. You need to explore *all* areas as the wild and crazy idea just might hold the essence of what's required to solve your problem.

Evaluation & decision making

Convergent thinking

The next part of the problem-solving process involves evaluating all the different ideas you've generated and deciding which are the ones that you'll take action on. This involves a different thinking style again, one of convergent (vertical) thinking. This is where you bring all those thoughts from different directions into a union or common conclusion. You categorise, analyse, improve and refine your ideas by using appropriate criteria and tools.

Don't dismiss the "out there" ideas. Consider what parts of them could be relevant to your problem. On the other hand, when it comes to selecting a solution, be aware not to jump to conclusions based upon a single criteria. Effective solution finding requires clear and explicit criteria and you may take into consideration things like time, cost, feasibility, your values, other people, material required, etc.

Stage **3**: Solution implementation

"If you're failing to plan, then you're planning to fail."
—SOME CLEVER BUNNY

Planning & ecology check

Solution implementation takes the idea you've selected as the best one and turns it into reality. So the first part of this stage is to plan the solution implementation and then check that it's going to work. You can save a lot of time, money and heartache by doing this part of the process properly. If the idea doesn't work, you want to find out as soon as possible so that you're not wasting precious time and resources on a bad choice. Set a time to review your solution once it's implemented.

> ### Thank You Very Much for Your Kind Donation
> A JOLT Challenge trainer, in a previous life had wanted to set up an art space that brought together different artists and create a community of creative spirits. However, he had no money of his own to do this.
> He explored his problem of having no money, no venue, and took his idea through the problem-solving process. He eventually went to a wealthy individual who was interested in creativity and got start-up funding. Through perseverance he achieved his goal and was richly rewarded in many ways as a result of it.

By being clear on the end point, you can now work out the steps involved in getting there. Identify the people, places, objects, times, reasons and actions that might help or hinder your implementation. By anticipating the likely and possible problems that may arise, such as who would resist this idea and what might they say, you can prepare your responses and actions that keep your solution alive and well.

You need to sell your idea to the people it's going to affect, whether it's your boss, your significant other or yourself! If you don't promote your idea and get the required buy-in, then chances are very high you'll hit stumbling blocks later down the line.

> ### The $75 Million Idea
> One of our corporate workout participants shared a story with us about the organisation he worked for blacklisting a small client in 2002 for some minor infringements. The blacklisted company had gone through many changes and in 2007, had 80 staff and turned over $200 million per annum.
> Our hero put together a 14-page document on why the organisation should reinstate this client now that the previous management had long gone, and even included the fact that other areas of the organisation regularly dealt with them and so did their own department, indirectly. *cont'd over*

By his calculations, if they dealt with the client directly rather than through external providers, then the client's business could be worth $75 million per annum to his company through both income and savings.

The result? Management changed the policy so that from then on no other company would be blacklisted for the same infringements, but refused to reinstate this particular client. Why? Unfortunately, the person who originally blacklisted them had also moved on without proper record on the matter. No one really knew exactly why they were blacklisted in the first place, and management decided to keep the status quo based on a technicality that didn't apply to this client – at the cost of $75 million each year!

So even your best idea that makes good sense to everybody may not be fully embraced if you don't get the decision maker on board.

Implementation & review

"Thinking is easy, acting is difficult, and to put one's thoughts into action is the most difficult thing in the world."

—JOHANN WOLFGANG VON GOETHE, POLYMATH

Now it's time for the final stage where you bring your idea to life. As the old adage says, "Plan your work and work your plan". Many people fall down at this stage as fear may rear its ugly head. It might be fear of the unknown, fear of failure or fear of judgement (Emotional Barriers: Week 5 Day 2). This can very easily lead to analysis paralysis. Don't be a slave to your decision making and research tools, you need to be courageous. According to Professor David Kreps, who has taught MBA and doctoral level courses in decision theory at Stanford University, the most effective decision makers are those who combine analysis with a healthy dose of intuition (Being in the Moment: Week 8 Day 2).

Once you've implemented your idea it's wise that you monitor it to see how it's going. In your planning stage you would have set a time to review your solution. Remember:

If your idea is going to fail, you want it to fail fast!

This above statement depends on the context of your idea. Obviously you don't want to be too quick to shut down your idea. Ensure you give it enough time to work. The nature of the problem often dictates how much time is required.

It's a little known fact that... the hit TV show *Seinfeld* was almost not picked up after the pilot was screened. It required a TV executive who believed in it to divert money from another budget to get the next four episodes filmed. The show was a slow success and took until the fourth season to break into the Nielsen Top 30 ratings. It then went on to win Emmy awards and became the most popular show in the United States.

So ensure you have built "failure time" into your idea. Failure time means you've given your idea a realistic and reasonable chance of success. It may be a day or it may be 10 years, depending on the idea.

REMEMBER:

1. There are two types of problem solving: proactive and reactive.

2. Idea generation is simply a numbers game.

3. Problem solving works best when logic and analysis meet intuition and creativity.

Week 8 summary map:

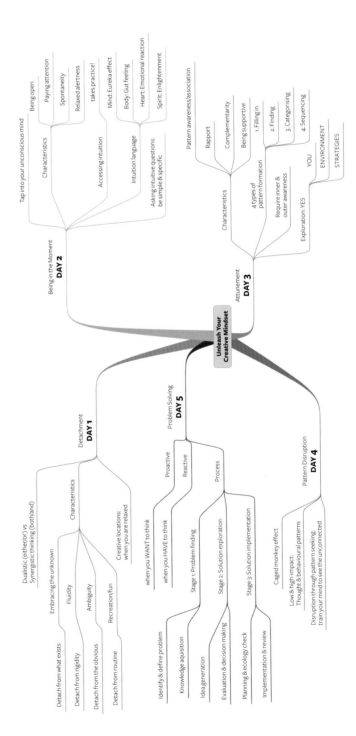

Unleash Your Creative Mindset

Being in the Moment — DAY 2

Tap into your unconscious mind

Characteristics
- Being open
- Paying attention
- Spontaneity
- Relaxed alertness
- takes practice!

Accessing intuition
- Mind: Eureka effect
- Body: Gut feeling
- Heart: Emotional reaction
- Spirit: Enlightenment

Intuition language

Asking intuitive questions: be simple & specific

Attunement — DAY 3

Pattern awareness/association

Characteristics
- Rapport
- Complementarity
- Being supportive

4 types of pattern formation
- 1. Filling in
- 2. Finding
- 3. Categorising
- 4. Sequencing

Require inner & outer awareness

Exploration: YES
- YOU
- ENVIRONMENT
- STRATEGIES

Detachment — DAY 1

Dualistic (either/or) vs Synergistic thinking (both/and)

Embracing the unknown

Characteristics
- Fluidity
- Ambiguity
- Recreation/fun

Creative locations: when you are relaxed

- Detach from what exists
- Detach from rigidity
- Detach from the obvious
- Detach from routine

Problem Solving — DAY 5

- Proactive: when you WANT to think
- Reactive: when you HAVE to think

Process
- Stage 1: Problem finding
- Stage 2: Solution exploration
- Stage 3: Solution implementation

- Identify & define problem
- Knowledge aquisition
- Idea generation
- Evaluation & decision making
- Planning & ecology check
- Implementation & review

Pattern Disruption — DAY 4

Caged monkey effect

Low & high-impact: Thought & behavioural patterns

Disruption through pattern seeking; train your mind to see the unconnected

Map Your Future

Purpose

To form a flexible action plan that lays the path towards your personal fulfilment.

Overview

Day 1: Exploration
Day 2: Current Reality
Day 3: Future Reality
Day 4: Tactical Mapping
Day 5: Embedding

Benefits

This week's experience in the Challenge guides you to:

- assess the steps that lead to achieving your desired outcomes
- make your desired outcomes more real and provide you with self-motivation
- organise and clarify your thinking on what is truly important to you
- improve your planning, taking the big picture into account
- see obstacles and create the necessary steps to overcome them
- approach your desired level of fulfilment in an easy and enjoyable way.

Week 9 Day 1: Exploration

> "If you don't know where you are going, all roads lead there."
>
> —ROMAN PROVERB

If you've read this far in the book, then you have the right attitude for success. Now it's time to explore, plan and create the life you'd like to live. All you have read so far has accumulated, and brought you to a point where this week will springboard you onto a path for a rewarding and enriching life.

Here's a very simple success strategy that all successful people follow.

You ready for it? Successful people know what they want. They set themselves goals and then achieve them. Yep, that's it.

Have you ever set a massive goal for yourself and not achieved it? Ever set a goal that you know deep down you won't reach? Ever set a New Year's resolution to stop smoking, lose weight, learn a language, spend more time with family, and then a few weeks down the track you're back to your old ways? Experiences like these may have convinced you that goal setting doesn't work. And in the traditional sense, it doesn't.

You might be thinking, *"Wait a minute! You first said successful people set goals and now you're saying goal setting doesn't work."* That's right. Goal setting done the traditional way doesn't work or bring long-term happiness. Remember, everybody achieves fulfilment differently. If you want to achieve your desired level of fulfilment, you need more than the traditional goal-setting method of writing down your goals, putting them in places where you'll see them daily and practising positive affirmations.

You need to map your future!

Future Mapping

Future Mapping is a more holistic take on the standard goal-setting method. It involves aligning your values to your desired outcomes and ensuring that it fulfils your purpose in life.

The **5** stages of Future Mapping:

1.	**Exploration**	– Are your values aligned to your purpose in life?
2.	**Current reality**	– Where are you starting this journey from?
3.	**Future reality**	– Where would you like to end up?
4.	**Tactical mapping**	– How do you get from your starting point to your destination?
5.	**Embedding**	– How are you going to keep yourself on track?

Why Future Mapping?

Setting and achieving goals is about achieving success, however you may define it. Future Mapping goes beyond achieving success. It's about living your purpose and achieving fulfilment. And certainly, goals are a part of that but they're not the end result.

We're not saying setting goals is bad. It's absolutely essential if you want to achieve the success you desire. You can call them whatever you want – goals, maps, visions, targets, dreams, objectives, outcomes – we use these words interchangeably. But there's more to life than just goals.

> *"The pain lies in what we think should happen and what actually happens."*
>
> —VERNON HOWARD, SPIRITUAL TEACHER

The quote above highlights why for many people, the phrase goal setting has negative connotations. Other reasons for this include:

1. Goals are missed.
People have a history of feeling defeated and unhappy for every unattained goal in their lives.

The term Future Mapping offers people a new approach to planning their lives differently.

2. Goals are temporary.
As soon as they are achieved, there is a need to set more of them.

Because Future Mapping takes into account your values and purpose, it is focused on the big picture.

3. Goals are rigid.
Goals are set by deadlines and therefore it's a win/lose situation, you either achieve them (win) or you don't (lose).

Future Mapping pays attention to the steps along the way, but you also remain fluid and detached from those steps so you can follow a new path if required/desired.

> *"Some of the world's greatest feats were accomplished by people not smart enough to know they were impossible."*
>
> —DOUG LARSON, RACER

Looking ahead
JOLT Challenge has helped you look at ways to overcome potential blocks and now it's time for you to realise your potential to plan, own and live your life. If you want to be successful then we suggest you make the time to plan your strategy. If you

don't, then in 10 years' time don't be surprised to find your dreams still being exactly that, dreams. Why haven't you written that book, started that hobby, mastered that language, founded that business, learnt that instrument, bought your dream home, gone to that country?

> *"I can teach anybody how to get what they want out of life. The problem is that I can't find anybody who can tell me what they want."*
>
> —MARK TWAIN, AUTHOR

Future Mapping provides you with a direction to improve your quality of life. You will be intrinsically motivated to achieve your desired level of fulfilment and have the peace of mind to enjoy it. Future Mapping in all areas of **The Big** **3** : Health, Wealth and Relationships, means that you are designing your life rather than leaving it up to chance.

> *"Life is like arriving late for a movie, having to figure out what was going on without bothering everybody with a lot of questions, and then being unexpectedly called away before you find out how it ends."*
>
> —JOSEPH CAMPBELL, MYTHOLOGY SCHOLAR

Cliff Says...
It's a little known fact that... many studies have proved that people who set goals achieve far more. At Harvard Business School researchers discovered that, 10 years after graduating, the 3% of the class that had set goals for themselves were earning 10% more than all the others in the class combined.

Foundation of Future Mapping

The foundation of Future Mapping is to know your values and purpose. This provides you with your *why* when it comes to your desired outcomes/goals. Having this foundation, you may even find that what were once your goals are no longer that important in your life.

> *"Most people live in a very restricted circle of their potential being. We all have reservoirs of energy and genius to draw upon of which we do not dream."*
>
> —WILLIAM JAMES, PSYCHOLOGIST & PHILOSOPHER

The exploration stage of the Future Mapping process is to discover that what you're seeking is actually what you want. If it's more money you want, then you'll know exactly why you want it. Is it to pay for your mortgage, to travel, to provide for your children, etc.? Keep chunking down by asking yourself *"What will I have when I get this?"*, until you come to the essence of your desire.

With a strong foundation your goals will be able to withstand the hammering they'll inevitably get from the obstacles that life throws at them.

> *"God gives every bird a worm, but he does not throw it into the nest."*
>
> —SWEDISH PROVERB

Knowing the *why* of your desired outcome will help you determine whether or not you are willing to pay the price to achieve it. If you were to list all the things you wanted to do in your life, you'd probably become depressed as you realise life is too short and there's not enough hours in the day to accomplish it all. Remember:

You don't have to have it all, you just have to have what is important!

Therefore, it's important to consider what you will sacrifice in order to live your desired life and where you will focus your energies in your day-to-day life.

The exercises and tools for today will give you the opportunity to explore the critical areas of your life.

The Big 3:

1. **Your Health** – mental, physical, emotional, spiritual
2. **Your Wealth** – career, business, savings, investments
3. **Your Relationships** – intimate, family, family of origin, friends, work

> *"Man is a goal-seeking animal. His life only has meaning if he is reaching out and striving for his goals."*
>
> —ARISTOTLE, PHILOSOPHER

Explore on the inside

When you are exploring what life you want to create for yourself, you need to tap into your inner wisdom. Like with setting your intention (Week 4 Day 2), you need to focus on what you do want rather than all the things you would like to eliminate from your life. Even if you managed to stop all the things you consider negative in your life, there's no guarantee that you'll end up with what you actually want. Remember the child in the lolly store (Desire: Week 5 Day 5) who said they didn't want licorice but didn't say what they did want – they got nothing!

At this exploration stage of Future Mapping, keep in mind that you're not working out a strategy to achieve your goals or trying to solve problems on the things that block you. You want to avoid complicating matters and simply use your imagination to delve into your mind and find the things that fulfil you mentally, physically, emotionally and spiritually.

REMEMBER:

1. You must spend time thinking about what kind of life you want to live, not the things you don't want.

2. You need to align your purpose and values in life with your goals.

3. You need all five stages of the Future Mapping process to achieve your fulfilment.

Week 9 Day 2:   Current Reality

"Man is what he believes."

—ANTON CHEKHOV, PLAYWRIGHT

You have learnt a lot about yourself doing JOLT Challenge so far and now you have the opportunity to bring that all together. But before you do, it's now time to re-evaluate your new perception of your reality. It wouldn't be uncommon for you to find that your actual current reality is different from the one you had when you started the Challenge. You may have experienced significant changes on this journey and with all the insight, knowledge and experience you have gained over the last nine weeks, it's important to know your new starting place. This ensures that your foundations are solid as you now move on to create and achieve the success you desire and deserve.

"Opportunity is missed by most people because it is dressed in overalls and looks like work."

—THOMAS EDISON, INVENTOR

Like a Rock

News reached an African farmer that someone had become rich by discovering diamonds on their farm. The African farmer sold his farm and headed off to the region so he too could become fabulously wealthy. He travelled for years, determined to find the diamonds, but to no avail. He eventually used up all of his savings, and with no money or friends, he died a poor, lonely desperate man.

The man who had bought the farm from the African farmer was out working the fields one day when his plough hit a stone. He picked up the stone and noticed how it captured the light in the most amazing ways. He showed a friend who recognised the stone as a diamond. They took it to a merchant who confirmed it was worth a lot of money and asked if there were any more. They went back to the farm to discover that beneath the topsoil the entire farm was littered with diamonds.

Your values, education, desires, family, friends, jobs, life experience both good and bad, are your diamonds that lie under the surface and have shaped who you are today. They are your resources and the things that will help you succeed. It is appropriate to know who you are and where you stand now, as you think about who you want to be. Of course you'll be you – but what kind of you is that? Too often people get stuck in the rut of day-to-day living without paying enough attention to the direction in which they're heading.

Know thy blocks

Knowing your current reality is important because any problems or blocks you have are rarely independent of each other. Due to the mechanics of the mind and the way you learn, there is a strong link between a cause and an effect.

EXAMPLE: One of our workout participants was always tired. She had problems getting out of bed in the morning. The cause of this was that she stayed up late on the internet chatting to friends on the other side of the world. The reason for this is that she felt she was missing out on things by going to bed and not being involved with her friends. She came to realise that she suffered from the "grass is greener" mentality and didn't truly appreciate the things she had in her life.

Until you know the root cause of a problem, you do not have a clear enough picture to know which problem to solve. Often seemingly unrelated problems stem from one or two core problems that cause all the others. Knowing your current reality helps you identify the core problems and gives you a direction for action. It also stops you from wasting time on irrelevant issues so your focus can be on creating a better reality.

Small detail vs Big picture

You have already explored Chunking (Week 4 Day 4), where you can chunk down and go into more detail or chunk up and look at the big picture. It depends where you are on this continuum as to how much impact these two frames of reference can warp your perspective on your current reality.

Small detail:

Obsessing too much on the small details of your life can cause you to focus purely on immediate events and miss how they fit into the overall scheme of your life. You end up being reactive rather than proactive in your daily activities.

Big picture:

Looking at your world where you only focus on the holistic overview and how it may look in the future, results in feeling overwhelmed and the meaning of current events in your life being lost. With the present out of focus, there can be a real lack of action in your life.

REMEDY:

Although you can make best use of both the small detail and big picture, look for the middle ground on this continuum where the relationship between events can be connected. There is only the present and it connects to the past and informs the future. Know your current reality now, understand how it came to be with an eye on where you are heading.

Two Camels

A mullah (Muslim priest) was out travelling with a sultan. However, the camel he was given was very slow indeed. The mullah didn't complain and soon into the trip he was left far behind. It wasn't much longer until the sultan was completely out of sight. Then the skies opened up and it began to pour down with rain.

The sultan got drenched. The mullah, however, got off his camel, disrobed, folded his clothes tidily and placed them under the camel as the storm raged. When the storm lifted, he put on his robes and made his way to the sultan's palace. The sultan was amazed that the mullah was completely dry as he had been unable to find shelter despite having a much faster camel.

"Thanks must go to the camel you gave me," said the mullah.

The next day the sultan gave the mullah the fastest camel he owned and took the slow one for himself. Again it rained and while the sultan got drenched once more, the mullah simply repeated what he had done the day before. When the sultan arrived at the palace he saw the mullah dry and content.

Again the mullah praised the camel. *"Thanks must go to the camel you gave me."*

The sultan was very angry and said between sneezes, *"This is all your fault for letting me ride the slow camel."*

The mullah simply smiled and said, *"Perhaps you must take the responsibility of staying dry."*

> *"Though no one can go back and make a brand-new start, anyone can start from now and make a brand-new ending."*
>
> —SOME SWITCHED-ON COOKIE

It's never late too late to succeed. Rather than lamenting over decisions you did or didn't make, reframe your situation (Choice: Week 6 Day 5), so that you acknowledge that everything you've done up to now has been for a reason. It's made you who you are today. Take these skills and knowledge that are unique to you and create your desired level of success.

"The size of your success is determined by the size of your belief."

Cliff Says...

It's a little known fact that... Colonel Sanders of KFC fame was 65 years old and totally broke when he decided to sell his chicken recipe. His social security cheque of $150 was enough to motivate him, and he was turned down 1009 times before he successfully sold his chicken recipe. Now that's perseverance!

"Which two, among a thousand wise men, will define success in the same words; yet failure is always described but one way. Failure is man's inability to reach his goals in life, whatever they may be."

—OG MANDINO, AUTHOR

REMEMBER:

1. Before selecting your destination, you must know where you are starting your journey from.

2. You have all the resources you need either within you or around you.

3. Knowing your current reality gives you a clear perspective on what aids you and what holds you back.

Week 9 Day 3: Future Reality

"When you arrive at your future, will you blame your past?"

—ROBERT HALF, ENTREPRENEUR

Your future reality is what you are creating right now. The good news is, you have the ability to create any reality you want. The bad news is, you're going to have to put some thought into it.

"Thinking is the hardest work there is, which is probably the reason why so few engage in it."

—HENRY FORD, BUSINESSMAN

You cannot afford to leave your life to chance – it's the only one you've got. You must be proactive in designing your life. Earl Nightingale, the man who is regarded by many as the father of the self-improvement industry, made a 20-year study of what made people successful. His research showed ultimately you become what you think about.

You gotta believe

That's why an important part of the Future Mapping process is ensuring that you believe you can achieve your desired outcome. If you set yourself a goal but deep down don't really believe you can achieve it – you'll be right! The good news is, you don't need evidence that you can achieve your goal, you just need faith.

Start replacing some of those 60,000 thoughts you have each day with ones stating you can achieve your goals, and notice how you'll start doing things differently and begin to create change in your life for the better.

Earl Nightingale's research also showed that the easiest way to reach your goals was to pretend that you've already achieved them. Think, feel and act like you're experiencing the success you desire. It's not lying to yourself if you plan to achieve that success, it's a strategy to help you make it a reality quicker.

"I don't care how much power, brilliance or energy you have, if you don't harness it and focus it on a specific target, and hold it there, you're never going to accomplish as much as your ability warrants."

—ZIG ZIGLAR, SALES COACH & AUTHOR

An archer had mastered his art and had reached legend status all around the land. People came and challenged him and in good humour he would accept their challenges to hit high targets, low targets, moving targets, stationary targets and even floating targets. One day a challenger took him to an empty field where there was no target in sight, just a wide open space with nothing but grass all around.

The challenger said, *"I challenge you to show to me this wonderful talent I have heard so much about."*

The archer replied, *"But you have set me no target."*

To which the challenger laughed, *"Ha! So you cannot meet my challenge then?"*

Before the challenger could say another word the archer had shot an arrow up into the air and it landed forty feet from where they were standing. The archer then shot arrow after arrow, each one of them landing on top of the previous arrow splitting it in two.

The smile left the challenger's face and was replaced with awe as he recognised indeed the mastery of the archer.

Even a master needs a target to show his skill and feel fulfilled. Creating a destination, a future reality for you to reach, is of vital importance for a happy and enriched life.

> *"If you want to be happy, set a goal that commands your thoughts, liberates your energy, and inspires your hopes."*
>
> —ANDREW CARNEGIE, BUSINESSMAN

Goals schmoals

Are there any reasons for not creating a desired future state? Any reasons you can come up with for not setting goals will come back to two things, fear and misunderstanding. If you don't appreciate the benefits of setting targets or aren't serious about living your purpose then you misunderstand the power of Future Mapping.

It may be you're afraid of failure and not setting any goals is a great way of staying within your comfort zone and getting through life unscathed. It may be that you're afraid of success and of taking responsibility for your life. Whatever the reason, it's robbing you of your life.

Be aware that as a general rule:

You judge others by their behaviour
but judge yourself by your situation

EXAMPLE: Someone cuts you off in traffic and you label them as rude and inconsiderate.

If you do exactly the same to someone else, it's different, because you're in a hurry or you would have given way if you had seen them.

EXAMPLE: If someone doesn't achieve their goal you may judge them as weak and unable to make a commitment. On the rare occasion you may not achieve something you set out to, then it's okay, because you had the best intentions but things just didn't work out.

By now you are more aware of your actions. So check in and see what it says about you. Are you someone you can trust, that others can trust to see a commitment through?

Put 'em up

In the movie *Fight Club*, Brad Pitt plays a character who puts a gun to the head of a Korean student who had dropped out of school and was working at a video store. He asks the student what he wants to be, and the student tells him *"a veterinarian"*. Brad Pitt's character tells him to restart his biology classes or else. Now that's inspiration! What could you achieve if someone held a gun to your head?

If it's that simple to set and achieve goals then why aren't people doing it every day? Well, some people are! Remember, it's those little S.U.C.C.E.E.D. steps every day (Week 1 Day 2) that count. Those people who have cultivated good habits reap the rewards of achieving what they set out for.

Done in 30 Seconds

Pablo Picasso was sitting in a café in France one day when a wealthy American woman asked him to draw a sketch of her. He agreed and within 30 seconds produced a magnificent sketch for her. Her joy soon turned to anger when he informed her that it would cost $3000.

"$3000?" she said outraged. *"$3000 for what? 30 seconds of work?"*

"Madam," he replied coldly, *"that sketch took me thirty years to produce."*

Keep in mind that you don't always see the effort people have put in to achieve their goals, just the end result.

So why do the rest of us find it hard to stick to and make our dreams come alive?

The reason we find it so hard is because it is so easy!

Three easy thoughts

If something is easy then human nature tends to think in one or a combination of the following ways:

1. There's limited value
2. There's plenty of time
3. There's excessive compulsion

Limited value:

If you think something is of limited value then you tend not to take action. You may know of someone who says they don't write down their goals because "*I know what I want,*" as they start tapping their head, "*it's all up here.*" Therefore they don't write down their goals. And sure enough, they don't achieve them. They can talk about their goals but they have nothing on paper, no map to follow.

Plenty of time:

How many times have you heard:

"*I'll start that up next week.*"
"*I'll stop doing that in the New Year.*"
"*I'll join the gym when I get some extra money.*"
"*I'm onto that as soon as the kids are older.*"
"*When summer hits, watch out!*"

These are all excuses that postpone action.

You may think it's not a matter of life or death if you don't start working on your goal straight away, but you're wrong. It is very much a matter of life – your life!

Excessive compulsion:

If the steps to take you towards your goal are easy, you may feel compelled to go further than you need to or can manage. If your goal is to get in shape, then rather than starting off small and doing S.U.C.C.E.E.D., you may go for a 10 km run, start a strict diet and go cold turkey on all soft drinks. This excessiveness may serve you well at first, but soon this simple goal of getting in shape (exercise and eat well?) becomes difficult and unrewarding. This self-imposed punishment takes all the shine off your goal, and when the goal no longer seems worth the effort, it ends up on the junk pile of past failures. Make sure you're not deliberately sabotaging yourself by making the process unnecessarily difficult.

The price is right

When it comes to creating your future reality you need to be honest with yourself. Are you really willing and prepared to pay the price to achieve your goals? There's no credit card where you can get your goal first and then pay back the hard effort afterwards.

What are you prepared to pay for your desired life?

🎥 Hello...

In the movie *The Princess Bride,* Mandy Patinkin plays the Spaniard Inigo Montoya, hell-bent on revenging the death of his father. He spends his entire life learning the art of the sword and even knows the exact words he will say when he finds the six-fingered man who murdered his Papa. *"Hello, my name is Inigo Montoya. You killed my father. Prepare to die."* Now that's commitment to a goal!

> *"Our lives improve only when we take chances – and the first and most difficult risk we can take is to be honest with ourselves."*
>
> —WALTER ANDERSON, ARTIST

If you smoke and know that you shouldn't, then you may have "give up smoking" as one of your goals. However, if you don't really want to give up, then forget about it. On the other hand, if you want to save money, be healthy and live long enough to see your children's children, then you will find within you what it takes to quit smoking. You have as much will power as the next person; you just have to tap into the motivating forces that are right for you. This is how you get leverage over yourself to drive towards your target.

📑 Scared Shipless

A warrior chief went to battle against an army that far outnumbered his own.

As his warriors arrived on the enemy's land, he ordered that they burn their own ships. Standing before his warriors he told them, *"We have no boats any more. We can no longer leave these shores alive unless we win this battle. Our choice is either to win or die!"*

They won.

Why is it that people who have been smoking for 30 years can quit for good when they have a health scare? What makes people leave abusive relationships suddenly after remaining in them for years? What makes people learn that skill, start that activity, reach for that goal after procrastinating for so long? It's because they stop the defence mechanisms (Choice: Week 6 Day 5) and have all tapped into the right desire, and gained the right mindset where they know they can no longer continue with their past behaviour.

In *Once Were Warriors*, Beth Heke can only take so much physical and emotional abuse from her husband Jake. It takes the suicide of her daughter to give her the courage to leave him.

Remember the Pleasure Principle:

All of your behaviour is designed to seek pleasure and avoid pain

The carrot and stick mentality (you reward your good behaviour and punish your bad), will only take you so far. Inspiration can run out when you find yourself stuck in the daily grind. The problem with the carrot and stick mentality is that when you use fear as a motivator and you move away from the stick towards the carrot you often find yourself becoming complacent and, before you know it, you're back needing the stick again.

Imagine you get told by your doctor you have high cholesterol. You start the necessary exercise and diet. A few months later you're told that everything is okay. What happens? You go back to your old ways because there's less motivation to act in a positive way now and you rationalise that you can always go back to your diet and exercise if you need to.

If you have truly tapped into what really gets you pumped, then your commitment and motivation to achieve fulfilment comes easily.

Take a Hike

A workout participant wasn't happy with being overweight and wanted to get into shape. However, he didn't enjoy going to the gym and lifting weights or the standard cardiovascular exercises that were on offer. He loved tramping in his younger days, so he started off getting up earlier and going for 30-minute walks around the neighbourhood daily. It wasn't much, but it was a start.

After a couple of weeks he felt he was fit enough to go for a medium-intensity tramp in the Waitakere Ranges. This has become a regular weekend activity with his wife who loves the quality time with her husband. Not only has he become a lot fitter, he did it in a way that he loved, and enjoyed spin-off benefits like improved communication and a deeper connection with his wife.

"Whoever wants to reach a distant goal must take many small steps."

—HELMUT SCHMIDT, PHYSICIST

The American oil billionaire H. L. Hunt said that you only need two things to succeed:

1. Decide exactly what it is you want (which most people never do).
2. Determine the price you are going to pay to get it and be willing to pay it.

> **Cliff Says...**
> *It's a little known fact that...* H. L. Hunt was the inspiration for the TV show *Dallas*. However, the producers had to play down many of the real family goings-on for believability's sake!

Once you have determined the price you will pay for your desired outcome, then commit to it and take action.

Your life story

Your life is a story that you are writing, directing, editing, producing and starring in right now. You have the lead role. Think about what kind of story you want your life to be? An epic adventure with romance, excitement and a happy ending? Or a dull, boring story with the same events happening over and over again and not even worth reading.

The time to be thinking about your future is *now*! What do you want when it comes to **The Big 3**: Health, Wealth and Relationships?

Who do *you* want to be? What kind of lifestyle do you want? What have you always wanted to do? Where do you want to travel to? Who do you want to surround yourself with? If you don't make these things happen, who will?

What story have you told so far? Is it the story you want to tell? If not, start re-writing it!

The universe does revolve around you, because without you there is no story.

REMEMBER:

1. Plan your future, don't leave it to chance.

2. You don't have unlimited time to achieve your goals, so get started now.

3. Decide what price you'll pay to achieve your dreams and then pay it.

Week 9 Day 4: Tactical Mapping

"Thinking without action is a daydream, action without thinking is a nightmare."

—JAPANESE PROVERB

If you want to get somewhere in life then it pays to have a map to work off. That way you'll definitely get to your destination and quicker too. There's no right or wrong way when it comes to creating your tactical map, your plan of action, that will help guide you. Some people will feel more comfortable with a detailed map while others need just a general guideline. One thing is for sure, a map is better than just trying to keep all the journey's details in your head. You need to find which is the best way of mapping for you and that will become obvious once you start putting one together.

"I have always found that plans are useless but the act of planning is indispensable."

—NAPOLEON BONAPARTE, POLITICIAN

Everybody has goals in some shape or form, whether it's to receive another week's pay or buy some new clothes or a desire for a holiday. The irony is most people will put more effort into planning a two-week vacation than their life. They'll take more time, do more research, cross more t's and dot more i's on those two weeks, than they ever will deciding what kind of life they want to live.

By now you know the power of Future Mapping and that to be someone who proactively creates their future you need to have your tactical map on paper in some form and not just in your head. The wording, timing and the way you structure your goal can make the difference between success and failure. You need to design your tactical map so that it's as simple as can be, it tells you when you're on and off track and it's a path that you can commit to.

"A man without a goal is like a ship without a rudder."

—THOMAS CARLYLE, ESSAYIST & HISTORIAN

Cliff Says...
It's a little known fact that... research into 50 start-up companies found those with a business plan had considerably outperformed ones without plans, even if the plan wasn't actually followed.

Writing your desired outcome helps you clarify what it is you want. Writing is a psycho-neuromuscular activity that connects the conscious and unconscious mind. It activates the reticular activating system (Neurons: Week 2 Day 3) and helps your unconscious mind seek ways to help you achieve your desired outcomes.

📖 Four Feet in One Day

The Moso bamboo plant is considered the most important bamboo species in China due to its versatility in use. Once it's planted, not much happens for the first four years. There are shoots but regardless how much you water and nurture it, there's very little growth.

However, in the fifth year, the Moso suddenly begins growing at a rapid rate of up to almost four feet a day, reaching heights of 80 feet! For the first four years all the growth is happening underground as the Moso lays its strong foundations.

🍺 Cliff Says...

It's a little known fact that... Moso (Mao Zhu in Chinese) means hairy bamboo. You can see Moso in use in the Jackie Chan movie *Rush Hour 2* where it's used not only as building scaffolding, but also as a stage for a kick-butt fight scene.

JOLT Challenge has helped you lay very solid foundations. When it comes to writing out your tactical map, ensure you keep S.U.C.C.E.E.D. (Week 1 Day 2) firmly in mind. It may seem that not much is happening, but just like the Moso bamboo, when the results start to kick in, they will show exponentially.

Isaac Newton's first law of motion, aka the "law of inertia", states that anything not moving will remain motionless until a force acts upon it. It also states that something in motion will not accelerate unless a force acts upon it.

This means if you're not moving towards your target, you'll remain where you are if you don't take action. It also means even if you are taking steps towards your goal, there will be no change in acceleration towards that goal unless you do something different to speed up the process of attaining it. In reality, if you're not moving then you're actually going backwards as others are moving forward.

Map writing

Think of writing your tactical map as the first step of breaking any inertia. It is the force that kick-starts you into action. Appreciate that your goals can be set on different scales. There's your life's goal, the destination you want to arrive at that's aligned to your values and purpose in life. Then there are smaller targets or signposts that you aim for that build up towards this bigger picture.

"A goal properly set is halfway reached."

ABRAHAM LINCOLN, POLITICIAN

For those who like to operate from a detailed map, then F-MAPS is a guide to increase the likelihood of you achieving your desired outcome. It will help you write the most effective map you can.

> **F** = **Flexible**
>
> **M** = **Measurable**
>
> **A** = **Achievable**
>
> **P** = **Positive**
>
> **S** = **Specific**

Be flexible
Your goals will change as you do. As you journey further down the path to your destination, you may find your priorities or the desired outcome has changed. Change your goal accordingly, rather than following an old dream you are no longer committed to.

> *"Obstacles are those frightful things you see when you take your eyes off your goal."*
>
> —HENRY FORD, BUSINESSMAN

Things will go wrong, accept this as it's part of the journey. The Chaos stage always follows a new challenge (Growth Cycle: Week 1 Day 1). Having obstacles to overcome makes reaching your destination all the more sweet.

Be measurable
You need to include your own signposts that show you whether or not you're still on the right path to your destination. These are things by which you can measure your success.

> *"What gets measured, gets done."*
>
> —PETER DRUCKER, MANAGEMENT ICON

EXAMPLE: If your target is to learn to play the guitar to a certain level, then you might have the following as signposts to highlight your progress:

- You know you can manipulate your fingers on the guitar when you can pick all the individual notes.
- You know you can strum well when you can hold all chords down and all strings sound clear while you strum.
- You know you can play simple chords well when you can change chords in rhythm and move your hands into position in time to the beat.

- You know you can read music well when you can read a line ahead of what you're playing.
- You know you can play well when you can listen to a recording and copy it note for note in the same style without making a mistake.

> *"A goal is a wish with a deadline."*
> —JANE POLLAK, ENTREPRENEUR

Be achievable

Like exercising a muscle, a goal has to stretch you to make you grow. If it doesn't stretch you at all, then you'll remain where you are. If it stretches you too much, it'll tear and cause pain, doing you more damage than good. Being achievable doesn't mean easy or reasonable, but simply that you can do it.

Be positive

Make sure your goals are positively framed and avoid the wanting state.

EXAMPLE: *"I am creating a fit, toned, healthy physique."*
Rather than: *"I don't want to be fat and unable to climb a flight of stairs without becoming breathless."*

EXAMPLE: *"I am finding a loving life partner."*
Rather than: *"I don't want someone who will cheat on me."*

Remember:

Say what you want, not what you don't want!

Be specific

The all-new K.I.S.S. philosophy – Keep It Simple Serves! If your goal isn't able to be written on the back of a business card then it's too complex. Keep it to one idea for one goal.

EXAMPLE: *"I am creating my financial freedom so I can enjoy a nice house and a boat ."*
Rather than: *"I want lots of money and to have nice things."*
The more you clearly define what you want and when you want it, then the better chance you'll have of knowing when you've achieved it. Avoid quantifier words like "some", "plenty" or "a little bit", which makes your target vague.

EXAMPLE: *"I am creating a healthy body to fit into my favourite pair of jeans."*
Rather than: *"I want to lose some weight."*

Note: F-MAPS isn't the only way to achieve goals. Some people who only have a rough idea of what they want and where they're going may not be able to have measurable and specific outcomes. They may find the following metaphorical story more helpful. Remember: there's no right or wrong – use whatever works best for you!

> *"It is good to have an end to journey toward, but it is the journey that matters in the end."*
>
> —URSULA LE GUIN, AUTHOR

The Hero's Journey

> *"It is not the mountain we conquer but ourselves."*
>
> —EDMUND HILLARY, MOUNTAINEER

Joseph Campbell, the mythologist who wrote the book *The Hero with a Thousand Faces,* found that every experience in life can be traced to what he called a "Hero's Journey". This journey applies across time, place and culture.

The Hero's Journey is a metaphorical way you can look at your goals if the detail of F-Maps seems too prescriptive for you.

The Hero's Journey (adapted):
Does this sound familiar? You are the Hero in your own Hero's Journey. You can think of this journey on the macro level (your life) or micro level (your job, relationship, hobby, etc.).

Ask yourself: What stage of the Hero's Journey are you at now?

In a Galaxy Far, Far Away

George Lucas was heavily influenced by the writings of the mythology professor Joseph Campbell when it came to writing the *Star Wars* movies. Watch any of the *Star Wars* movies and you'll see the Hero's Journey in action.

> *"What you get by achieving your goals is not as important as what you become by achieving your goals."*
>
> —JOHANN WOLFGANG VON GOETHE, POLYMATH

So relax safe in the knowledge that detours, roadblocks, potholes, and dead ends are all part of your journey. As long as your map is sound, you will ultimately find your way to your destination.

REMEMBER:

1. Writing a tactical map immediately increases your chance of success.

2. Understand the need for strong foundations without expecting immediate results.

3. Obstacles are required for you to achieve your goal.

Week 9 Day 5:   Embedding

"Goal begins with 'GO'."

—BIL KEANE, CARTOONIST

No matter how you set your goals, you must continuously embed them until they are scorched into your mind. You can't set a destination and then never look at your map again. Well, actually you can but that's called procrastination or dreaming. Tactical maps and signposts need to be reviewed regularly and your commitment to them must be strengthened. Only then, will you see the journey out to the end and attain your goals. The more challenging the goals, the more you must embed them. There are a number of ways for you to reinforce your commitment to your desired outcome.

EXAMPLES:
- Design your own mental rehearsal (Visualisation: Week 4 Day 3) that you run through before you go to sleep at night and do first thing in the morning.
- Employ S. U. C. C. E. E. D. (Week 1 Day 2) and make sure that you are continuously taking small steps to achieve your goal.
- Display the final written goals where you will see them daily – by your computer, mirror or shower.
- Practise self-hypnosis through autosuggestion (Beliefs: Week 6 Day 1) and give yourself positive encouragement and suggestions.
- Set yourself mini goals on a daily or weekly basis that move you forward.
- Visualise the end goal, see it in detail and detach from the path you took to get there.
- Practise the Make Your Day tool (Intention: Week 4 Day 2).
- Establish a group of supporters and mentors (Modelling: Week 4 Day 5) that you check in with on a regular basis.
- Keep a journal that tracks your progress.
- Paint a picture or make a sculpture of you achieving your desired outcome.
- Create a Vision Board and meditate on it.
- Spend 10 minutes before you go to bed to review your day and note where you succeeded and where you can do better.
- Create anchors (Senses: Week 2 Day 5) to keep you at the top of your game.
- Any other way that works for you!

> **📖 A Ritualistic Dragon**
> Siimon Reynolds, the millionaire advertising expert who featured in the Australian version of the *Dragon's Den* TV show, has a daily ritual that he does every morning. First thing he does is a meditation and prayer. Then he has a bath where he writes out his goals and reads about his future self and what he aspires to become. He focuses on how he'd like to be seen by people in his life and finishes off by thinking of a couple of things he's grateful for.

Sense your target

It helps to develop a multi-sensory visualisation for your target (Visualisation: Week 4 Day 3). This involves seeing your desired outcome as reality now, hearing what you and others are saying, what you're doing and feeling and any smells or tastes involved. Create your own visualisation and use it to help you when you feel the rigours of daily life are getting on top of you. It re-engages your senses and helps you tap into feeling the excitement and pleasure you'll get from achieving your target.

Target support

Remember to find someone or surround yourself with people who will support you. It will help you stick to your tactical map and reach your desired target. Sports psychologists know that even with individual sports such as triathlons, training and results are greatly improved when athletes train together. Being a part of a team increases your commitment to the goal.

> *"Great spirits have always encountered violent opposition from mediocre minds."*
> —ALBERT EINSTEIN, PHYSICIST

And likewise avoid anyone toxic that may poison your goal. There are plenty of people who don't have the courage to live their life to the full and may gain pleasure in bringing you down. They may ridicule, tease, discourage or even get angry with you. Know what you want and be true to yourself. If you don't have family, friends, supporters, mentors or coaches who positively support you then actively seek these people out.

> *"Talk doesn't cook rice."*
> —CHINESE PROVERB

And... Action!

You've explored your desired future state, you've taken check of your current reality and you've glimpsed into the future and mapped your strategy to get there.

It's now time for you to take action.

Knowledge isn't power. APPLIED knowledge is power!

You're not going to achieve your desired destination in one single step. So rather than suffer analysis paralysis, just get moving. You're not going to know how it ends up. This is where detachment (Week 8 Day 1) is so important. Not detachment from your desire but detachment from the way you achieve your goals. You're not going to have all the green lights in your favour but you've got to put yourself into gear and start the journey. It's better for you to take action with a rough map than no action with a detailed map. Action gives you momentum and being flexible means you can always change direction when required.

> *"Knowledge must come through action. You can have no test which is not fanciful, save by trial."*
> —SOPHOCLES, PLAYWRIGHT

Start her up!
In the movie *Collateral*, Jamie Foxx plays a taxi driver with a burning ambition to own his own limousine service. He knows the name of the business, has scoped out all the cars, knows exactly how they'll be fitted out and even who the clients will be. However, because he has never taken any action it remains a dream.

> *"When all is said and done, there is too much said and not enough done."*
> —SOME MOTHER'S CHILD

We've provided you with the knowledge to help with Overcoming Internal and External Barriers (Week 1 Days 3 & 4) and Procrastination (Week 1 Day 5) that stop you from taking action. The important thing to realise is that ultimately the only thing that can stop you from achieving your fulfilment is you.
Remember:

There are only two moments in life: NOW and TOO LATE!

When good maps go bad
It's much easier if you just accept now that things won't always go your way. Expect the glimmer of your goals will fade at times and the discipline required to achieve anything worthy will at times take a beating.

> *"If you're going through hell, keep going."*
> —WINSTON CHURCHILL, POLITICIAN

It's natural to get discouraged. If fulfilment was easy then everyone would be walking around happy. Living a fulfilling life takes commitment. When you do feel overwhelmed or discouraged – use the knowledge in this book to explore, discover and help guide you through any bad waters, and keep you on your desired track. Look at the big picture, think where you'll be in a year's time or five years' time, reframe the situation, do whatever it takes – just never give up.

> *"Never give in. Never give in. Never, never, never, never – in nothing, great or small, large or petty – never give in, except to convictions of honour and good sense."*
>
> —WINSTON CHURCHILL, POLITICIAN

If you believe you're on the right path then keep persisting. Persistence is a form of genius. Think back to the stories in this book of people like Thomas Edison and Colonel Sanders who kept on pursuing their dream and never gave up. Adopt the belief that there is always a way, and you will live a life of fulfilment and enjoy the journey along the way.

> *"When you come to the end of your rope, tie a knot and hang on."*
>
> —FRANKLIN D. ROOSEVELT, POLITICIAN

Your life doesn't have to be perfect. You're setting way too high expectations if you think it does. But just because it's not perfect doesn't mean that it can't be wonderful. Continue to take action, continue to learn and no matter what obstacles life throws at you, you will get to your desired destination. In tough times, remember the Japanese proverb "Fall seven times, stand up eight".
Remember:

You are the Hero on your Hero's Journey. Keep on moving!

> *"Genius will not; unrewarded genius is almost a proverb. Education will not; the world is full of educated derelicts. Persistence and determination alone are omnipotent. The slogan 'Press On' has solved and always will solve the problems of the human race."*
>
> —CALVIN COOLIDGE, POLITICIAN

Hitting the target
When you achieve a goal, take the time to enjoy the satisfaction of having done so. Don't be in a hurry to set another one immediately or focus on the ones that haven't been achieved yet. Reflect upon what you have learnt, how you feel and reward yourself appropriately.

Celebrate success, even small wins!

Savour small victories, because they always reflect something much larger.

Look back on that particular journey and see what you can learn from it. You may want to ponder on:

- How easily did you achieve the target and should they be made easier or harder?
- How does achieving this objective affect your other ones?
- What skills did you gain or have to gain in order to have achieved this desired outcome?

Remember:

There is no failure, only feedback!

So take any lessons and inspiration you can and feed it into your Future Mapping process.

Keep in mind that your targets will shift as you get older, learn more and live your life. Ensure that you remain in charge of your future map and that it doesn't dictate to you. The aim of Future Mapping is not to bully you but rather to bring you pleasure and happiness in life and a sense of fulfilment and peace.

REMEMBER:

1. You must constantly reinforce your tactical map so that you reach your destination.

2. You will have rough patches – don't quit! Keep on moving!

3. Celebrate your successes and see how they can further benefit you.

Week 9 summary map:

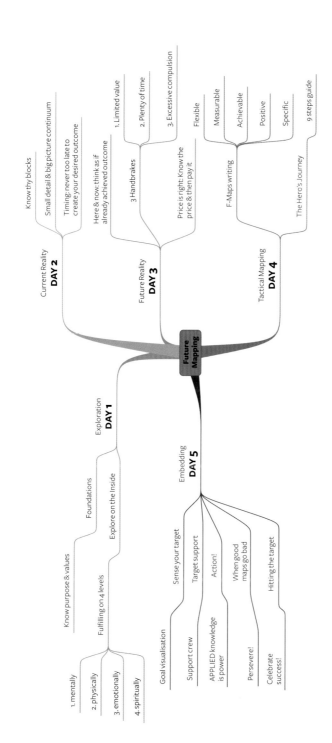

We'd like to finish with Johann Wolfgang von Goethe's famous passage that beautifully sums up what happens when you commit to action.

"Concerning all acts of initiative, there is one elementary truth, the ignorance of which kills countless ideas and splendid plans: the moment one definitely commits oneself, then Providence moves too. All sorts of things occur to help one that would never otherwise have occurred. A whole stream of events issues from the decision, raising in one's favour all manner of unforeseen incidents and meetings and material assistance which no man could have dreamed would come his way. Whatever you can do or dream you can do, begin it. Boldness has genius, power and magic in it. Begin it now."

Our Philosophy

JOLT Challenge program, which includes the book, the journal, the class and the self assessment module, has been researched and developed since 2004 and follows the "something old, something new" philosophy. The very best of different disciplines have been and will continue to be researched, adapted, tested and culminated into an accessible format to improve your life and give you what you need to achieve your desired level of fulfilment. Where such exercises and tools did not exist to bring the theory to life, we created and tested them ourselves on focus and trial groups.

JOLT Challenge draws on and combines theories, strategies, tools and exercises from the following areas:

Psychology
Behavioural, clinical, evolutionary, organisational, social

Education
Accelerated learning, assessment and evaluation, experiential training, learning styles, multiple intelligence

Leadership studies
Behaviour, communication, creativity, goal setting, motivation, storytelling, values

Therapeutic arts
Art of improvisation, autogenic training, cognitive behavioural therapy (CBT), hypnotherapy, kinaesiology, neuro linguistic programming (NLP), physiotherapy, visualisation

Science
Anatomy and physiology, biochemistry, neuroscience, nutrition

Philosophy
Eastern, Indigenous and Western cultures

These different areas have been integrated into a model based on the following seven philosophies:

1. Mind/Body learning
The mind and body are two parts of the same system. You cannot affect one without affecting the other. There are plenty of ways of working out your body, so the focus of JOLT Challenge is to work out your mind. We recommend that you do a minimum of 30 minutes of physical exercise daily throughout this Challenge.

2. Self-directed learning

JOLT Challenge provides you the opportunity to find your own answers. It is not prescriptive, telling you exactly what to do and what to think. Instead, it offers experiences and opportunities for you to discover what works for you, so you can achieve your desired level of fulfilment.

3. Neuroplasticity

Neuroscience tells us that your brain is incredibly malleable and is constantly rewiring and sorting itself until the day you shift off this mortal coil. That means you can learn new behaviours, change old beliefs and pick up new skills and talents. So you *can* teach an old dog new tricks and the proverbial leopard *can* change its spots. Some things may take longer to change than others depending on what's required to learn. However, positive change IS possible for you.

4. More options

JOLT Challenge offers you a wide range of options and experiences to increase the likelihood of you achieving the change you desire. Not all of the JOLT Challenge is going to float your boat. That's why it's a Challenge with a capital C! It will challenge you on many different levels; emotionally, cognitively, creatively and more. The key is to experiment with all the exercises and tools. Implement them into your daily life. If they work, keep them and if they don't, get rid of them. But make it an informed decision not to use them rather than a pre-judged one.

5. S.U.C.C.E.E.D. – Stepping Up Constantly & Consistently Each & Every Day.

Do just a little bit at a time. Rather than read the whole book from start to finish, follow the guidelines – just a little bit each day. In fact, not even each day. Just five days a week. Only by bringing in a little bit at a time can you make positive change that actually lasts. We believe in reinterpreting the old K.I.S.S. principle into – Keep It Simple Serves!

6. The learning is in the doing

We recognise that the JOLT Challenge book is packed full of useful information. The companion journal and workouts help you to make that information relevant, by putting it into practice.

Our philosophy is: information is not knowledge until you do something with it.

7. Experiential learning

This is the way to turn the information into knowledge. JOLT Challenge is a multi-modality learning experience. This means that has an impact on the three ways you learn – visually (seeing), auditory (hearing) and kinaesthetically (doing).

There is more on the power and benefits of experiential learning in the JOLT Challenge journal. (see www.joltchallenge.com for more information)

Testing JOLT Challenge

All the information, tools and exercises in JOLT Challenge were tested against these three questions:

1. Is knowing this going to improve my life?
2. Is this simple to understand?
3. Is this effective?

If it's confusing, unresourceful or doesn't work, then you won't find it in JOLT Challenge.

Of course, deciding what information is useful or not, or which exercises and tools are beneficial, is a very subjective thing. Just as there will be exercises that may horrify you or you think are a waste of time, there will be others that will have a profound impact on you and resonate with you on a deep level.

> *"Everything should be made as simple as possible but no simpler."*
>
> —ALBERT EINSTEIN, PHYSICIST

Nonetheless, the content has been used and critiqued by thousands of people in both corporate and public workshops since 2004, so we know everything in JOLT Challenge works on some level for everyone, including you.

Our advisory panel

We have an international advisory panel of experts that have scrutinised the program to ensure it is robust and ecologically sound.

The JOLT Challenge advisory panel is:

Dr Rich Allen

Dr Rich Allen is a highly regarded educator and master trainer, with a PhD in Educational Psychology. His cognitive learning theory research, which provided understanding on how the brain receives, processes, stores and recalls information, forms the basis for his approach to teaching, presenting and facilitating. In the 20-plus years he has been taking his ideas around the world, he has worked with senior managers, corporate training divisions and education departments in the United States, Canada, the United Kingdom, Australia, New Zealand, Hong Kong, Singapore, Brunei, Russia, Jordan and Brazil.

A former off-Broadway actor, Rich was a director and lead facilitator for Super Camp, an accelerated learning program for teens, before focusing on teaching brain-based learning strategies. He is the author of a number of best-selling education books including: *Impact Teaching*, *TrainSmart* and *Green Light Classrooms*. Rich can be contacted at www.drrichallen.com

Dr Jim Bartley

Dr Jim Bartley is an Auckland ear, nose and throat surgeon. He is a senior lecturer in surgery at the Auckland Medical School and has fellowships in both surgery and in pain medicine. Trained in Wellington, Hamilton and Auckland, Jim did further post-graduate work in London before doing a fellowship in sinus surgery in Philadelphia. Jim currently has his own practice and works at the Auckland Regional Pain Service and at Counties-Manukau District Health Board. He has published over 30 papers in the scientific literature and two books, *Breathing Matters* and *Healing Headaches*.

Dr Peter Blyde

Dr Peter Blyde is the founder of CATALYST4 – a consulting organisation that stimulates development in the areas of vision and strategy, leadership and people change. Peter's PhD examined Executive Perceptions of Leadership in New Zealand and Australia. His work was highly commended by international leadership expert Barry Posner, author of *The Leadership Challenge*, *Credibility*, and *Encouraging the Heart*.

Peter is the lead designer and facilitator of the Hillary Leadership Program (an 18-month, cross-sectoral leadership program for senior executives) with Excelerator: The New Zealand Leadership Institute, part of the University of Auckland Business School. This is New Zealand's most significant public leadership development program and is attracting a lot of attention and support from the Gallup Institute, Duke University, and INSEAD.

Peter spent two years with the Hay Group in Sydney, and within one year was selected as the Australasian representative for the Hay Group Global R&D Network. This recognised his innovative program design and depth of experience and created the opportunity to keep up to date with global best practice in leadership development and emotional intelligence.

Dr Helena Cooper-Thomas

Dr Helena Cooper-Thomas is a Senior Lecturer in Industrial Work and Organisational Psychology at the University of Auckland. With a PhD in Psychology, her focus is on applying an understanding of psychology to explain and improve the performance and well-being of people at work. She has published her research in a number of respected applied psychology journals.

Helena is a Chartered Psychologist in the UK and is registered with the NZ Psychology Board. Prior to returning to academia and emigrating to New Zealand, Helena worked both as an independent consultant and for consulting firms, working mostly in the UK and France. Helena has consulted to companies including Accenture, Shell, Lloyds TSB, and Hilton Hotels, as well as a number of UK government agencies including the Ministry of Defence and the Department for Education and Employment.

Dr David Hopcroft

Dr David Hopcroft is an experienced family medicine practitioner with a special interest in diabetes and nutrition. Prior to completing his medical degree he undertook a PhD in cell biology, publishing several papers on the cellular interactions within insulin-secreting pancreatic islets, for which he was awarded the ANZ Society of Cell Biology Young Scientist of the Year.

David is presently involved in a number of GP research activities, continues in part-time general practice, and also has a nutritional medicine clinic. He is a member of the Australasian College of Nutritional and Environmental Medicine and a Fellow of the Royal NZ College of General Practitioners. He can be contacted at david. hopcroft@ihug.co.nz

Dr Ken Hultman

Dr Ken Hultman received his BS and MA degrees from Arizona State University, and his doctorate in counselling psychology from Rutgers University. He has over 30 years of experience helping individuals, teams, and organisations identify and overcome barriers to effective performance.

Ken is the author of six books, including *Making Change Irresistible: Overcoming resistance to change in your organizations*, and *Balancing Individual and organizational Values: Walking the tightrope to success, Values-Driven Change: Strategies and tools for long-term success*, and *Becoming a Genuine Giver: Overcoming relationship barriers*. His article *"Evaluating Organizational Values"* was selected as the 2005 outstanding *Organization Development Journal* paper of the year. Ken, who is a registered organisation development professional, and a licensed clinical professional counsellor, can be contacted at www.kenhultman.com

The JOLT Challenge measurement component was designed by Davidson Consulting Limited.

Dr Jane Davidson

Dr Jane Davidson is the director of Davidson Consulting Limited, an Auckland-based evaluation and organisational consulting firm. Jane returned to New Zealand in 2004 from the United States where she served as Associate Director of the internationally recognised Evaluation Center at Western Michigan University. There she launched and directed the world's first fully interdisciplinary PhD in evaluation.

Jane is author of *Evaluation Methodology Basics: The Nuts and Bolts of Sound Evaluation*, which is used internationally as a graduate text and practitioners' guidebook, and co-editor of the free-access online *Journal of Multidisciplinary Evaluation*. She was the 2005 recipient of the American Evaluation Association's Marcia Guttentag Award, awarded to a promising new evaluator within five years of completing their doctorate.

Jane received her PhD from Claremont Graduate University, California, in organisational psychology with substantial emphasis on evaluation, her MA in psychology from Victoria University, undergraduate degrees in psychology and chemistry from Massey and Canterbury universities, respectively, and a Diploma of Teaching from the Christchurch College of Education.

Where to from here?

Take the next step on your Self Intelligence journey and get yourself a copy of the JOLT Challenge journal.

This companion journal is packed with the latest tools and exercises relating to each weekly theme. Visit www.joltchallenge.com to view sample pages and stay up to date with the latest information on courses, news and articles.

About Mind Warriors Limited

For more information on Mind Warriors please visit our website:

www.mindwarriors.com

Contact us:
PO Box 56-263
Dominion Road
Auckland 1446
New Zealand
Email: info@mindwarriors.com

Recommended Reading

Rather than a bibliography, which would be a mini-book in itself, we've provided a list of recommended reading and a brief commentary on six books for each week plus a reference on where to find more stories. This compilation includes everything from classic books to not so well-known ones, small and easy-to-read books through to university textbooks.

Week 1   Strengthen Your Foundations

Allen, D. (2001). *Getting Things Done: The art of stress free productivity.* New York: Penguin.
Simple strategies are provided to help you become more productive. Of course, with anything, it's the doing that counts. Experience tells us that the techniques in this book work.

Allen, J. (1992). *As A Man Thinketh.* New York: Barnes and Noble, Inc. (Original work published 1902).
The small classic on the power of thought. Although published in 1902, its words still ring true today. A book that you can read many times and will serve you greater with each reading.

Mann, C. (2005). *The Myths of Life and the Choices We Have.* Surrey Hills, NSW: Koromiko Publishing.
A book on existential psychology that challenges those barriers that may be hindering you. With some exercises included, it's a good book to get you thinking about who you are and what you do.

Maurer, R. (2004). *One Small Step Can Change Your Life: The kaizen way.* New York: Workman Publishing Company.
A small and powerful book on the Kaizen way. It provides a user-friendly approach to change in an easy-to-read style.

Peck, M. S. (1990). *The Road Less Travelled.* London: Arrow Books. (Original work published 1983).
Another classic. This one explores the attributes that make up a fulfilled person and covers areas such as discipline, love, growth and grace.

Tracy, B. (2001). *Eat That Frog! 21 Great ways to stop procrastinating and get more done in less time.* San Francisco: Berrett-Koehler Publishers.
This book provides different ways to overcome procrastination. It's simple and the techniques are useful.

Week 2   Discover Your Amazing Brain

Carter, R. (2000). *Mapping the Mind.* London: Phoenix.
A technical book on the brain and mind, full of fascinating facts, stories and diagrams. If you're interested in human behaviour and the role of the brain behind it, then this is the book for you.

Cash, A. (2002). *Psychology for Dummies.* Hoboken, NJ: Wiley Publishing, Inc.
One of the most user-friendly introductory books on psychology available. It gives a great overview and is humorous which helps makes the information more accessible. Although it looks a big book, it's actually quite easy to read.

Dispenza, J. (2007). *Evolve Your Brain.* Deerfield Beach, FL: Health Communications, Inc.
If you read just one book on the brain and the mind – make it this one. It gives great detail on the brain, the impact of emotional addictions, the science behind why change is so difficult and describes the art and science of mental rehearsal and how it creates positive change for you. Although very technical at times, it makes you very familiar with what you're working with in between your ears.

Hannaford, C. (1995). *Smart Moves: Why Learning Is Not All In Your Head.* Salt Lake City: Great River Books.
This has a focus on children's education but don't let that fool you. Written by a neurophysiologist, it gives the science behind the mind/body connection and the role of emotions. Also, a must for any parent.

Luria, A. R. (1973). *The Working Brain: An introduction to neuropsychology.* (Translated by Basil Haigh). New York: Basic Books.
Written by the famous Russian neuropsychologist, this book is not for the faint of heart. Very technical, and it gives a solid introduction to the intriguing topic of neuropsychology.

Ornstein, R. & Thompson, R. F. (1985). *The Amazing Brain.* London: Chatto & Windus, The Hogarth Press.
A very informative book on the brain with lots of pictures. Probably the best book to start with if you're interested in understanding your brain.

Week 3   Maximise Your Energy

Bartley, J. with Clifton-Smith, T. (2006). *Breathing Matters: A New Zealand guide.* Auckland: Random House.
An excellent book on best breathing practices, this will definitely make you think about the way you breathe. A little technical in places when it goes into physiology and anatomy detail,

but the information is easy to understand and can have a great impact on your health.

Blaylock, R. (1997). *Excitotoxins: The taste that kills.* Albuquerque: Health Press NA Inc.
This book comes from a neurochemistry angle, highlighting all the dangers of consuming MSG, aspartame, and other food additives. Although technical in nature, it is easy to understand. A warning though – you may end up reading food labels after reading this book.

Campbell, T. C., & Campbell, T. M. (2006). *The China Study: Startling implications for diet, weight loss, and long-term health.* Dallas, TX: BenBella Books, Inc.
Research from the largest nutrition study is put into this book, which makes a case for a whole food, plant-based diet. Like all things, experiment and see what works best for you.

Pinel, J. P. J. (2006). *Biopsychology* (6th ed.). Boston: Allyn & Bacon.
A university textbook that is more of a reference book to sit on your bookcase than your bedside table. Nonetheless, it contains riveting information not only on sleep, but covers everything from human evolution to psychiatric disorders. Read a page and people will marvel at your genius when you can drop interesting facts into conversations.

Sears, B. (1995). *Enter the Zone.* New York: HarperCollins Publishers, Inc.
If you've ever had trouble losing excess weight – then read this book. It will open your eyes and mind to a new way of eating that's easy to incorporate into your day-to-day life. Not so much a diet but rather a way to create sustainable healthy eating habits.

Weeks D. & James J. (1998). *Secrets of the Super Young: The scientific reasons some people look ten years younger than they really are – and how you can, too.* New York: The Berkley Publishing Group.
This book is in two parts. The first part provides the science of staying healthy and fit plus interviews with celebrities who have remained young at heart, of mind and in appearance. If that doesn't grab you, jump straight to the second part that is full of practical and useful tips for staying sharp both mentally and physically.

Week 4   Action Your Success Strategies

Arntz, W., Chase, B. & Vincente, M. (2005). *What the Bleep Do We Know? Discovering the endless possibilities for altering your everyday reality.* Deerfield Beach, Florida: Health Communications Inc.
The book is based on the award-winning documentary of the same name. It helps make quantum physics more accessible and explains the science behind setting your intention.

Chopra, Deepak. (1996). *The 7 Spiritual Laws of Success.* London: Bantam Press.
A simple and profound book. One that you can read over and over again and appreciate more fully with each reading.

Dyer, W. (2004). *The Power of Intention.* Carlsbad, CA: Hay House, Inc.
For the more open-minded reader, as this book is esoteric in parts. Inspired by Carlos Castaneda, this book offers different steps for you to achieve inner peace and fulfilment.

Fanning, P. (1994). *Creative Visualisation* (2nd ed.). Oakland, CA: New Harbinger Publications, Inc.
Probably the best book to start with when it comes to visualisation. It has lots of exercises, helps you find your inner guide and gives lots of excellent suggestions.

McTaggart, L. (2007). *The Intention Experiment.* New York: Free Press.
More reader-friendly than her other book *The Field*, which was fascinating but harder to grasp due to the complex nature of the topic. *The Intention Experiment* picks up where *The Field* left off but you won't suffer for not having read the first book. It provides hard data on human intent and gives you the steps to set your intention.

O'Connor, J. (2001). *NLP Workbook.* London: Thorsons.
This is one of the better neuro linguistic programming books out there in bookstores. It provides some useful tools and techniques to aid you achieve whatever it is you seek in life. It also includes the background to NLP, and which people and what studies influenced its founders, which all helps to de-mystify NLP.

Week 5   Master Your Emotions

Ekman, P. & Friesen, W. (2003). *Unmasking the Face.* Cambridge, MA: Malor Books.
Although this book is about recognising emotions on people's faces it also has plenty of good information on the primary emotions. An excellent introduction to emotions.

Gilbert, D. (2006). *Stumbling on Happiness.* New York: Alfred A. Knopf, Inc.
Harvard professor Daniel Gilbert has written a cracker of a book that is enlightening and really will make you think differently about the world you live in. It's very humorous and keeps you engaged right to the end.

Goleman, D. (1996). *Emotional Intelligence.* London: Bloomsbury Publishing.
One of the classics on the subject of EI that illustrates emotional intelligence in action. It provides excellent illumination on the role of emotions and their effect in our day-to-day lives.

Klein, S. (2002). *The Science of Happiness.* New York: Marlowe & Company.
A very well-written book that explores the science and psychology behind happiness. This one just pips *Stumbling on Happiness* as our top recommendation if you were only going to read one book on happiness. Of course, we recommend that you read both.

Pert, C. (1997). *Molecules of Emotion.* New York: Simon & Schuster.
Part autobiographical, part leading-edge science, this book explains the mind/body connection in the most engaging way. It covers the biochemistry of emotions while providing insights into the world of leading scientists.

Seligman, M. (1991). *Learned Optimism.* New York: Alfred A. Knopf, Inc.
From the father of positive psychology comes this classic on the effects of optimism. It provides cognitive behavioural therapy techniques at the end of the book. This is a must-read if you think you're a "glass half empty" kind of person.

Week 6   Explore Your Behaviour

Covey, S. R. (2006). *The 8th Habit: From Effectiveness to Greatness.* New York: Free Press.
A book on personal leadership that picks up where *The 7 Habits of Highly Effective People* left off. Although both great books, we prefer this book to its predecessor because it goes into much more detail around self-efficacy.

Glasser, W. (1999). *Choice Theory: A new psychology of personal freedom.* New York: Harper Perennial.
This hammers home the power of choice we have every moment of our lives. It's an excellent book by the founder of Reality Therapy that shows how choice can work in our personal life, our relationships, and at work.

Helmstetter, S. (1986). *What to Say When You Talk to Yourself.* Scottsdale, AZ: Grindle Press.
A light, easy-to-read book on the power of the inner voice. It may seem a little dated now in parts but has practical advice and some good tips to follow.

Henderson, M. (2004). *Finding True North: Discover your values, enrich your life.* Auckland: HarperBusiness.
An excellent book on helping you find your values in life. There are plenty of exercises presented in a simple fashion that can simplify your life on your path to fulfilment.

Hultman, K. (2001). *Balancing Individual & Organizational Values.* San Francisco: Jossey-Bass/Pfeiffer.
Probably *the* book to read if you want more information on values and how they affect your life at home and at work.

Robbins, A. (2001). *Awaken The Giant Within: How to take control of your mental, emotional, physical and financial destiny.* New York: Pocket Books.
Largely a reinterpretation of NLP principles, it covers a wide range of personal development areas, such as beliefs, emotions, decision making and how you talk to yourself.

Week 7   Align Your Needs

Csikszentmihalyi, M. (1998). *Finding Flow: The psychology of engagement with everyday life*. New York: Basic Books.
A small and powerful book by the professor who has studied peak performance for many decades. It also shows you how you too can reach the flow state.

Ellis, A. & Harper, R. A. (1975). *A Guide to Rational Living* (3rd revised ed.). Chatsworth, CA: Wilshire Book Company.
The classic rational emotive behavioural therapy book first published in 1961. Although particularly suitable for people who suffer from depression, it provides a wonderfully different perspective of looking at how we go through life.

Frankl, V. (1985). *Man's Search For Meaning*. New York: Pocket Books.
This classic book explores Viktor Frankl's time in the Nazi death camps and the type of new psychotherapy that emerged as a result. This is a must-read if you've ever wondered what the meaning of your life is.

Gallwey, W. T. (1999). *The Inner Game of Work* (1st ed.). New York: Random House.
This book provides great tips on how to focus your attention to get into the flow state and has a very user-friendly methodology of creating positive change in your life, especially as the title suggests, at work.

Ruiz, D. M. (1997). *The Four Agreements: A practical guide to personal freedom*. San Rafael, CA: Amber-Allen Publishing, Inc.
Based on ancient Toltec wisdom, it imparts an inspiring message for you to achieve inner peace and the bonus is – it's small and easy to read! This is definitely a book you could read over and over again to maintain a heightened sense of awareness.

Sieger, R. (2004). *Natural Born Winners: How to achieve happiness and personal fulfilment* (New ed.). London: Arrow House.
A personal development book with a very authentic tone and not one of those over-the-top self-help books.

Week 8   Unleash Your Creative Mindset

Aleinikov, A. G. (2003). *Mega Creativity: 5 steps to thinking like a genius*. Singapore: John Wiley & Sons (Asia) Pte Ltd.
If you want to develop the mindset for creativity, then this is the book for you. It gives your brain a wonderful workout and provides plenty of tools and strategies for you to put immediately into action.

Cushnir, R. (2005). *How Now: 100 ways to celebrate the present moment*. San Francisco: Chronicle Books.
A beautiful book with 101 simple exercises on being more present. One of those books you can pull from the bookcase, turn to a page and do an exercise.

Sofo, F. (2004). *Open Your Mind: The 7 keys to thinking critically*. Crows Nest, NSW: Allen & Unwin.
A book to challenge your habitual thought processes and get you out of stuck thinking. More theoretical in nature, it provides ways to tap into your natural creative talent.

Thompson, C. (2007). *What A Great Idea! 2.0: Unlocking your creativity in business and in life* (Rev. ed.). New York: Sterling.
A great book on creativity with lots of handy tools and techniques. It's simple to read with a gem on every page.

Tolle, E. (2001). *Practicing the Power of Now: Essential teachings, meditations, and exercises for living the liberated life*. Sydney: Hachette Australia.
This is the follow-up and action book to *The Power of Now*. It was a little tough to get into at first but warmed up later on. Upon further re-readings it became much more favourable with our researchers.

von Oech, R (1998). *A Whack on the Side of the Head: How to be more creative* (3rd ed.). New York: Warner Books, Inc.
This book helps you overcome ten of the biggest mental hurdles when it comes to being creative. It's light in tone, very easy to read and is a must-read for those who wish to improve their creative output.

Week 9   Map Your Future

Fritz, R. (2003). *Your Life As Art*. Vermont: Newfane Press.
The basic concept behind this book is that you create your life as an artist creates art. It goes into detail about understanding your goals with an excellent chapter on why patterns keep repeating in your life.

Johnson, S. (1999). *Who Moved My Cheese?: An amazing way to deal with change in your work and in your life*. London: Vermilion.
A parable that uses cheese as a metaphor for what you want to have in life. It's short but has a great impact on helping you adapt to change.

Loehr, J. (2007). *The Power of Story: Rewrite your destiny in business and in life*. New York: Free Press.
This book looks at your life as a story and takes you through a journey where you explore your stories around your health, work and relationships. A well-written personal

development book that is easier to read than *Your Life As Art*.

Ray, M. (2005). *The Highest Goal: The secret that sustains you in every moment*. San Francisco: Berrett-Koehler Publishers, Inc.
There are many important life messages in this excellent book, a crucial one being: have the courage to be yourself and walk your own path and arrive in harmony.

Smith, H. W. (2001). *What Matters Most: The power of living your values*. New York: Fireside.
This book guides you to find what is most important to you and imparts an important discover, plan and act model. Great, practical information with excellent stories shared as case studies and examples.

Seuss, Dr. (2003). *Oh, the Places You'll Go*. London: HarperCollins Children's Books.
Buy this book and read it often – even if you don't have kids. It carries the secret to a fulfilling life amongst classic Dr Seuss rhymes and illustrations. It reminds you that in order to achieve life fulfilment you must take action.

Stories

The stories throughout this book are a culmination of personal experiences from our trainers and participants, stories passed around and stories from books. Stories have their own life so please take these stories and re-tell them your way.

If you're looking for books with stories then we recommend the following:

Canfield, J. & Hansen, M. V. (1993). *Chicken Soup for the Soul: 101 stories to open the heart and rekindle the spirit*. Deerfield Beach Florida: Health Communications, Inc.

Owen, N. (2001). *The Magic of Metaphor: 77 stories for teachers, trainers & thinkers*. Carmarthen: Crown House Publishing.

Owen, N. (2004). *More Magic of Metaphor: Stories for leaders, influencers and motivators*. Carmarthen: Crown House Publishing.

Index